Robert Mundell, Nobel Prize in Economics in 1999, Professor of Economics, Columbia University:

"Currency board systems have become more popular since the collapse of the Soviet Union and with good reason: they provide a good option for monetary policy formation in countries where a suitable anchor currency is available. Warren Coats's well-told account of the establishment of a currency board in war-torn Bosnia and Herzegovina is fascinating and insightful reading. His mastery of detail and intimate knowledge of that unusual environment, both political and economic, challenge and deepen our understanding of monetary systems and policies."

Richard Rahn, Director of Cayman Islands Monetary Authority, former Chief Economist of the U.S. Chamber of Commerce, and syndicated columnist and author:

"If you were going to build a monetary system that would heal the wounds of a civil war-devastated country and help lay the foundation for economic recovery and development, what would you do? Warren Coats provides the answer given for Bosnia and Herzegovina in his well-told story of the establishment of the Central Bank of Bosnia and Herzegovina. Readers of his book will follow the detective-like uncovering of the workings of the unique Yugoslav banking and payment system and the challenges faced and overcome in replacing it with a modern, market based system."

Mario I. Blejer, Former Governor of the Central Bank of Argentina (2001–2002) and Senior Advisor in the IMF (1980–2001). Currently Director of the Centre for Central Banking Studies at the Bank of England:

"Warren Coats describes and analyzes the very complicated and extremely relevant process of the establishment of Bosnia's present monetary system in clear, highly readable prose. His book not only clarifies potentially obscure economic concepts for the layman but also illuminates the important interconnections between the economic and political aspects of post-conflict reconstruction."

SLOVENIA

Zagreb ★

Karlovac

Sisak

C R O A T I A

HUNGARY

Pécs

Osijek

Vukovar

Vojvodina

(autonomous province)

Novi Sad

Danube

Ruma

Prijedor

Slavonski
Brod

**Federation of Bosnia
and Herzegovina**

Bihać

Republika Srpska
Banja Luka

Brčko

*(The status of Brčko will be
determined by arbitration.)*

Belgrade ★

Doboj

Bijeljina

Šabac

Udbina

*Inter-Entity
Boundary Line (IEBL)
(Dayton agreement line)*

Ključ

Tuzla

B O S N I A

Knin

Glamoč

Zenica

A N D

H E R Z E G O V I N A

Srebrenica

Žepa

S e r b i a

Užice

Šibenik

Sarajevo ★

Pale

**Federation of Bosnia
and Herzegovina**

Gorazde

Split

Otok Brač

Mostar

**Republika
Srpska**

Otok Hvar

Ploče

Otok Korčula

Neum

M o n t e n e g r o

Nikšić

CROATIA

Dubrovnik

Kosovo

*(autonomous
province)*

A d r i a t i c

S e a

Tivat

Podgorica ★

Scale: 1:2,270,000

*Lambert Conformal Conic Projection,
standard parallels 40°N and 56°N*

0   40 Kilometers

0   40 Miles

Serbia and Montenegro have asserted the formation of a joint
independent state, but this entity has not been formally
recognized as a state by the United States.

Lake
Scutari

A L B A N I A

Bar

Shkodër

ONE CURRENCY FOR BOSNIA

CREATING THE CENTRAL BANK OF BOSNIA AND HERZEGOVINA

Warren Coats

JAMESON BOOKS
2007

Titles from Jameson Books are available at special discounts for bulk purchases, for sales promotions, premiums, fund raising or educational use. Special condensed or excerpted paperback editions can also be created to customer specifications.

For information and other requests please write Jameson Books, Inc., 722 Columbus Street, P.O. Box 738, Ottawa, Illinois 61350.

Direct Orders:	800-426-1357
Telephone:	815-434-7905
Facsimile:	815-434-7907
Email:	jameson@jamesonbooks.com

Printed in the United States of America.

Map of Bosnia courtesy of the University of Texas Libraries, The University of Texas at Austin.

Jameson Books are distributed to the book trade by MidPoint Trade Books, 27 West 20th Street, Suite 1102, New York, NY 10011. Bookstores please call 212-727-0190 to place orders.

Bookstore returns should be addressed to MidPoint Trade Books, 1263 Southwest Boulevard, Kansas City, KS 66103.

ISBN: 0-915463-99-7 · 978-915463-99-2

6 5 4 3 2 1 · 10 09 08 07

Library of Congress Cataloging in Publication Data

Coats, Warren L.
     One currency for Bosnia : creating the central bank of Bosnia and Herzegovina / by Warren Coats.
     p.   cm.
     Includes bibliographical references and index.
     ISBN-13: 978-0-915463-99-2 (alk. paper)
     1. Banks and banking, Central—Bosnia and Hercegovina.   2. International Monetary Fund.   I. Title.   II. Title: Currency for Bosnia.   III. Title: Creating the central bank of Bosnia and Herzegovina.
HG3239.A7C63 2007
332.1'10949742—dc22
2007025955

CONTENTS

SIDEBARS

PREFACE

I owe a deep debt of gratitude to many people, without whom this book could not have been written. First and foremost I would like to thank members of the International Monetary Fund, which made the experiences I relate possible, and the many IMF colleagues and other experts I worked with in Bosnia and Herzegovina. From the IMF these include Juan José Fernández-Ansola, Tobias Asser, Scott Brown, John Dalton, Bruno de Schaetzen, Haizhou Huang, Gary O'Callaghan, Marco Rossi, Philipp Rother, Chris Ryan, and Alessandro Zanello. The talented and dedicated experts who worked with me under IMF contracts include Jean-Luc Couetoux (Bank of France), Howard Crumb (formerly Federal Reserve Bank of New York), Leonard Fernelius (formerly Federal Reserve of Minneapolis), Benjamin Geva (York University, Canada), Simon Kappelhof (De Nederlandsche Bank), Hugh O'Donnell (Bank of Ireland), and Chaiha "Kim" Rhee (formerly IMF). They also include the first two governors of the CBBH, Serge Robert and Peter Nicholl.

I am also deeply indebted to the officials who sat across the table for enriching my life and helping to rebuild an integrated and efficient financial system. These include local members of the Board of the CBBH, Manojlo Ćorić, Kasim Omićević, and Jure Pelivan; the Vice Governors, Enver Backović, Dragan Kovačević, and Ljubiša Vladušić; staff of the CBBH in Sarajevo, Banja Luka, and Pale; CBBH Payment System Coordinator and Director of the Mostar Main Unit Anka Musa; Directors of the Federation and RS Payment Bureaus Maruf Burnazović and Ranko Travar, and their staff; Minister and Deputy Minister of Finance of RS Novak Kondić and Gorolana Čenić Jotanović, and their staff; Minister of Finance of the Federation Dragan Bilandzija; Director of the Banking Agency of RS Simeun Vilendacić; and Director of the Federal Banking Agency Zlatko Barš.

Warren Coats
Washington, DC
April 2007

INTRODUCTION

A success has many fathers and a failure has none. The Central Bank of Bosnia and Herzegovina has many fathers and I am proud to be one of them.

For twenty-six years I was an economist with the International Monetary Fund (IMF). For most of the decade following the collapse of the Soviet Union, I led technical assistance missions to countries (or territories) to advise central banks, or to help establish them. Most of my work has been in former Soviet Republics or other so-called transition economies—those attempting to transform themselves from centrally planned to market economies. My goal as an employee of the IMF had been to help establish in these countries the institutional structures and expertise that are needed for stable and efficient monetary and banking systems compatible with market economies. My work, and the work of others in this grand endeavor, has been fascinating, taking me to previously unknown corners of the world and of economic analysis.

In this book I share some of my experiences and explain some of the more interesting economic issues we confronted and attempted to resolve when establishing the Central Bank of Bosnia and Herzegovina. My goal is to share with you how we came to understand the issues we confronted and how we attempted to resolve them as events unfolded, and to introduce some of the people and places I was privileged to encounter. Most things are obvious after the fact. I want you to see how issues and events looked to us as they were unfolding and still mysterious, as well as our more informed understanding after the fact.

Key economic concepts and principles, which may be beyond the interest of the average reader, are explained in boxes or relegated to appendices to allow the narrative to flow uninterrupted. The boxes and appendices provide a summary of the important monetary policy concepts at play and lessons learned in establishing the Central Bank and should be interesting to students of money. In some instances boxes add economic content to the narrative; in other instances they provide brief summaries of concepts elaborated in the text. I attempt to place the Bosnia-specific issues in this broader monetary policy context and provide you with an overview of modern monetary policy and central banking. The expositions are intuitive rather than technical.

The story of creating the Central Bank of Bosnia and Herzegovina involved many more people than I write about. The Office of the High Representative (OHR), the World Bank, USAID, and their contractors, and many others played very important roles. My account is personal and thus reflects what I was directly involved with. Such a presentation is of necessity historically unbalanced, but I hope that it will be interesting and provide a useful historical record from one insider's perspective.

The storytelling is uneven because my records and notes are uneven, though I have attempted to give it some overall structure and coherence. Parts were written at the time as diaries, but most of it was reconstructed later from memory and notes. The story is told only very roughly chronologically. In keeping with my desire to share with you the development of economic issues, most of the story is grouped into topics, thus undermining a purely chronological format.

I meant to keep a diary, as several friends advised, knowing that my adventures would be interesting. Regrettably, the long hours we worked during our visits, which we call "missions," made it very difficult to keep a diary beyond our missions' official reports. I have never been good at keeping a diary anyway. Its great advantage over my filtered official reports is the preservation of officially unimportant but often very intriguing human details about people or events. I have tried to remember as many as I can. I hope that I can make interesting and alive the difficult issues we faced and the huge effort we made at the IMF to bring monetary stability and free markets to as much of the world as we could. I believe that we were right to try.

1 SARAJEVO

Because all the passenger seats were taken, I was sitting on a bench in the cockpit of a C-130 Hercules, behind the pilot and the co-pilot, as we began our descent through sheets of rain. I could barely see the giant turboprops, two on each wing, churning the air. They were pulling a plane so large it could transport utility helicopters and six-wheeled armored vehicles.

Somewhere below was the Sarajevo airport. As I strained to see the landing strip, a dark shape suddenly loomed to our left. A mountain. It rose several hundred meters above our altitude, so close that even with the rain I could make out individual trees. I thought fleetingly about Ron Brown, who was killed in a crash a few months earlier while trying to land at Dubrovnik, not far from Sarajevo. In the rain. The accident report had just been published, citing pilot error among other things. I glanced to my right and left. These two guys seemed to know what they were doing. The pilot, dark-haired with cold gray eyes, looked at me and grinned. "Don't worry. It's down there." I relaxed and thought about tomorrow. I had important things to do on the ground, on which I fully expected to land safely. It was July 23, 1996.

After months of waiting, the Bosnian Serbs had finally indicated that they were ready to start discussing the draft of a central bank law I had helped prepare many months earlier. I cancelled a visit with my family in California in order to participate in the first joint meeting of Bosniac, Croat, and Serb representatives to discuss our draft. I was finally going to see this war-torn but beautiful country.

Scott Brown had quickly organized the meeting of all three sides with the IMF and was sitting below in the hull of the Hercules transport plane with Alessandro Zanello and Simone, Alessandro's cat. Scott was the IMF mission chief for Bosnia and Herzegovina from our European I Department, and was thus responsible for negotiating any financial assistance the IMF might provide. Alessandro was another Fund colleague and was on his first visit to Sarajevo to take up his post as the IMF's first resident representative. Alessandro wore thick glasses, had thinning curly brown hair, and a whimsical smile. He always wore a suit or coat and tie that somehow looked casual and proper at the same time. He was the type who thrived on a challenge. Alessandro would thrive in Bosnia.

As the Fund's "oldest hand" on Bosnia, Scott knew the territory well. He had come to the IMF from the U.S. Treasury and the U.S. State Department where he had served during the Reagan administration. Scott was intelligent, energetic, determined, and possessed by widely varying moods. (He later miraculously survived the bombing of the Canal Hotel in Baghdad that took the life of Sergio de Mello, UN Special Representative in Iraq, on August 19, 2003, but permanently lost most of the use of his left arm.)

Scott and I had spent the previous evening together in the Croat capital of Zagreb talking over the problems we would face in Sarajevo. We rendezvoused at an outdoor cafe near the large, central square. The streets had been full of young people, many of them quite good-looking. It was hard to imagine that the city had been shelled (rather lightly) only a year earlier (May 2 and 3, 1995). Many of the young women wore miniskirts—the local version of fashion according to Scott—and might easily have been mistaken for hookers in Paris or London.

Sipping our beers, we had pondered the trip ahead. Would the upcoming meeting be a breakthrough? Would we be able to build one of the common institutions that had been specifically provided for in the Dayton peace accord? What positions and attitudes would each of the three sides bring to the table? Would the meeting even take place? Scott had been disappointed many times before. Now, as the plane touched down on the landing strip, I realized we were about to learn the answers to these questions.

Our C-130 Hercules Transport from Zagrab to Sarajevo—June 1996

2 DAYTON

My involvement with Bosnia and Herzegovina (BiH) had begun in the fall of 1995 when the IMF was asked to prepare a background note for a U.S. negotiating team that was helping to draft a new constitution. The new constitution was a part of the agreements that finally ended the war in that tragic country. The negotiating team had sought our advice on the type of monetary system to establish in light of the strong distrust that existed (and that we could assume would continue to exist after the war ended) among the ethnic and nationalist factions involved. The episode exemplifies the quick response to needs for which the IMF staff is proud.

BACKGROUND

Bosnia and Herzegovina was one of the six republics making up the Socialist Federal Republic of Yugoslavia (SFRY). Following Slovenia and Croatia, which declared independence in the summer of 1991 (and later Macedonia), the Republic of Bosnia and Herzegovina (BH) declared its independence from the SFRY in March 1992. The UN and most of its members quickly recognized the new nation, but its independence was promptly challenged by the Yugoslav National Army and local Serb militia, who launched a war in April that continued until the last of many cease-fires on October 10, 1995. In the midst of these hostilities, which generated some of the most brutal fighting ever seen in Europe, armed conflict also erupted between forces in the Croat-majority area of BH and the Republic (Muslim-majority area) army, a conflict that lasted from early 1993 until February 25, 1994. The death toll of these combined conflicts in BH is estimated at about 250,000 and about three million of the country's 4.4 million inhabitants were displaced from their homes. (About one million became refugees abroad).

Bosnia and Herzegovina had existed since the Middle Ages under a variety of foreign rulers (Ottoman, Austro-Hungarian). Over most of its history it had been a multi-ethnic region. Sarajevo, where Catholic and Orthodox churches, Jewish synagogues, and Muslim mosques have peacefully coexisted for centuries, has particularly thrived in such an environment. The three principal ethnic groups—Croats (Catholic), Bosniacs (Muslims), and Serbs (Orthodox)—lived in close proximity throughout the country. Racially the three groups were indistinguishable. They were differentiated only by religious identification.

By the end of 1995, Bosnia's three ethnic majority regions had become more homogeneous as a result of the ethnic cleansing that had taken place during the recent wars, and each region had its own government, army, and currency arrangements. While German marks were in use throughout the country, the Croat majority area also used Croatian kuna (HRK), the Serbian majority area used the new Yugoslav dinar (YUD), and the Bosniac majority area used the Bosnia and Herzegovina dinar (BHD) issued by the National Bank of Bosnia and Herzegovina (NBBH). The BHD was the only domestically issued currency still in use in the country at that time.

Peace between the Croats and Bosniacs following their war in 1993 was formalized by the Washington Agreements of August 1994, which resulted in the creation of the Federation of Bosnia and Herzegovina. In reality, the Croat and Bosniac majority areas remained substantially separate. When we first arrived in 1996 each region of the Federation continued to operate separate payment systems and use different currencies (kuna and BHD). Thus Bosnia and Herzegovina consisted of two so-called "Entities": the Federation and the Republika Srpska.

The issues behind the war and its resolution were so complex, the fighting so fierce, and the conditions of the population so horrible, that I had specifically decided during the wars not to follow these events reported so graphically on TV and in newspapers every day. To my surprise, I discovered from other foreigners working in Bosnia and Herzegovina that I had not been alone in blocking out the reports of the horrible events there. During the conflict I was working in Bulgaria (next door) and Kazakhstan and Kyrgyzstan (in central Asia) and later in Moldova and the West Bank and Gaza Strip, so my hands were full trying to understand their histories and institutions. Once I became a part of the international effort to reconcile and rebuild the historically multi-ethnic country called Bosnia and Herzegovina, I wasn't sure that a better knowledge of Balkan history would have helped.

The simple part of the story was the desire of many in the Serbian majority area of the Republika Srpska to merge with the Serbian part of Yugoslavia, the desire of many in the Croat majority area of Herzegovina to merge with the newly independent Croatia, and the desire of many in the Bosniac (Muslim) majority area to keep the country together. The deeper issues and causes of the prospective break up (beyond the ambitions of Slobodan Milosević in Serbia and Franjo Tudjman in Croatia) were a mystery to me.

After three-and-a-half years of bloody war, on September 8, 1995, the foreign Ministers of BH, Croatia, and the Federal Republic of Yugoslavia (FRY—consisting of the remaining two republics—Serbia and Montenegro) signed the "Agreed Basic Principles" for a peaceful settlement of the war. This was followed on September 26 by "Further Agreed Basic Principles" and on October 10 by the final cease-fire. "Proximity Talks" among the Presidents of BH, Croatia, and the FRY on a peace agreement—and a new constitution reintegrating the regions of Bosnia and Herzegovina—began on November 1, 1995, in Dayton, Ohio under the sponsorship of the United States. These talks resulted in the initialing on November 21 of a General Framework Agreement for Peace in Bosnia and Herzegovina that included a constitution for the continued existence of the country. These talks were followed by an

What is the IMF?

Anticipating the end of World War II and the need to rebuild a more secure and healthy international economic and monetary order, delegates from the Allied countries met in Bretton Woods, New Hampshire, July 1–22, 1944, to design the three international institutions that would (1) oversee the physical reconstruction of Europe and Japan (the International Bank for Reconstruction and Development—the World Bank), (2) the promotion of free trade (now the World Trade Organization), and (3) the free flow of capital to finance trade (the International Monetary Fund). The IMF's role among these three so-called "Bretton Woods Institutions" was to monitor member countries' exchange rate policies and to provide balance of payments financing (foreign currency loans) where appropriate to promote the financing of freer trade without the competitive devaluations experienced during the 1930s (so-called, "beggar thy neighbor policies").

The Fund's Articles of Agreement (the treaty between nations under which it operates) came into force December 27, 1945, when 29 of the 44 countries that had drafted and signed them had formally ratified the Articles. It started operations at its headquarters in Washington DC on March 1, 1947. Its first loan was extended on May 8, 1947 (to France). Its first large loan was to the United Kingdom. It now has 185 member countries.

The IMF's Web site summarizes its purpose as follows: "The IMF ... was established to promote international monetary cooperation, exchange stability, and orderly exchange arrangements; to foster economic growth and high levels of employment; and to provide temporary financial assistance to countries to help ease balance of payments adjustment."[1] In a world in which capital moves across

—continued on page 9

international peace conference in Paris at which the final agreements were signed on December 14, 1995.

IMF ROLE

My employer, the International Monetary Fund (IMF), is an international organization created after World War II to promote the orderly financing of international trade. Its 184 member countries cooperate through the IMF to promote exchange rate stability and orderly exchange arrangements. It is one of the three so-called Bretton Woods institutions, which also include the World Bank and the World Trade Organization. The IMF may provide temporary financial assistance to its member countries to help ease balance of payments adjustments. It also provides technical assistance to its members in developing the capacities of their central banks and finance ministries to formulate and implement the sound macroeconomic policies needed for exchange rate stability and to ensure their ability to repay the IMF. I began my work providing technical assistance to central banks as an IMF staff member with the collapse of the Soviet Union, first in Kazakhstan and Kyrgyzstan, then Moldova.

Leading up to the Dayton discussions, the IMF's First Deputy

Managing Director, Stanley Fischer, met on October 17, 1995, with the IMF's Executive Directors from the G7 member countries, to discuss issues related to Bosnia and Herzegovina and their possible future membership in the Fund. On behalf of the G7 (the US, Germany, Japan, UK, France, Italy, and Canada), the Directors requested that the IMF prepare a brief note for the upcoming Dayton peace talks outlining the requirements of viable fiscal and monetary structures in confederacies.

Since I had just recently overseen the preparation of a paper for the UN on the Minimal Requirements for Money and Payments in Post Crisis, Post Conflict Countries, I was assigned to prepare my department's contribution to the note (i.e., the monetary part). The goal was to find an arrangement for satisfying the monetary and payment needs of Bosnia and Herzegovina that would facilitate the economic recovery of the country and would provide a proper basis for an IMF supported stabilization program and that would be acceptable to the warring factions. The monetary arrangements should also contribute to the economic reintegration of the divided economy, if not country, and should be capable of becoming operational very quickly. (See Appendix I.)

national boundaries more freely than in the 1950s and the major economies' exchange rates are more flexible and market-determined, the Fund has refined its functions into *surveillance* (review of member countries' exchange rates and macroeconomic policies that affect their balance of payments with each other), financial assistance (so called "balance of payments" loans to member governments in order to facilitate orderly exchange rate adjustments without resorting to restrictions on trade), and technical assistance (to central banks, banking supervisors, and finance ministries in the design and implementation of good monetary and financial policies).

The IMF's members vote and can borrow when they qualify in relation to their financial contributions to the Fund (determined by each country's quota). The U.S. quota, for example, is 16.83 percent of the total and Russia's is 2.7 percent. The Fund's 185 member countries are represented by 24 Executive Directors who meet almost daily in Washington to approve loans and policies to fulfill the IMF's purposes. These meetings provide a valuable forum for addressing international financial issues in a cooperative way.

In recent years the Fund has extended large loans, sometime criticized as bailouts—to Russia, Turkey, Argentina, Brazil, Thailand, Korea, and Indonesia, to name some of the largest—to support the orderly adjustments of their exchange rates in the face of financial crises. Many of these exchange rate crises were accompanied by banking crises. While the main purpose of these loans was to minimize the domestic economic cost of these crises from dislocation and lost output, IMF financial support often allowed these countries to repay a larger share of foreign bank loans than would otherwise have been the case. For this reason IMF lending has sometimes been criticized for

—*continued on page 10*

lowering the risk of international private sector lending, thus creating a moral hazard of excess lending. To minimize this potential moral hazard, the IMF only lends when borrowing countries agree to policy conditions that are meant to address the underlying cause of the crises and thus to enable the borrowing country to repay the IMF. Typical Fund "conditionality" includes limits on government deficits and monetary growth in order to reduce inflation, removal of trade and capital restrictions, and strengthening of financial sector prudential supervision.

My work in Bosnia and elsewhere is an example of IMF technical assistance to member governments' central banks.

It was clear to me and my colleagues that these objectives would best be served by a unified monetary system. In its simplest and purest form, a unified monetary system is one in which everyone uses the same currency. But the world has produced many examples of variations on this theme. The essential requirement for a viable unified monetary system is that the money supply for the area as a whole be under proper control (an uncontrolled supply of money would result in uncontrolled inflation). This control requires, first and foremost, that there be no more than one monetary policy. I had grappled with this issue several years earlier (1992) in connection with the break up of the Soviet Union and the disintegration of the ruble that followed over the next two years.[2] If there is more than one monetary authority, there must be very clear and binding rules that link their activities together to ensure that the quantity of money is well determined and controlled.

These considerations suggested to us that the most promising options for the country were to choose a foreign currency as its legal tender, to adopt a national currency board, or to adopt two (or three) regional currency boards with the same currency peg and exchange rate. The first option, a foreign currency, had one great advantage: No central bank had to be put in place to issue a currency and control its quantity. It was an option that to some extent was already in place. It was the option I was to recommend for Afghanistan some years later (during a visit to Kabul in January 2002).

While each of the three ethnic majority areas used its own currency (Bosnian dinar) or the currency of the neighboring country defining its ethnicity (Croatian kuna and Yugoslav dinar), all three also used the German mark. The country could "dollarize" with German marks. While retiring the Bosnian dinar (the only currency in BiH issued by a central bank operating in the country) would need to be organized, the kuna and Yugoslav dinars could be exchanged in the market for German marks since they could be used in Croatia and Yugoslavia respectively. It was not clear, however, that the German central bank would agree to the official designation of its currency as legal tender in Bosnia and Herzegovina. Whatever its immediate advantages, this option came with several costs. The seigniorage (profit) from issuing money would be earned by the foreign country whose currency was used, rather than by the domestic central bank, if a domestic currency were issued. Furthermore, the use of a foreign currency might not contribute to reintegration and nation building in the same way that a national currency might.

The case for a currency board— the second and third options—had seemed obvious to us from the first. The conditions normally required for the successful establishment of a currency board (a healthy banking sector and sound public finances) did not exist in BiH. Bosnia's banking sector was in shambles because many of its borrowers had been bombed out of existence, and the rest suffered from the general collapse of the economy. Government revenues at the state (countrywide) level

What is a unified monetary system?

Modern means of payment can be highly complex. They are generally made to look simple because, for domestic payments at least, payment by whatever means is generally in the same currency. If I pay you $100, you receive $100 (somehow). I don't need to convert or exchange the currency I pay into the one you receive. That feature is the key property of a unified monetary system. It should have the feature that the bank notes issued by the Central Bank are acceptable and are legal tender anywhere within the territory serviced—in this case anywhere in Bosnia and Herzegovina.

Another and perhaps fuller meaning of a unified monetary system is that the primary means of payment—transfers of bank balances as well as cash—function throughout the system. This would require the ability to submit a payment order (or a check) at one location (or to one person or business) and have it delivered to any other location (or person) throughout Bosnia and Herzegovina.

Modern technology is reducing, but not fully eliminating, the importance of operating within a unified monetary system. I can use my credit card almost anywhere in the world. My hotel bill in Kazakhstan will be billed and charged to my card in tenge (Kazakhstan currency), but I will be billed and pay at the end of the month in U.S. dollars. The dollars I pay are converted into the tenge my hotel receives out of sight but with an exchange rate risk and an exchange cost.

were not well established as yet and were heavily dependent on donor grants. However, the only remaining domestically issued currency, the Bosnia and Herzegovina dinar (BHD), was fully convertible into German marks at a fixed rate.

The BHD was issued by the NBBH basically following currency board rules already. Thus the sort of discipline and stability provided by

Dollarization

Dollarization refers to the direct use of another country's currency. Examples are Panama's use of U.S. dollars—Panama mints its own coins called Balboas but uses U.S. dollar bank notes—and Kosovo's use of euros (initially the German mark). Fully dollarized economies have no currency of their own and thus no "monetary policy."

In fully dollarized economies—many are partially dollarized—the price level is largely determined by prices in the country whose currency is used. This is because any significant departure of the price of a traded good in the local market from its price abroad would result in importing the cheaper foreign good or exporting the cheaper domestic good until their prices were about the same (except for the cost of transportation).

The exogenously determined price level and the level of domestic output determine the demand for money. Thus the supply of money is brought into equality with its demand through market forces. The usual case—the money supplied by the central bank causing the price level to adjust until demand equals the central-bank-determined supply—is turned upside down. If people hold more dollars than they demand at the imported price level, their additional spending on investments abroad or import will eventually reduce the number of dollars domestically to the desired level (or vice versa). In gold standard days (a form of dollarization), this was called the "specie flow mechanism." Gold (dollars) flowed from one country to another (gold standard country) until supply equaled demand globally as well as in each country.

a currency board was already well understood and accepted. Furthermore, a currency board is easier to set up and to operate than a full-fledged central bank and could thus be put in place quickly. Perhaps more importantly, the high level of distrust among the three major ethnic groups and/or the three previously warring regions of the country would make it very difficult to gain their cooperation with a discretionary central bank. Since a currency board has little or no discretion, surrendering authority to a national currency board should be far more acceptable to the three regions than to any other form of monetary authority.

The second and third options, one national or several regional currency boards, would fulfill equally well the criteria of stable, non-discretionary monetary policy, and administrative simplicity. The option of a national currency board was the marginally more efficient of the two (establishing one institution rather than several) and would contribute more to nation building, if the three regions were prepared to embark in that direction.

CURRENCY BOARD ARRANGEMENTS

Following the founding of the Sveriges Riksbank in 1668 (the Swedish National Bank), considered the world's oldest central bank, and the Bank of England in 1694, the central banks of nation states gradually acquired the exclusive right to issue their country's currency. For several centuries these monopolies over the printing and circulation of money were more a source of government finance than monetary stability. Hyperinflations can only be produced by central banks. However, when properly focused on preserving the stability of the value of their currencies, central banks can contribute to the economic well being of their countries and increasingly have done so.

The value of money depends on its quantity relative to its demand. While properly defining the quantity of money and discerning the factors influencing its demand (largely income and interest rates) can be complex, the simple supply-must-equal-demand paradigm is powerful and insightful. Modern central banks control the quantity of their currency in their economies. They control its value (given the public's demand) by controlling its supply.

In a simplified world without banks, where money is synonymous with currency, doubling the supply of currency will double all prices (thus cutting the value of money in half). The idea that printing too much money is inflationary is widely understood. The relationship between the quantity of money and its value has been immortalized in the famous

Seigniorage

Seigniorage is the name given to the profit central banks make from their monopoly issue of currency. This profit results from the fact that the cost to the central bank of issuing (and maintaining) currency is less than the value of the assets it can purchase with the currency issued. Currency notes do not pay interest; thus the cost of issuing them is the cost of printing, distributing, and safekeeping them. The profit can be measured in several ways and has a stock and flow aspect. Intuitively, if the central bank can print currency at a lower cost that its value in the market, it can invest the difference. One measure of profit is the interest return on those investments after deducting the costs of the currency. If currency is issued to buy domestic bills or bonds, the profit is the net income from those bonds over time. If it is issued for foreign currency, as in the case of a currency board, the profit is the net income from the foreign investments of the central bank's reserves.

Counterfeiters, when successful, profit by the difference between their cost of printing their bank notes and of using them to buy goods and services. Central banks are in business for the long haul, however, and must also include the cost of maintaining the stock of its currency over time (replacing old and damaged notes with new ones). In addition, the costs of issuing currency include the vaults in which it is stored and the teller and security staff that issue and safeguard it. Nonetheless it is hard not to profit from the currency monopoly if the supply of currency is limited enough to preserve its value. Profits increase as the rate of supply increases, and this has been the underlying cause of many inflations. However, as with any monopoly, beyond some point further inflation reduces profits more than the additional supply adds to them and net profit declines as the rate of printing and issuing new notes expands beyond that maximum.

equation of exchange, the heart of the quantity theory of money. (See Appendix II.)

In its purest form, a currency board buys and sells (issues and redeems) its monetary liabilities against a specific foreign currency at a fixed exchange rate. The board must maintain full backing for its monetary liabilities in the same foreign currency. In fact, the first requirement of "passively issuing and redeeming its monetary liabilities against a foreign currency" ensures fulfillment of the second requirement of "full backing"—if the resulting reserves are invested so as to preserve their value and to generate net income sufficient to cover the operating costs of the currency board. Unlike true central banks, which are sometimes called the bankers' bank, the purest form of currency board accepts no deposits from banks (or anyone else). However, there are very few existing currency boards that take this pure form. The Cayman Islands Monetary Authority is one.

The purest currency board will only issue bank notes against foreign exchange. However, most existing currency boards are also central banks, i.e., they accept deposits from banks with which banks may settle interbank payments, and thus play a role in the non-cash payment system. All currency boards, however, operate within strict rules, either automatically, having no discretion at all, or within very narrowly constrained limits.

In a recent article on currency boards in the Federal Reserve Bank of San Francisco Economic Letter, Mark Spiegel defined a currency board as "a fixed exchange rate regime whose currency is fully backed by foreign reserves." There is a subtle, but important, difference between these two definitions. The fixed exchange rate version hints at a more active institution subject to strict rules rather than a purely passive one.

Conceptually, central banks exist because of the belief that individuals through markets are not able to adjust to monetary and other economic and financial shocks as well as governments. A full-fledged central bank is expected to exercise its judgment over the magnitude and sources of shocks and execute interventions (e.g., open market operations, foreign exchange interventions, reserve requirement adjustments) that neutralize or mitigate their disrupting effects at lower social cost than would result from the private sector's adjustments to the same shock.

Experience has taught, however, that the nature and magnitude of shocks are not so easily diagnosed at the time they occur and that other objectives and bureaucratic inertia (or conservatism) of government bodies often operate to undercut the potential advantage of government over the private sector in this area. The last half-century is rich with examples of monetary shocks delivered by or magnified by central banks or of monetary stability sacrificed for government revenue or other objectives. Historically, rather than the after-the-fact conceptual justification given above, the first central banks were created to finance their governments. Hyperinflation was an invention of central banks.

To maximize the benefits and minimize the dangers, full-fledged central banks have increasingly been made "independent" of the government by making them accountable to parliament for the achievement of price stability. The evidence to date indicates that independence has improved central bank performance, especially in developed countries. However, achieving public confidence (credibility) in a central bank generally requires a long track record. A reputation of virtue is not easily obtained, and can be quickly lost.

The primary attraction of a currency board, along with its operational simplicity, is the strong public certainty that can be attached to the policy that it will follow. Currency boards have no discretion (or very limited discretion) and are thus better protected from political interference or their own misjudgments. Unlike a gold or some other

Currency Boards

Currency boards were first established by the United Kingdom in its colonies in the mid-nineteenth century. They were government authorities that issued a local currency at a fixed exchange rate with the pound sterling. These boards passively sold their currency for sterling or bought it back (redeemed it) for the same amount of sterling and invested the sterling in the UK. Currency boards allowed the country or territory to enjoy the national symbol of its own currency and its seigniorage without the risks of inflation so common with central banks (beyond the inflation created by the Bank of England). By the end of World War II there were about 50 currency boards in operation.

A currency board is the next step beyond dollarization. It prints and maintains its own currency (usually by contract with an established printer) and the facilities for exchanging it with banks or the public. It cannot lend to government, banks, or anyone else. In its purest form it does not accept deposits. By the nature of its limited and passive operations, its currency is fully backed by the foreign currency to which its exchange rate is fixed and it has no monetary policy. Thus the supply of its currency is determined by market demand. The value of its currency is determined largely by the value of the currency to which it is pegged.

commodity standard, which puts monetary policy in the impartial hands of mother nature, a currency board arrangement entrusts monetary policy to the central bank that issues the currency to which the board's currency is fixed. To be credible, the commitment of a currency board to its rules must be as strong and as difficult to reverse as possible, and the public must be frequently reassured that the rules are being adhered to.

Under a currency board arrangement, the money supply adjusts to the economy's demand for it through market mechanisms. The passive issuance or redemption of domestic monetary liabilities at a fixed exchange rate ensures a well-defined quantity of money that adjusts to the public's demand (given income, interest rates, exchange rate, etc.,) automatically. Anyone who wants more domestic money may buy it (ultimately) from the central bank for foreign currency and vice versa. Rather than an exogenous quantity of money determining the price level, given the public's demand for money, an exogenously determined price level (via the fixed exchange rate and price level in the country of the currency peg) and international interest rates determine the public's demand for money to which the supply adjusts.

The disadvantage of a currency board is the need to give up the potential (but often unrealized) advantages of central banks, i.e., the ability to offset shocks through market intervention. Under a currency board arrangement, the economy must adjust fully to shocks through markets. The speed and ease of such adjustments depend on the efficiency of those markets, the flexibility of prices, and the degree of factor mobility. Consider in turn a shock to reserve money (monetary base) and a shock to the money multiplier.

Look first at the case of a capital outflow (residents investing abroad or foreign investors withdrawing their money). As domestic money is exchanged for foreign currency and transferred abroad, the monetary liabilities of the currency board (so called "reserve money") and its foreign assets will fall by the same amount, thus preserving the full backing of its diminished monetary liabilities. The resulting monetary contraction will increase domestic interest rates until the relative advantage of investing abroad and thus the capital outflow is eliminated. The monetary contraction will also put downward pressure on domestic prices and nominal income, which should eventually improve the country's current account or trade balance with the rest of the world. That is to say, the fall in domestic prices and demand will increase exports and reduce imports, diminishing the initial outflow of money. Automatic market adjustments in interest rates and prices will eventually stop the initial currency outflow. The immediate liquidity squeeze, which would normally be offset or softened by a central bank, must be dealt with by an increase in short-term borrowing abroad by banks or by the liquidation of some of their foreign assets. If short-term borrowing abroad cannot be easily obtained, or if price level and current account adjustments are slow, domestic interest rate increases are likely to overshoot with adverse consequences for investment and output. On the other hand, if a central bank prevents a sufficient adjustment in interest rates or attempts to maintain rates at an inappropriate level, adjustment will be delayed resulting in a larger capital outflow than otherwise.

Bank runs produce a very different shock. In the case of an increase in the public's preference for cash relative to bank deposits (e.g., as a result of a loss of confidence in banks in general), the monetary liabilities (and foreign currency assets) of the currency board don't change, but banks lose balances in their reserve accounts with the central bank. Currency held by the public increases and bank deposits with the central bank decrease. This process reduces the deposits created from a given amount of reserve money and thus reduces the quantity of money over all. Again a monetary contraction (from a reduction in the so-called "money multiplier") results in an increase in interest rates and downward pressure on income and prices. The contraction will generally be moderated by a capital inflow in response to the higher interest rates and a trade balance improvement as a result of fall in prices of domestically produced goods and the resulting improvement in export competitiveness. The short-term liquidity squeeze must be dealt with by an inflow of foreign exchange, because the liquidity shortfall is systemwide.

An adjustment to a change in the money multiplier with no change in aggregate money demand will surely be more costly when made through market interest rate and price level adjustments than when made by a central bank adjustment in reserve money. The neutralization of shifts in the money multiplier probably represents one of the clearest cases for the potentially positive role of a central bank as a "lender of last resort."

FINAL AGREEMENT

On October 19, 1995, I e-mailed Scott Brown a two-page note for my department's contribution to the Dayton background note (the monetary part), which introduced the idea of a currency board. Over the next five days, working with Scott, who was also coordinating the preparation of the fiscal side of the note, we developed a note containing the above three basic options (with several variants) and supporting arguments. On October 25, we delivered the requested note and a note on Bosnia's external debt and financial workout scenarios to the U.S. Treasury for use in Dayton.

A thank-you note to Mr. Fischer from Jeffrey R. Shafer, Assistant Secretary for International Affairs of the U.S. Treasury, dated November 2, 1995, stated in part that

> Both papers are already playing major roles in shaping discussions on Bosnia's future. The paper on options for a financially viable federal republic in particular is already being used by Contact Group officials in negotiating new constitutional arrangements.

The Constitution of Bosnia and Herzegovina, which was initialed in Dayton on November 21, 1995, and formally adopted in Paris on December 14, contains the following section on monetary arrangements:

> Article VII
> Central Bank
> There shall be a Central Bank of Bosnia and Herzegovina, which shall be the sole authority for issuing currency and for monetary policy throughout Bosnia and Herzegovina.
>
> 1. The Central Bank's responsibilities will be determined by the Parliamentary Assembly. For the first six years after the entry into force of this Constitution, however, it may not extend credit by creating money, operating in this respect as a currency board; thereafter, the Parliamentary Assembly may give it that authority.
> 2. The first Governing Board of the Central Bank shall consist of a Governor appointed by the International Monetary Fund, after consultation with the Presidency, and three members appointed by the Presidency, two from the Federation (one Bosniac, one Croat, who shall share one vote) and one from the Republika Srpska, all of whom shall serve a six-year term. The Governor, who shall not be a citizen of Bosnia and Herzegovina or any neighboring state,

     may cast tie-breaking votes on the Governing Board.

3. Thereafter, the Governing Board of the Central Bank of Bosnia and Herzegovina shall consist of five persons appointed by the Presidency for a term of six years. The Board shall appoint, from among its members, a Governor for a term of six years.

Aside from imbedding the currency board arrangement in the Constitution, the above Article had several unusual provisions that became the source of considerable discussion when we were drafting the central bank law.

3 DEVELOPING THE CENTRAL BANK LAW

Our Hercules C-130 landed safely, of course, on that first trip (and every other one). Sarajevo is surrounded by beautiful mountains. In fact, most of Bosnia and Herzegovina consists of spectacular mountains and winding rivers. The winter Olympics were held near Sarajevo in 1984. World War I is said to have begun there with the assassination of Archduke Ferdinand in 1914. The airport terminal was still a shambles on this first visit and for some time to come. It was surrounded by minefields and the rows of high rise apartments just beyond had taken a very heavy beating during the several months of Serbian shelling near the end of the war and were uninhabitable. A forklift drove up the tail ramp and removed our luggage from the belly of our plane. The forklift sat the luggage for us to retrieve outside the temporary tent waiting room.

A car and driver from the World Bank office in Sarajevo drove us to the Hotel Bosna in the heart of the city. The traditional old city center of Sarajevo was seven or eight miles from the airport. Within a few hundred meters from the airport we passed several gutted tanks on the edge of the road. We fell silent.

As we approached the old city, the destruction tapered off rapidly. Our hotel was on the edge of the central market place and pedestrian walkway, and half a block from the National Bank of Bosnia and Herzegovina. The central pedestrian area is the jewel of Sarajevo. Except for a few famous mortar hits, it had not been seriously damaged by the war. One of those famous shells had landed on the open-air vegetable market called Markale, killing 68 people. It was this attack that finally brought the United States into the war. Mortar shells leave an easily recognizable footprint in the pavement where they explode. The craters from this and the other mortar hits that had taken lives in Sarajevo had been filled in with a red plastic substance that both repaired them and immortalized the event.

Markale vegetable market in Sarajevo where 68 people died from a 120-mm shell fired from nearby hills in Republika Srpska on February 5, 1994.

OUR FIRST MEETING

The Hotel Bosna had been the favorite hangout during the war for news correspondents. A CNN crew came and went during our stay. For us, the attraction of Hotel Bosna was that it was half a block from the National Bank, though we did very much appreciate the convenience of walking into the central market a few blocks away. Though the rooms were very warm in the summer and chilly in the winter, the hotel almost always had electricity and usually had warm water.

On this occasion, being there with Scott and Alessandro rather than a team of technical experts, I had a regular room rather than the suite I usually commanded as the chief of a technical assistance mission in need of a space for meetings with my team. The room was tiny. It had a standard, Soviet-style, twin bed, a small table on which sat a TV, and a wooden chair. I generally worked on my laptop sitting on the bed. There was a phone in the room, but the system did not permit me to connect my computer to the Internet.

A message was waiting at the hotel for Scott to call the U.S. State Department political officer stationed in Sarajevo, who wanted us to join him for dinner. We were picked up outside our hotel and driven what seemed to me a considerable distance to a restaurant in a basement. It was "guarded" by a motorcycle inside the front door at the top of the stairs and a large sleeping dog near the bottom of the stairs. On later visits I realized that the restaurant, Café Jez, was quicker and easier to reach from our hotel on foot than by car.

Scott and our host were old friends, perhaps from Scott's days in the State Department, but at least from Scott's earlier trips to Sarajevo. Scott is a very quick study and knows the right people in short order. I listened carefully to the conversation of these two "old Bosnia hands," absorbing all that I could and grateful that few questions came my way. I seemed, through Scott, to have fallen into the center of things, though as in most other countries in which I worked, I rarely had contact with the U.S. Embassy staff (other than those working directly in the technical assistance area) in Sarajevo.

The next morning I met Scott downstairs for breakfast. Following breakfast we walked the half-block to the National Bank building where the meeting with our counterparts would take place. The NBBH had been the central bank of all of Bosnia and Herzegovina before the war. During the war, the Serbian majority area set up its own central bank, the National Bank of Republika Srpska (NBRS) headed by Manojlo Ćorić. They separated their part of the payment bureau system I was still to learn about from the rest of Bosnia and Herzegovina but maintained its link with the Yugoslav system. In fact, the SPP, as the payment bureau was called in the Republika Srpska, was a technically integral part of the Yugoslav payment system. And, of course, the Yugoslav dinar was the currency used in that area. (I will explain the unique and troublesome payment bureau system later.)

The Croat majority area broke away as well, severing its part of the payment bureau system from the rest and using Croatian kuna and German marks. Unlike the NBRS, which continued to function as a branch of the National Bank of Yugoslavia, the Croat majority area had no central bank and no relationship with the National Bank of Croatia (as it was called then). Its payment bureau system, the so-called ZAP (the same name used for the payment bureau system in Croatia) was not linked in any way to the Croatian ZAP. Thus, the Croat majority area ZAP took on some quasi-central bank-like functions. As a result of these wartime changes, the NBBH during and after the war was de facto the central bank only for the Muslim majority area and its bank notes, the BH dinar, circulated only in the Bosniac region. We were in Sarajevo to establish a new central bank that would replace existing complex arrangements, including the NBBH and the NBRS.

The National Bank occupied 25 Marsala Tita, the main street of Sarajevo, off of which one block away started the pedestrian walkway through the heart of the old city. The building looked like the central bank that it was—unimaginative, but solid and apparently safe. A mortar splat on the sidewalk in front and some shrapnel and pock marks on the facade were the only evidence of the war. The building rose, unassuming, five stories from the street like a solid rock. Its basement housed the currency vaults one expects to find in a central bank. We climbed the few steps to the front door, announced IMF, and were waved through by "security," to climb the remaining steps to the first (ground) floor. The first floor had very high ceilings and a large banking hall in the center, now filled with clerks sitting at tables and chatting with each other. I followed Scott up the broad stairs to the second floor and the governor's office, a path I was to take many times over the next few years.

Scott took me to the office of Kasim Omićević, Governor of the NBBH. Like almost everyone in the Balkans, Kasim was a heavy smoker. He was in his early sixties, I would guess, and had the weathered look excessive smokers tend to acquire. He spoke English well enough for casual conversation and to understand what he wanted to understand. He rarely relied on an interpreter, even in our official meetings and conversations. Scott's assessment of people tends to be very accurate and he liked Kasim (I tended to like most of the people we met in the Balkans, whether they deserved it or not). Neither of us knew how far to trust him, however, or at least I didn't. I don't think Scott trusted anyone very much. Kasim was crafty. I never felt that I really knew his real agenda. His moods and rhetoric swung widely from the very smooth and flattering to the very harsh and damning. I was a recipient at one time or another of all of his moods.

Kasim Omićević (Governor of the NBBH and Bosniac member of the board of the CBBH)

At this point, Kasim was still governor of the NBBH. He had held the monetary system of Bosnia together through the wages of war, with (it would seem) only minor indiscretions, fully understandable in the context of war. The value of the BH dinar of DM = 100BHD continued to hold, and the liabilities of the NBBH were more or less fully backed with German marks. In many respects Kasim was at the peak of his glory. The times ahead would not be easy for him, and he knew it. While the creation of a new countrywide central bank would mean the end of the NBBH and Kasim's position as its governor, he professed to be fully supportive of the new bank and seemed sincere. Indeed, such a position was fully consistent with the Bosniac commitment to keeping the whole country together.

Scott introduced me. We exchanged brief pleasantries during the time it took Kasim to smoke several cigarettes, and then proceeded from his office directly into the boardroom of the NBBH for the start of our meeting. A large, long boardroom table that could seat twenty-two people filled the room. A large mural depicting aspects of life in Bosnia covered the wall opposite Kasim's office entrance. Kasim pointed out several small holes in the mural created by fragments of the mortar that had exploded on the sidewalk just outside the second-story room. Over the next three years, I was to spend many hours sitting at that table.

Organizing a meeting with participants from the three previously warring areas of BiH was still not easy in the summer of 1996. Phone connections between the three areas were not yet restored, except for several special lines in the Office of the High Representative (OHR), the highest civilian authority placed in BiH by the United Nations to oversee the implementation of the Dayton Accord. The first High Representative to BiH was Carl Bildt, a former Prime Minister of Sweden.

More importantly, travel outside one's own area was not considered safe. The Serb representatives coming to the meeting were entering Sarajevo for the first time since the war and required military escorts. Several armored cars and soldiers were provided by the French contingent of the Implementation Force (IFOR), the multi-national military force of the countries that had supplied soldiers to help end the war and secure the peace.

Kasim was there for the Bosniacs, and I no longer remember who attended for the Croats. But the two men attending for the Serbs were not whom Scott had expected. As they walked into the boardroom, Scott's face turned pale and then reddened. They were mid-level technicians, who clearly would not have the authority to negotiate anything. Scott spoke carefully and calmly as he welcomed everyone, but his anger was unmistakable. We had dropped everything and traveled thousands of miles for nothing. I presented an overview of what the law contained and how the Central Bank it would create would function. A plum brandy, Slivovica, popular in the region, was served, officially signaling the end of serious discussions, and we adjourned to a luncheon hosted by Kasim.

THE SECOND MEETING

Scott and I returned to Washington, but Alessandro remained in Sarajevo to establish his resident representative office. From there he continued the efforts, which were mainly proceeding at higher political levels, to advance the dialogue on the Central Bank and banking law drafts we had prepared. It took almost three months before all three groups agreed to resume discussions on the two draft laws. The agreement was a result of stern messages from the international community—expressed through the OHR and other channels—that the locals had better get on with implementing Dayton or no aid would be forthcoming. Two other big-ticket issues that were "moving" too slowly were agreement on a new flag for BiH and on the design of new car license plates that would not reveal the home area of the car. Such license plates were considered important to lower the risks to the locals of traveling between regions of the country.

Alessandro pushed for the establishment of technical working groups authorized to discuss the texts of the two drafts. Our second meeting on the draft laws, which would be held with the technical working group on the banking law, was agreed for September 20, 1996, and Scott and I returned to Sarajevo.

Everything about organizing these meetings and doing official business in BiH was always complicated by the need to be even-handed with the two Entities and the three ethnic majority areas. It is not clear to me to this day whether the hard fought U.S. policy of creating the Federation of Croats and Bosniacs was a help or a hindrance. The idea was to join the Croats and Bosniacs in a united front against the Serbs, following the end of the war within the war between the Croats and Bosniacs. Especially following their brief but unbelievably vicious war with each other in 1993, the Croats and Bosniacs hated, or at the very least distrusted, each other as much as they each hated and distrusted the Serbs. One visible result of the arrangement was that the Republika Srpska was quicker and better organized in responding to almost every situation. The Federation had to first fight everything out within their so-called coalition. For several years the union existed primarily on paper.

In any event, in the interest of equal treatment, the second meeting was planned for the city of Duboj, on the RS side of the Sava river, which marked the border between the Serbian majority area (RS) and the Bosniac majority area. As an aside, we always had difficulty knowing how to refer to these regions. No one formulation was acceptable to all three groups. The terminology of "this or that ethnic majority area" was adopted by the international community and generally accepted by our local counterparts when they were in a cooperative mood. The unambiguous terminology most often used by our counterparts was "the territory occupied by this or that army."

On this trip, I sat in the fuselage of the NATO Hercules C-130 that flew us from Zagreb to Sarajevo. From there, sitting in webbed rope seats hanging from the ceiling maybe 15 feet above and facing one another in two long rows on each side of the fuselage, I was surrounded by soldiers. We could not see out as the little round windows were well above our heads. A Norwegian Air Force officer (this was a Norwegian Air Force NATO plane) served us coffee.

On arrival in Sarajevo I could already notice some gradual improvements to the airport. On this occasion they were limited to removing some of the war damage rubble. But on each subsequent visit at least a few things were changed as the airport was very slowly restored. For a while the most noticeable change was the ever-changing arrangements for retrieving our luggage, which eventually moved inside of the terminal building and then from one location and arrangement to another. In the end, we also arrived in and left from the terminal building (again from ever-changing locations) rather than the tent that had been used initially.

After a day of meetings in Sarajevo, Scott, Alessandro, and I gathered at the NBBH building early on the morning of September 20; and—with Kasim and Enver Backović, a Vice Governor of the NBBH— we entered the two cars that would take us to Doboj. Though we had been offered a military escort for the drive, we chose to use the two cars available to us with UN license plates (Alessandro's resident representative car, and Kasim's governor's car). Such plates were still essential to avoid complications at roadblocks and the border crossing between the three areas of the country.

Enver was a Bosniac war hero. He was young, early forties I would guess, handsome, and articulate. He spoke English well and seemed to us the voice of reason when, as so often happened, Kasim was being unreasonable. Enver was someone you could enjoy spending time with, a slap-on-the-back kind of guy who always greeted us warmly and had good stories to tell. Several years later, following a nasty shouting match between Enver, dressed all in black, and Avdo Ajanovic, the Deputy Director of the Federation payment bureau (ZPP), I whispered to him that he looked and acted like Michael Corleone from "The Godfather" movie. He smiled approvingly and said that he had to behave like that sometimes to keep them in line and that I could always smooth things over afterward (good cop/bad cop). Enver later proved to be a big disappointment.

The drive to Doboj was my first through the beautiful countryside of Bosnia and Herzegovina. The natural beauty of the mountains and the rivers was undercut by the shocking devastation of almost every structure along the way. The destruction of virtually every bridge was understandable (we crossed the rivers where necessary on one lane, temporary, steel bridges erected a few months earlier by NATO forces). The heavy damage to industrial plants was to be expected. But the destruction of virtually every house we could see along the way was a shock to us. It is hard to imagine a military purpose for such systematic and complete destruction. The many subsequent trips along these roads were marked by the gradual restoration of most of the residential structures.

We arrived in Doboj after the three-hour drive and stepped out of the cars and stretched. The length of these trips varied a great deal depending on the weather and the length of the waits at border crossings. Enver, especially, seemed nervous. He was in former enemy territory for the first time since he had fought the Serbs in the war.

In a letter sent to us in Washington preceding this meeting, the National Bank of Republika Srpska (NBRS) had proposed a single central bank that would share most of its responsibilities with the NBRS and a proposed National Bank of the Federation. This indicated that they were thinking about creating a new central bank, indeed taking the proposal seriously (as was required by Dayton) but were not moving in an acceptable direction. Building the required consensus for the kind of central bank we hoped to establish was not going to be easy.

A room in a restaurant had been reserved for our meeting and most of the other participants had already arrived. We proceeded to discuss the draft banking law, paragraph by paragraph for about three hours, then broke for lunch. My intention was to return to the central bank law draft after lunch. The lunch was friendly, and old adversaries were beginning to relax and loosen up some. After about an

Meeting with the Federation Payment Bureau: from left to right: Enver Backović (Vice Governor NBBH/CBBH), and the author—February 1997

hour and a half, as I was beginning to think we should be getting back to work, out came the Slivovica; and the work was clearly over for the day. With little accomplished, Scott and I returned to the United States.

Thousands of miles and several days of travel, jet lag, and work disruption, for three hours of work, seemed a very slow pace to me. However, it was a start, and Alessandro continued the pressure by chairing inter-entity working group discussions of the two drafts in the coming weeks. He called or emailed me to clarify the intent of various passages from time to time, and generally maintained some amount of dialog among the members of the group.

NOVEMBER MEETINGS
PROSPECTIVE CENTRAL BANK BOARD

The big breakthrough came October 29, 1996, clearly in response to mounting political pressures, when Bosnia and Herzegovina's Joint Presidency appointed the governor and the three ethnic members of the Board for the future Central Bank of Bosnia and Herzegovina (CBBH). The Dayton agreement had stipulated that the IMF would nominate the governor from outside the country or surrounding countries. The IMF's Managing Director nominated Serge Robert, a former French banker, who at the time was a resident advisor to the Governor of the Central Bank of Haiti as part of our technical assistance program there. The Bosniac member was Kasim Omićević, as expected. Manojlo Ćorić, governor of the NBRS, was appointed the Bosnian Serb member. The third ethic member of the Board was Jure Pelivan, the Croat of the group, who had been an earlier governor of the NBBH before the war. These four were to be our counterparts in subsequent discussions of the draft central bank law. They all had legitimate professional claims to their new positions, which gave us hope.

I grew to respect all three local Board members and the honesty of their good intentions. But all were acting on behalf of their respective constituencies, particularly at the beginning. Only shortly before, the people each of them represented had been in a particularly ugly war with each other. It was to be expected that they did not trust each other, and

I didn't know how independently each was able to operate as members of the Board of the new central bank.

The formal appointment of the Board signaled the
beginning of serious discussions of the draft central bank
law. I returned to Sarajevo on November 10, 1996, with
my IMF colleagues Chris Ryan and Tobias Asser. Chris
was a capable and affable Australian economist who had
returned to my department for a second try at working
in the IMF. After another several years he gave up living away from home, and returned again to Australia.

*Manojlo Ćorić (Governor of
the NBRS and Bosnian Serb
member of the board of the
CBBH)*

He worked closely with me for the next year in Bosnia. Tobias was one
of the IMF's senior lawyers, from a distinguished Dutch family. He had
worked with me on the draft law in Washington and had the primary
responsibility for the legal drafting.

Thus on November 11, I again found myself at the long boardroom
table in the NBBH building in Sarajevo, this time with high expecta-
tions of serious progress. Mr. Ćorić arrived with a colleague from Pale,
the little skiing village next to Sarajevo near the site of the 1985 Winter Olympics. Pale was evolving into the headquarters city in the *Republika Srpska* for most government functions as the hard liners, mostly
located in the south, strengthened their hold on the RS government.
Actually Mr. Ćorić was living in Belgrade, after having fled Sarajevo
during the war. Mr. Pelivan entered from his office in the building.
Kasim entered from his private entrance that connected his office to the
boardroom. Serge Robert, the IMF-chosen Governor-designate, chaired
the meetings. Serge was himself just getting to know the other newly
appointed members of the Board.

As our work was to faithfully transform the monetary framework
provisions of the Dayton agreement into reality, we were in some formal sense working on behalf of the OHR. Thus Thomas Schiller from
the OHR participated in all of our meetings on the central bank law.
Thomas was in his early thirties. He was a very warm and engaging
young German with a handsome, welcoming, and enthusiastic smile.
He was there, working hard, because he cared and wanted to make a
difference. Working with such people was one of the great pleasures of
my job.

The meeting opened with gentle words of greeting to everyone from Serge. Serge was a Frenchman and had all of the charm that a French-man is expected to have. The others spoke in turn. Since the meeting was being held in the NBBH building, Kasim as unofficial host was first. He was at his diplomatic best. Neither Manojlo Ćorić nor Jure Pelivan spoke English so interpreters were used when anyone spoke. Mr. Ćorić wasted no time in expressing his displeasure at meeting in the NBBH building and insisted that the meeting be held in the more neu-tral office space of the OHR (also in Sarajevo) and that the meetings be rotated between the Entities. He stated that he was not authorized to negotiate in this Bosniac building. This was followed by a stern lecture from Kasim about the need to be cooperative now that the war was over. This speech brought a rebuttal from Ćorić. My heart was sinking.

Following this factious opening, Serge, using all of his considerable diplomatic skills, suggested that he would endeavor, subject to practi-cality, to spread the meeting locations, but that as we were where we were, we should proceed today, even with informal discussions. With that, the meeting proceeded. We began our long trip through the draft, paragraph by paragraph. We continued to meet in the NBBH building each day and arranged for the final meeting on Friday to take place in Pale, in Paradise Lodge, the seat at that time of the Republic of Serbia's government.

Every day began with some kind of political diatribe by a different Board member. Each day two of them were the paradigms of coopera-tion and reason and the third was difficult and unreasonable. These roles rotated. But each day the initial diatribe grew shorter and softer (until the last difficult day in Pale).

POLITICAL AND SYMBOLIC ISSUES

The detailed economic issues that must be addressed when designing the structure of a currency board consumed most of the time we spent on drafting the law in Washington and almost none of our time dis-cussing and refining it with our counterparts in Bosnia and Herzegov-ina. What might be called the more political issues of power and symbols, which took up almost none of our time in Washington, dominated at

Sarajevo and Pale. An inappropriate choice of words (to one of the three ethnic Board members) could erupt into an hour of sharp exchanges over issues I could hardly understand.

Our goal was to implement the Dayton agreement, which was meant to keep the country together while respecting its ethnic diversity. A single monetary system with a single currency was one of the important elements for holding the country together and facilitating its economic recovery. The officials in the Federation and the RS, on the other hand, were very concerned with ensuring that the structure being put in place would not prevent them from functioning separately in the event of separation (with or without another war).

"Glasses"

Obviously, the national currency to be issued by the new Central Bank would need a name and a design for its bank notes, and we knew that agreement on these would be difficult. However, these issues could be saved for the end, since they had no implications for the central bank law itself. In the discussions of the draft law with our counterparts, we used the name "glasses" (my imagination was running thin at that time) for the unnamed new currency to facilitate our discussions of the law.

Intense discussions ensued over the meaning of a single currency and of legal tender. The Bosnian Serbs wanted their own version of *glasses,* which would be issued by their branch of the Central Bank but would be legal tender throughout the country and fully interchangeable with the Federation version. This, in their view, was consistent with the essence of a single monetary area and system. Manojlo presented us with a number of lessons in the great diversity of currency arrangements in the world, in order to fortify his argument that a single currency could have two versions. He liked the example of the Scottish pound in the UK. We pointed out that the twelve different versions of Federal Reserve notes in the United State resulted from the fact that the twelve Reserve Banks were legally separate entities and that the branches of the new central bank would not be legally separate. Furthermore, the differences between the twelve versions of Federal Reserve notes are barely noticeable (and with the new dollar notes issued in the U.S. in the late 1990s,

Varieties of single currency arrangements

American currency[1] is issued by its central bank, the Federal Reserve. However, as a legal and technical matter, the U.S. actually has twelve central banks—The Federal Reserve Bank of Boston (District 1 or A) through the Federal Reserve Bank of San Francisco (District 12 or L). Nonetheless the U.S. only has one monetary policy overseen by the Board of Governors of the Federal Reserve System in Washington DC and the Presidents of the individual Reserve Banks. Until 1996 each Reserve Bank issued its own version of these Federal Reserve Notes. However, few Americans noticed the subtle differences between these notes (the name, seal, district number, and letter of the issuing bank) because to the casual eye they were identical. These differences have now largely vanished, with only the district bank's letter surviving in each note's unique serial number.

The earlier history of American currency is much more complicated and diverse. The original colonies each issued their own paper currencies starting with the Massachusetts Bay Colony in 1690. In 1775 the Continental Congress authorized the issue of paper currency, infamously known as continentals (as in "not worth a Continental"). Following the short lives of the First and the Second Banks of the United States (1791–1811 and 1816–1836) individual banks freely issued their own currencies during what became known as the free banking era. Over 8,000 banks issued their own notes during this period. Under the National Bank Act of 1863, the Federal government licensed banks that issued their own notes under more organized and supervised conditions. The one dollar silver certificates (originally redeemable for silver) were issued by the U.S. Treasury from 1876 to 1963.

—continued on page 35

are now gone altogether). We argued that the Belgian (and Canadian) bank notes provided a good model of reflecting their countries' ethnic diversity by emphasizing one group and language on one denomination and the other on another denomination, but with only one version of each denomination.

There was indeed more diversity in the world's monetary arrangements than I had realized. Even the monetary history of the United States was full of diverse arrangements, which Manojlo thankfully did not cite. We were getting to know one another and what different words and concepts meant to each of us through the intermediation of interpreters. It was not easy to clearly and definitively understand each other, especially when I suspect not everyone wished to be clearly understood all the time. To test whether a single currency with two designs was really a single currency in the minds of the Board members, I pointed out that non-cash *glasses* (deposit balances) had no design at all, only amounts that could not be distinguished in terms of which branch had issued them. To my relief, this was understood and accepted by all without hesitation.

It was particularly important for the Bosnian Serbs that the new monetary arrangements would not interfere with their close financial ties with Yugoslavia (Belgrade). The Yugoslav dinar was legal tender in the RS and domestic payments were made in Yugoslav dinar and settled through the Yugoslav-wide payment bureau system. However, the Yugoslav dinar was not a freely convertible currency. Thus, the introduction of a new national currency, which would be the sole legal tender in both the Federation and the RS was an important and sensitive issue. It was fully accepted by everyone that people would remain free to transact in the currencies of their mutual choice. Nonetheless, only *glasses* would be legal tender. We had lengthy discussions with our counterparts about what legal tender meant, leading to a long and unique article in the law setting out the implications of legal tender.

Upon its establishment in 1694, the **Bank of England**[2] began issuing notes, which following the practice of the time were individually issued to depositors of gold and silver coins in the precise amount of the deposits for which (in whole or in part) they were redeemable. From 1745, Bank of England notes were generally issued in standard printed amounts but were personally signed by the issuing Cashier. It issued the first fully printed notes only in 1855. The Bank's notes were made legal tender in 1833 and the adoption of the Bank Charter Act of 1844 was the beginning of its eventual monopoly on note issue in England and Wales.

Scottish banks[3] provide yet another example of the diversity of currency arrangements and were specifically referred to by the Serb representatives to the central bank law drafting sessions. Starting in 1704, Scottish banks began to print their own pound notes. The Bank of Scotland, the Royal Bank of Scotland, and Clydesdale Bank continue to do so today. The notes of each bank look nothing like those of the other banks. The Banknote Act of 1845 established British control over all note issues in the United Kingdom and permitted the continued but regulated issue of notes by Scottish banks. Scottish bank notes are redeemable for the same value of Bank of England notes.

Branches

The role of branches was also a hotly debated issue. Having relaxed somewhat the initial position that there should be separate central banks in the two Entities, Manojlo sought to preserve as much autonomy as possible for the Entities by assigning important powers to the branches of the Central Bank that would be established in each Entity. There was even a discussion of whether the foreign exchange backing required by the currency board arrangement would be owned by and invested separately by each branch.

The Bosnian Serb position was a mix of symbolism and substance. Indeed the issues on which all three representatives took strong positions were often a mix of symbolism and substance. The Bosnian Serbs had long insisted that the branches be named "central banks," even if they were subordinate to the Headquarters of the Central Bank in Sarajevo. They did not wish, it seems, to see the words "Central Bank of Bosnia and Herzegovina" on the branch office in the RS. Of greater substance, they fought for the law to explicitly delegate significant authority to the branches. We resisted.

The Board

The constitution adopted in Dayton had several unusual provisions that became the sources of considerable discussion when drafting the central bank law. The first of these was the sharing of one (Federation) vote by the Bosniac and Croat members of the Board. Did this mean that if they disagreed no Federation vote would be cast or that opposing half votes would be cast? In fact, there is no circumstance under which it would matter which interpretation was given. However, considerable discussion arose over the difference of treatment of the RS member and the Federation members. The Dayton agreement specified the ethnicity of the two Federation members of the Board, but did not do so for the RS member. Could, for example, a Bosniac (Muslim) from Banja Luka hold the RS seat? It would be interesting to know what was said during the discussions in Dayton that resulted in that language. To my mind, it was the result of the fundamental peculiarity of dividing Bosnia's three ethnic majority regions into two Entities. The central bank law that was finally adopted, with the agreement of the Office of the High Representative (OHR), ignored this asymmetry, and provided for a Croat and a Bosniac from the Federation, and a Serb from the RS.

The Dayton agreement also states that the Governor may break tie votes of the Board. However, this statement provoked another controversy—one of the last issues resolved before the central bank law was approved—and that was whether the Governor was a regular member of the Board. If so, the Governor could create a tie and then break it. As a member of the Board, the Governor would also be entitled to vote. Thus, if the Federation members disagreed (and either split their vote or cast no vote) and the Governor and the RS member disagreed, the Board would be tied and the Governor could then cast another vote to break the tie and the Governor's views would prevail. Under the other interpretation, the Governor would only vote when there was a tie and the same configuration of votes as in the preceding example would result in the Serb's views prevailing. The interpretation that won out in the Central Bank Law—the interpretation we gave to the Dayton agreement—was that the Governor was a regular voting member of the Board.

There was also a difference of views among the members of the Board over whether they should have executive powers or not. Though practice varies among central banks, our view was that the Board should only approve policy and monitor its implementation. A conflict of interest could arise if Board members also executed policy. Furthermore, as the Board members had more explicit ties to the government, central bank autonomy would be enhanced if they had no executive powers. The difference of views among the Board members had mainly to do with their personal desires to be devoted full time (or not) to the work of the CBBH and the related salary implications. The Central Bank Law finally adopted does not give executive powers to the Board.

SUBSTANTIVE ISSUES

As I mentioned earlier, the above topics overwhelmingly dominated our discussions with the Board. There is, of course, another set of issues having to do with the monetary responsibilities of the currency board, which occupies most of the academic discussion of currency boards. As I noted earlier, these issues were primarily debated among ourselves in Washington.

CBBH bills

The most important protection of the Central Bank from misuse was to forbid in the law any central bank credit to anyone. Thus the CBBH would not be permitted to lend to the government nor to banks. With no lender of last resort, a banking system that needs liquidity in the aggregate (i.e., needs additional balances in its reserve/settlement accounts with the central bank) can sell foreign exchange or domestic assets to the central bank. But the sale of foreign currency assets held abroad (a central bank operating under currency board rules can only sell reserve account balances for the foreign currency it is required to hold as backing) can only be settled with two-day value (one day at best when attempting to correct a reserve shortfall late in the day). Thus, the sale of foreign exchange is not an option for a bank that discovers it needs additional liquidity late in the day. If, however, the central bank could buy domestic assets as long as it did not violate its 100 percent foreign exchange cover requirement, the settlement of such a transaction could be confirmed immediately, giving rise to an immediate credit to the selling bank's reserve account.

We considered several options for providing banks with this kind of instrument for liquidity management. One approach would be to permit the CBBH to purchase domestic government securities to the extent that it held foreign exchange assets in excess of its backing requirement. Another, which has been adopted by Bulgaria's currency board, would be to allow the CBBH to extend settlement credit (by a separate department of the Bank) to the extent that it held foreign exchange assets in excess of its backing requirement. We chose to permit the CBBH to issue and to buy back its own bills and to require it to include its bills held by the public in its monetary liabilities that required foreign exchange backing. Serge favored this approach, which was working well in Haiti. This was a very conservative approach to giving the market a liquidity management asset that could be highly useful for very short-term liquidity adjustments (in either direction). The CBBH could not be expansionary via this instrument, because it could only buy back bills that it had previously issued and the issuance (sale) of its bills was itself contractionary. The public could purchase CBBH bills with foreign exchange. In that case, both monetary liabilities and assets of the CBBH would increase by the same amount. The public could also buy CBBH bills with domestic cash or bank deposits (both monetary liabilities of the CBBH). In that case, the mix of the CBBH's monetary liabilities would change, but not the total.

Reserve requirement

We also recommended a reserve requirement uniformly applied to all bank deposits. The instrument had two purposes. By increasing or decreasing the requirement ratio, the CBBH could affect the money multiplier and thus wholly or in part neutralize monetary shocks, thus providing an instrument of limited monetary control. Once the required ratio had been reduced to zero, however, its expansionary potential would have been spent. We recommended that the required ratio of reserves to deposits be set and held at a moderate level (say 10 percent) and adjusted downward only in the event of a sudden and temporary contraction of liquidity. Required reserves were to be remunerated at market interest rates.

The more important purpose of the requirement, which was to be met on an average basis over each month, was to provide an additional instrument to banks for liquidity management. Required reserves could be used on any day for the settlement of that day's payments, as long as appropriately higher levels were held on other days. For example, this option could be exercised while waiting for the delivery two days later of the proceeds of a sale of foreign exchange.

Gross assets and liabilities and borrowing

As noted above, we had proposed a gross monetary assets and liabilities approach to the foreign exchange backing requirement because it was easier to define and because it opened the possibility for the Central Bank to borrow foreign exchange abroad to maintain the required backing.

We preferred a comprehensive definition of monetary liabilities in order to provide no exceptions to the backing requirement. The draft law we prepared defined gross monetary liabilities of the CBBH as the sum of:

1. all outstanding bank notes, coins, and debt securities issued by the Central Bank; and

2. the credit balances of all accounts maintained on the books of the Central Bank by account holders.

IMF deposits

Other modern currency boards exclude deposits due to the IMF from the central bank's liabilities that must be backed with foreign exchange.

These deposits reflect the local currency counterpart of any purchases of foreign exchange by the country from the IMF.[4] Normally the government sells the foreign exchange it purchases from the IMF (or anyone else, for that matter) to its central bank in exchange for a deposit of an equivalent amount of domestic currency. The domestic currency deposit of the government can then be used to provide the IMF with the funds it must hold in its deposit with the central bank. The operation enlarges the foreign exchange reserves of the central bank and its monetary liabilities to the same extent. Thus, such an operation has little point for a currency board.

Often, however, purchases from the IMF are used to supplement the government's budget resources, in which case the government borrows the domestic currency from the central bank that it must transfer to the IMF as the counterpart of its purchase. In such cases the central bank then acquires a claim on the government matched by its liability to the IMF (the IMF's deposit). The argument in favor of this exception to the rule of no central bank credit is that the credit, while expansionary, is embedded in and controlled by the conditionality of the economic policy arrangement supported by the IMF. Those of us working on Bosnia and Herzegovina argued within the IMF that no exceptions to the currency board rules against central bank credit should be introduced, not even for the IMF. This view was accepted but not without a struggle with the IMF's Treasurer's Department (now called the Finance Department).

Government deposits

The definition of monetary liabilities that we proposed also included government deposits. Increases in government deposits at the central bank normally result from the payment of taxes or of other obligations of the public to the government. Thus, bank reserves (and reserve money) drop by the amount of the increase in government balances with the central bank. Though the shift of the central bank's monetary liabilities from deposits of banks to deposits of government does not change its total liabilities, it significantly changes the liquidity of the banking system. Most "smoothing" operations of central banks are directed at neutralizing this effect so that the normal fluctuations of government balances do not translate into fluctuations in banking sector liquidity and the money supply.

We debated for a while whether or not to exclude government deposits (thus adopting a definition that would coincide with reserve money, i.e., the monetary base). The case for excluding them (reducing the banking sector liquidity consequences of fluctuations in government deposits) also underlies the definition of reserve money as the aggregate that results in a more stable money multiplier (central government deposits are generally not included in the definition of reserve money or broad money.) If we excluded government deposits from the backing requirement, an increase in such deposits would reduce the CBBH's monetary liabilities with no change in its foreign exchange assets. This reduction would automatically open a surplus of foreign exchange assets over liabilities that might be used to offset the drop in reserve money. The resulting excess of foreign exchange would allow a limited range for stabilizing activism by the Central Bank that might strengthen the functioning of the currency board arrangement.

Government deposits can also increase from the proceeds of foreign borrowing, in which case there is no decline in reserve money to neutralize. In addition, excluding government deposits from the backing requirement would allow offsetting temporary fluctuations in reserve money only if it were accompanied by limited open-market operations or lending in domestic currency. This approach seemed to us to open too many doors that might result in abuse, thus undermining the currency board arrangement. While in some settings such an instrument might be defended, we concluded that in Bosnia and Herzegovina, with the high degree of distrust of each side toward the others, we should stay closer to the pure form of currency board arrangements. Thus in the end we rejected the idea and included government deposits in the definition of monetary liabilities, while recognizing that dealing with the liquidity consequences of changes in reserve money induced by the behavior of government deposits would be an important challenge for the system.

Foreign borrowing

As already noted, the use of gross rather than net assets and liabilities opens the door for a central bank to borrow abroad in order to cover any foreign exchange backing shortfall (as might occur if the central bank's operations incurred a loss or from investment losses in the value of the bank's foreign exchange assets). This possibility might also be abused if, for example, the central bank could extend credit as long as it had foreign exchange backing. Thus, we proposed two safeguards. The primary one was the absolute prohibition against the Central Bank extending credit of any kind. A secondary one was a limit on the amount of foreign borrowing by the Central Bank of 50 percent of its capital and reserves.

SUCCESSION OR NEW BANK

We briefly discussed whether the new Central Bank would succeed the NBBH and thus acquire all of its assets and liabilities, or be established as a completely new institution. Serge and Kasim thought that succession was the way to go. However, we did not have a clear idea of what the NBBH's assets and liabilities were; and I did not want the new bank encumbered by the legacies of the old one. Furthermore, the NBRS did not fit easily into a succession model, which would raise unnecessary problems. I argued that the CBBH should be a new institution (with the extra legal work that that would entail) and take over only those assets and liabilities from existing institutions that were appropriate to its monetary function. This proposal was quickly accepted. We would start with a clean institution with a clean balance sheet. The subsequent problems with the liquidation of the NBBH, after it transferred its monetary liabilities and equivalent German mark assets, proved the wisdom of this choice.

The new Central Bank was to replace all existing ones. The RS and the Bosniac part of the Federation both had their own central banks, the NBRS and NBBH. The Croat majority part of the Federation had no central bank; but its payment bureau, the ZAP, performed some central bank functions. Thus the NBRS and the NBBH were to go out of existence by transferring their monetary liabilities to the new Central Bank along with German mark assets of equivalent value with which to back these liabilities. The NBBH's monetary liabilities consisted of its Bosnian dinar deposit liabilities to banks and to the government and Bosnian dinar bank notes in circulation. The NBRS's monetary liabilities consisted of its Yugoslav dinar deposit liabilities to banks and to the government. Transferring these liabilities to the CBBH raised different issues for the NBBH and the NBRS.

In addition to these two central banks, the payment system in each of the three ethnic majority regions in Bosnia and Herzegovina was dominated by its own unique payment bureau (the ZPP in the Bosniac majority area; the ZAP in the Croat majority area; and the SPP in the Serbian majority area). As I will explain in more detail in the next chapter, each successor payment bureau in BiH had (in practice) a monopoly over domestic non-cash payments in the area it served. As a wartime measure, the ZAP and ZPP also permitted the public to deposit German mark bank notes and to make domestic payments by transferring them within the payment bureau system.

In principle, the payment bureaus should have had no monetary liabilities, operating purely as third-party payment-order processors for banks. However, the ZPP had started accepting DM deposits from the public during the war and had held them in DM bank notes in their vaults. These deposits were more like lock box operations, and we referred to them as "custodial deposits." They were fully backed with German mark bank notes by their very nature. Furthermore, the ZAP, which was performing some central bank functions for its area, had DM and kuna liabilities to banks and the government. The ZAP held DM bank notes equivalent to its DM deposit liabilities and kuna bank notes and claims equivalent to its kuna deposit liabilities to banks and the government. These kuna claims were the source of its quasi-central bank function. All of these deposit liabilities with the ZPP and the ZAP were to be withdrawn. We assumed that a significant amount of the public's DM deposits with the ZPP would be placed with banks and that most of the banks' DM and kuna deposits with the ZAP would be placed with the CBBH in the form of *glasses*. As kuna was a freely usable currency, we assumed that some amount of those deposits would be converted into *glasses* and deposited with the CBBH. For this purpose the kuna would first need to be exchanged for DM in the market.

The NBBH was the only institution in Bosnia that had issued its own currency, the Bosnian dinar. The NBRS had issued its own currency for a short period in 1993 and '94 but it was wiped out by hyperinflation at the same time the old Yugoslav dinar was wiped out, and it was never replaced. The NBBH would transfer to the CBBH its Bosnian dinar bank note liabilities and its Bosnian dinar bank notes in its vaults, plus an amount of DM equivalent to issued Bosnian dinar (those in circulation rather than in the vaults of the NBBH). The Bosnian dinar in circulation would then be exchanged for the new bank notes of the new Central Bank once these were available.

The NBBH had issued its dinar at the exchange rate of DM = 100 dinar and had operated (most of the time) as a currency board. Thus that was clearly the rate at which the German mark counterpart to be transferred to the CBBH would be determined and at which the bank notes in circulation would ultimately be redeemed for the new notes of the CBBH. Similarly, bank balances of Bosnian dinars with the NBBH would be transferred to the CBBH with an equivalent value of DM using the same exchange rate. Banks would receive an equivalent value of deposits at the CBBH in *glasses* (still nameless). This was all straightforward and uncontroversial.

The situation with the NBRS was more complicated. The NBRS had no bank notes of its own in circulation, but had "issued" Yugoslav dinars (YUD) against German marks or debits to banks' YUD accounts at the NBRS. It exchanged the YUD bank notes for DM at official exchange rates, which were significantly out of line with street rates. The NBRS acquired the YUD bank notes from Belgrade by selling DM to the National Bank of Yugoslavia (NBY) at the official exchange rate. Unfortunately most of the DM bank notes in the NBRS's vaults had been sold to the NBY for this purpose and were being kept there (in Banja Luka) for the NBY to avoid physical shipment. In short, they no longer belonged to the NBRS. Thus the NBRS did not have sufficient DM bank notes to back its YUD monetary liabilities. In fact, the NBRS was more accurately thought of as an agent for the National Bank of

Yugoslavia for the issue of YUD. Its YUD liabilities to banks were, in principle, backed by claims on the NBY in Belgrade.

There was a brief debate over whether the NBRS should be permitted to transfer its monetary liabilities to the CBBH with an equivalent value of YUD. The proposal by Manojlo assumed that the amount of YUD required for this purpose would be determined at the official exchange rate. I argued that YUD could not be accepted even at the street rate because the CBBH should only hold German marks against its monetary liabilities and the YUD was not a freely usable currency that the CBBH could exchange into German mark. I maintained that the CBBH should only accept and hold German marks and that the NBRS (and the ZAP) would need to convert any other "foreign" currency that it held (YUD and kuna) into DM first. The Bosnian Serbs were obviously not very happy with this proposal, since it forced them to recognize that the NBRS was insolvent.

Manojlo announced that the monetary liabilities of the NBRS could not be transferred (deposit liabilities to banks and government with an equivalent value of DM) until the end of the six-year currency board period. Rather than insist on the impossible (or at least the improbable), we agreed that as long as the NBRS closed its operations, transferring its deposit liabilities somewhere, banks in the RS would only be required to hold deposits of *glasses* with the CBBH to the extent of the reserve requirement. It was also clear that government deposits in the RS would never be placed in the CBBH, and there was no point in insisting on it.

Because the kuna was freely useable in the market with a market determined exchange rate, we anticipated no serious problems to the proposed unwinding of DM and kuna deposits with the ZAP. Down the line, reality proved to be more complicated.

FRIDAY, NOVEMBER 15, 1996

As agreed on the first day of this visit, the last meeting was held in Pale. Pale is almost a suburb of Sarajevo—a drive normally of fifteen minutes from the NBBH. Tobias, Chris, and I gathered in the morning with

Serge, Kasim, and Jure at the NBBH for the short drive. Ms. Vashkun-lahti from the OHR also joined us. Thomas Schiller, who had been sitting in on all of our meetings from the OHR had temporarily returned to his home in Frankfurt the day before. We also took two of our interpreters.

In the intensity of our work, I often forgot what our local counterparts were going through. The two interpreters were young ladies from Sarajevo. One was a Croat whose life-long Sarajevo home was currently occupied by Bosniacs. Both of them had been to Pale many times to ski but not since the start of the war five years earlier. I noticed them conversing nervously and it belatedly occurred to me that there might be a security concern in their minds about the trip. Indeed there was, but they were more curious to visit their old haunt than concerned about security, so adventure won out.

It had snowed in the night and continued to snow lightly in the morning. Our short trip first took us past the famous Vijecnica library that had been deliberately burned down at the very beginning of the war. Then we climbed up the mountain on the edge of Sarajevo toward Pale. There was a tunnel just before the border, which had been damaged during the war and was under repair. On the many trips to come between Sarajevo and Pale we sometimes had to drive around the tunnel, sometimes through it, using a single lane. On this occasion we had to drive around on a dirt road older than the tunnel, a treacherous route in the snow. Not far from the tunnel on the Pale side, the NATO soldiers at the border saw our UN license plates and waved us through.

On the outskirts of Pale we turned right and proceeded up the final hill to Paradise Lodge. The lodge had been a favorite place with skiers who did not want to stay in facilities on the slopes themselves. It was small but had a beautiful view of the surrounding area. From a security point of view it was ideal. It was now the headquarters for Momčilo Krajišnik, the Serb Joint President. The entrance was guarded by Bosnian Serb soldiers who checked our passports but were expecting us. I was surprised that security seemed so relaxed.

We parked our cars and walked into the relatively open building. Though soldiers were standing around, they seemed to pay no attention to us. We were greeted by Manojlo, now on his home ground (though he is actually from Sarajevo but currently living in Belgrade) and ushered into a relatively small conference room with a commanding view of a snow-covered Pale below. Manojlo and his Serbian colleagues joined us and the room filled with smoke as the meeting began.

Since this room was smaller than the boardroom in the NBBH, and since all of our counterparts puffed on cigarettes almost continuously, the room filled with smoke rapidly. In addition to this unpleasantness, the Serbs provided their own interpreter. She was a young girl with a seriously disfigured face—the result of some horrible war incident—who sat quietly facing us. She said nothing throughout the day until TV cameras were brought in for an afternoon meeting with President Krajišnik. His office was next to our conference room.

During the week we had narrowed the areas of disagreement to a few key issues, which we hoped to resolve during this final meeting. Our goal was to have an agreed draft that the Board could present to the Joint Presidency for adoption. We were to be disappointed. Early in the day Manojlo backtracked on some earlier agreements. Jure, who normally said little, but on occasions played the peacemaker by offering sensible interpretations or compromises, began uttering things none of us could really comprehend. Clearly the three of them had had detailed discussions with their political bosses. Manojlo had the advantage because the President, his boss, was in the office next door. Manojio called for several breaks during the day, to consult with his superiors. At the time, I assumed that he desired to accept several of the compromises his government had opposed and was attempting to get the people next door to change his instructions.

The smoke in the room was unbearable. At one point Tobias stood up and went to the closed window (as it was very cold outside), opened it and stuck his head out for a few minutes of fresh air. He whispered to me that he had been close to passing out. Throughout the day the disfigured Serbian girl faced us, adding to the already high tension.

At one point in the afternoon, when Manojlo backtracked on yet another earlier agreement, Tobias went ballistic, declaring that we would then go back to the beginning and withdraw all of the concessions we had made during the week. I heard myself demanding that Tobias (my senior, but a subordinate on this mission) be quiet. He only half honored my instruction. We were tired, discouraged, and choking on smoke; and I was developing a headache. The meeting careened toward total collapse. It became clear that we would not achieve our objective, and I began to formulate our fallback position in my mind.

We had agreed upon most of the provisions of the draft. We agreed that afternoon that the IMF would publish the version of the draft supported by my team, in light of the agreements that had been reached during the week, and issue a report on the few issues of remaining disagreement. Serge would continue to work toward their resolution after our departure.

With matters up in the air, we were taken into President Krajišnik's office in front of TV cameras to receive little silver medals and a statement of his appreciation for our work. As we walked into his office, Tobias whispered to me that he was inclined to make a citizen's arrest of a war criminal. In our exhausted condition at the time, I couldn't tell how serious he might be. Several years later the War Crimes Tribunal in The Hague indeed indicted Krajišnik as a war criminal. He was arrested by French troops of the NATO Stabilization Force (SFOR) on April 3, 2000, and turned over to the War Crimes Tribunal.[5]

The next day I flew back to Zagreb and on to Frankfurt, from where I would fly home to Washington the next day. As I was walking through the Frankfurt airport toward the hated but oh-so-convenient Airport Sheraton Hotel, I spotted Thomas Schiller coming toward me. He was, he explained, on his way to meet his wife on an incoming flight. I won't even speculate about the odds of such a chance meeting in such a large place. I started to report to him on the final meeting that he had missed. No need, he said, Ms. Vashkunlahti had already emailed him a full report.

4 THE PAYMENT BUREAU SYSTEM

BANK PAYMENT SYSTEMS

I had first met Thomas Schiller a few months earlier in connection with our work on the payment system. I had liked him immediately. He knew little about payment systems, but he understood the importance for economic integration of the ability to make payments across the boundaries of the three ethnic areas. He also had a very practical mind, understood the normal day-to-day needs of everyday life, and was a tenacious problem solver. Thus when I first met him during my September 1996 visit to Sarajevo, he was already at work on what became the only inter-regional means of "non-cash" payments for over a year.

A "payment" consists of transferring the ownership of a mutually acceptable asset. The standardization of the assets used for this purpose resulted in the "invention" of "money." An asset becomes "money" because of its widespread acceptability as a payment asset (e.g., gold). For example, when I buy a grandee cappuccino from you, I pay you by handing you a dollar. However, cash payments are generally made only face-to-face—hand-to-hand. Even the post office warns us never to send cash in the mail. If I wish to make a payment more indirectly, a more complex means of payment is needed.

It would take a great deal of our valuable time to make all payments in cash face-to-face. Even if we outsourced the work to runners, it would be very expensive for someone to walk to the power company or the phone company with cash to pay the monthly bill. Paying someone to drive to New York City to deliver cash to pay for our subscription to *Newsweek* would swamp the cost of the subscription. The evolution of payment systems, like much else in the economy, is motivated by the desire to reduce the cost of the activity (i.e., of making payments). Banks are first and foremost places for the safekeeping of cash and for facilitating the making of payments with cash. The systems of payment they have developed are designed to minimize the cost (time, and money) and maximize the safety and convenience of making payments (generally by transferring claims to bank balances rather than cash). However, every step to reduce the number of face-to-face cash payments introduces some risk into the process. Speed and cost saving, thus, must be balanced against maintenance of adequate safety. The added risks must be limited and properly managed.

Non-cash payments consist of transferring ownership of deposits of money in banks and can be made across time and space. If I buy a *Dungeons and Dragons* game software from your Web site, I might pay you by mailing you a check for $50 (or an electronic check over the Internet). The check is an order to my bank to transfer $50 to you via your bank. In banking systems around the world such transfers are ultimately made (settled) by transferring bank deposit balances that banks maintain with their central banks. When you deposit my $50 check in your bank, your bank needs some way of collecting it from my account at my bank. Your bank does this (ultimately) by transferring $50 from my bank's deposits with the central bank to its own account with the central bank. For this purpose very specific rules and procedures have been developed and put in place. However, between countries (or between the war-separated regions of Bosnia and Herzegovina) there is no one "central bank" on whose books the ultimate transfer can be made.

For purposes of cross border payments, a common depository is needed for the transfer of deposits between the two banks. Correspondent banking provides one such arrangement. If your software business is in England (never mind that it can be accessed on the World Wide

Web from anywhere in the world), you will collect my $50 check using a correspondent bank. If my bank in the U.S., the Bank of Washington, maintains balances of U.S. dollars in a London bank, say Citibank of London, in which your English bank, Standard Charter, is also prepared to hold U.S. dollars, my payment to you in England can be made by electronic messages between the Bank of Washington and Standard Charter (and Citibank of London) that result in a transfer from the Bank of Washington's account at the Citibank of London to Standard Charter's account at Citibank. This procedure abstracts from the need to exchange one currency (U.S. dollars) into another (U.K. pounds) that is often involved in cross-border payments.

Depending on the monetary and exchange rate regime of the countries involved, a payment between parties in two countries that involves the exchange of one currency into another can also ultimately result in transfers between their respective central banks (e.g., the Federal Reserve Bank and the Bank of England). Central banks hold reserves of other countries' currencies for this purpose (or of a "reserve" currency country, whose currency is widely used in the world, such as U.S. dollars or euros). In an earlier day, gold was held and transferred for this purpose. The arrangements described above render it possible to make a payment to someone in another location without a face-to-face delivery of cash.

The next huge cost saving in the systems that have evolved comes from "netting." Banks do not settle each and every payment individually. In the above example, the Bank of Washington may also be receiving payments for its customers from Standard Charter depositors. In fact, banks send and receive hundreds to many thousands of payments to and from other individual banks each day. Depending on the size of each payment (very large ones are usually settled individually), most of these payments and receipts are accumulated over the day and only the net amount owed by, say, the Bank of Washington to Standard Charter (or vice versa) is settled at day's end. If at the end of the day the Bank of Washington has paid more to Standard Charter than it has received from Standard Charter, it issues one payment instruction to Citibank of London for the net amount due, thus settling all of the payments between the two that day.

The cost saving of netting is enormous. The risk is that the Bank of Washington might fail during the day before final settlement of its net payments. If Standard Charter credits your account with my $50 in the morning (before actual net settlement at the end of the day), it is, in effect, extending you a loan for that amount on the expectation of collecting it at the end of the day from my bank (via its account with Citibank of London). If the Bank of Washington fails during the day and thus is unable to make the end of day net payment, Standard Charter is out the money that it will not be able to collect (or it may attempt to reclaim the $50 it put in your account). Thus such systems need to be designed carefully to clarify and minimize these risks.

THE POST-WAR SYSTEM IN BOSNIA

It was not generally possible to make a phone call from one of the three regions of Bosnia to another in 1996. The banks in one region had no correspondent banks in the other regions through which to make cross-regional payments. Some cross-regional payments were being made, however, through the use of foreign correspondent banks in Frankfurt, London, and New York.

During the war, the common currency of Yugoslavia gave way in each republic to the newly independent republic's own currency (the kuna in Croatia, and the Bosnia dinar in Bosnia and Herzegovina). The one exception was the Serbian majority area of the Republika Srpska, which continued to use Yugoslav dinars. However, during the Bosnian wars, each of the three regions also gave some quasi-official status to the German mark. Thus the DM was widely used in all three regions for making domestic payments during and following the Bosnian wars. Payments across regional boundaries could thus be made in German marks through a correspondent bank in Germany or elsewhere. Such foreign currency payments, which were performed for their customers by banks directly, were expensive and thus limited to relatively large amounts.

I have yet to explain the very complicated system of domestic payments that we found in Bosnia and Herzegovina. Understanding it was one of the most difficult challenges of our work there. Its true character seems to have been misunderstood by almost everyone. I remember getting my first totally confusing explanation from Maruf Burnazović,

Chairman of the Federation Payment Bureau, during the luncheon hosted by Kasim following our aborted first meeting on the central bank law in June. In that first go around, I was not very clear about who could or who had to make their payments through the payment bureaus, what kinds of deposits the bureaus held, which currencies were used, or what kinds of services were provided. More importantly, I didn't understand what assets and liabilities the payment bureaus really had.

The system of domestic non-cash payments that we found in BiH grew out of the Yugoslav Service for Social Bookkeeping (*Služba društvenog knjigovodstva*—SDK). SDK was a system designed to maximize state control over economic activities in a centrally planned economy. All domestic non-cash payments (deposit transfers) were made through the SDK. It had a legal monopoly on such payments. All enterprises were required by law to make their domestic payments through the SDK, except for wage payments, which they made in cash withdrawn from their accounts with the SDK. Cash was generally deposited and withdrawn from SDK offices, which outnumbered the offices of banks. Payment instructions (payment orders) were given at the offices of the SDK, and statements of account balances were picked up there. Each enterprise had a particular SDK office with which it did business. Banks did not seem to be involved.

The real confusion arose over the nature of the accounts maintained by the payment bureaus. My attempt to discuss and understand the system was not helped by the need to communicate through interpreters. But even if we had all been speaking in English (or Serbo-Croatian), we would have had difficulty understanding each other because my counterparts understood their system in different terms than I came to understand it.

The key to understanding the system is to realize that generally the payment bureau had no deposit liabilities and no assets of its own resulting from the deposits or withdrawals made at its teller windows. The exceptions were the wartime measures taken by the ZPP to accept DM deposits from the public and by the ZAP to provide some central bank functions for its banks by accepting DM and kuna deposits from banks and the government. Despite Maruf's insistence that the ZPP had its customers' deposits during the day, it was "merely" the bookkeeper and payment instruction executor on behalf of banks. The public similarly misunderstood the system. Because they went to their payment bureau office to make deposits and withdrawals and to issue payment instructions, they also thought of the bureau as having their money.

In fact, every customer dealing with the payment bureau had a "contract" with a bank, and every bank had a settlement (and required reserve) account with the central bank. Thus, any cash brought to the bureau was really being deposited in the customer's bank with the bureau acting as agent for the bank. The bureau recorded the customer's deposit with the customer's bank and credited that bank's account with the central bank. While the cash usually remained in the vaults of the bureau, it was actually owned by the central bank with the bureau acting as agent safekeeping the cash for the central bank. The Giro[1] account balances through which the system operated was a complicated bookkeeping system for tracking simultaneously the customers' deposit balances and those of their banks, as balances were transferred between customers (and their banks). At the end of each day, the net differences of the amounts paid from and received by each bank (and by their customers), were settled by transferring bank balances with the central bank from banks in deficit to those in surplus.

Though banks were not involved in providing domestic payment services, the payment bureaus had no deposit liabilities of their own and no assets against the Giro account balances they maintained for the public (except for the wartime measures already noted). All payment orders submitted by customers were accepted by the payment bureau only when the customer's Giro account had sufficient funds and were cleared every afternoon. The resulting net payment or receipt by each bank (on its own account or on account of its customers) increased or decreased each bank's Giro account balance. Though the payment bureau had no assets and liabilities of its own as a result of these activities, the public tended to think of their money being with the payment bureau and thus being safe. They would have been quite shocked had they lost money they "deposited" at a bureau office because their bank failed.

This was the way the system worked throughout Yugoslavia before the wars. It was one integrated system and unlike anything I had ever encountered before. However, with the wars and the independence of one republic after the other, the system began to break up into separate republican "systems." When war erupted in Bosnia and Herzegovina, its SDK offices in what is now the Federation, separated from the Yugoslav system that still operated in Republika Srpska (called the Serbian Payment Bureau—SPP) to form two separate systems, one in the Croat majority area (called the ZAP after the system in Croatia) and the other in the Bosniac majority area (called the ZPP). During the wars, these payment bureaus developed differently in each region, and they began to use different currencies (plus DM) so that when we arrived, there was no homogenous technical and operational base for the installation of a countrywide non-cash system of payment. This fact introduced the need to develop a means to make and settle payments across Entity borders.

CASH SETTLEMENT

Thomas had been discussing with the authorities in all three areas a less costly way of making such payments

> ### The Yugoslav system of payments—the SDK
>
> The *Služba Društvenog Knjigovodstva* (SDK) processed all payment orders that transferred deposit balances the public held with banks to other depositors within Yugoslavia. Each bank office (branch) had its unique SDK office through which its payment orders entered the nationally centralized system and from which it received payment orders from other banks or branches of its own bank on behalf of its customers. Thus the SDK had computer records of all payments made with bank deposits within Yugoslavia. The system was technically advanced and efficient.
>
> With regard to payments, the public dealt with the SDK rather than their own bank. They presented payment orders to the local office of the SDK and could "deposit" and withdraw currency from the same office. They could also check their bank account balance with the same SDK office. These arrangements led to general misunderstanding of the role of the SDK. The public (even some SDK officials) thought of the SDK as a deposit-taking institution like a bank. They tended to think of the deposits they thought they maintained with the SDK as a liability of the SDK. In fact, all deposits were with banks; the SDK actually had no deposit liabilities to the public. The SDK maintained shade balances of the public's bank accounts. The SDK was the accounting back office for the state-owned banks. If a bank had failed, the funds that the public thought they held with the SDK would have been reduced or lost as part of the liquidation of the failed bank.

than the use of foreign correspondent banks described above. The alternative of delivering German marks face-to-face across the borders between the three ethnic groups in Bosnia and Herzegovina would be much more costly. In addition, in 1996 Bosnians were generally afraid to cross from their own region into a neighboring one. At that time their car license plates clearly identified exactly where they were from. Thomas led the design of a payment order form for making payments in German marks using the payment bureaus that could be used by all three bureaus. The format, bank and customer identifiers, and other design features of the payment orders then in use, were no longer compatible among the three regions and their now-separate payment bureaus. Thus electronic messages of the type used within each system could not be used to send cross-border orders. The payment orders using the common form designed by Thomas were thus faxed between the headquarters of the three systems in Mostar, Banja Luka, and Sarajevo. Because telephone (fax) communication between the regions had not been fully restored and was very unreliable, Thomas arranged for the use of one of the few dedicated phone lines that had been set up for the Office of the High Representative.

A payment order from the Hotel Ruza in Mostar to pay DM to its napkin supplier in Sarajevo would result in a debit to the hotel's account in its bank in Mostar (Hypo Alpe-Adria Bank) and to Hypo bank's "due to banks in other regions" account with the Mostar ZAP (since that system had no central bank). When received by fax in the Sarajevo ZPP, the information would be entered into the ZPP system, resulting in credits to the napkin supplier's account with its bank (Central Profit Bank of Sarajevo) and to Central Profit Bank's "claims on banks in other regions" account with the ZPP. If there had been one central bank for the two areas, the interbank transfer would have taken the form of a debit of Hypo bank's account with the central bank and a credit to Central Profit bank's account with the same central bank. The central bank's liabilities would not change from this transfer of balances from one bank to another. This is an important point from the perspective of the operation of a currency board, which cannot extend credit to banks. But there was no such central bank yet. There was the central bank in Sarajevo (the NBBH) and the payment bureau in Mostar (ZAP) playing the role of a central bank. If the payments between the regions netted out to zero (if as many DM went from Mostar to Sarajevo as came from Sarajevo to Mostar), everything would be OK. But there was no assurance that such would be the case. The challenge was to find a way to make transfers between the ZAP and the ZPP (and the SPP) that would settle any net differences in the amounts of the interregional flows.

What if, in the above example, the central bank in Sarajevo (the NBBH) credited the account of Central Profit bank (and Central Profit credited the napkin suppliers account) by the amount of Hotel Ruza's payment? This would be an increase in the NBBH's deposit liabilities. What would be the matching asset? If the NBBH did not receive DM from Mostar to match the increase in its deposit liabilities to its banks, it would implicitly have extended a loan to the bank whose account it credited. Thus the matching asset would be an increase in credits to banks. Such a credit would violate currency board rules.

Having digressed to explain the above point, I would like to elaborate on it to include a way in which such a credit could come about even under a single central bank, because it was a major concern we had when setting up the CBBH. The payment bureau system of the area, whether one integrated system or three separate systems, used end-of-day net settlement. This means that all payment orders submitted during the day were cleared through the system on a provisional basis. At the end of the day, the net amount received by or paid out by each bank on behalf of itself and its customers was computed and those net amounts were settled. As already explained, those end-of-day settlements (within each central bank) were made by transferring bank balances within the central bank.

What if one bank did not have enough in its account with the central bank to pay for the net amount it owed all other banks that day (i.e., after taking into account all that it had received that day from other banks)? If the central bank credited all banks with the net funds due them, and debited the accounts of all of the banks that owned money on net, except for the bank that didn't have enough, the central bank would have implicitly loaned that bank the money it needed for the settlement. Where else would the money credited to the other banks come from? The central bank's liabilities would have increased. If the bank that is short of funds is unable to borrow them from other banks in time, the settlement could not take place for the system without the central bank's implicit loan to that bank.

Net settlement payment systems

The net settlement of payments through a clearinghouse can be very efficient. Generally every bank both makes (on its own account or on account of its depositors) and receives many payments each day. The inflow and outflow of funds to some extent at least offset each other. With periodic settlement of the net amounts due rather than the final settlement (irrevocable transfer of funds from one person or bank to another) of each individual payment, the number of actual funds transfers can be dramatically reduced. Only the net amount due to or from each participant and all others in the clearinghouse are "settled" periodically. Net settlement might occur once a day or several times during the day.

Net settlement suffers from complications when one of the participants does not have sufficient funds to complete the full amount required for net settlement. It is a mistake to think that the amounts due to or from everyone else can be recorded without overdrawing the central settlement account (usually at the central bank) of the deficient member. Net settlements must add up to zero for the group. If the central bank or one of the other participants is not able to lend the needed funds to the deficient bank, the net settlement cannot go forward (without removing at least some of the payments from the deficient bank and recalculating everyone's net position).

Modern electronic payments are reducing the cost savings of net settlement, but at the cost of more demanding liquidity management.

With a currency board that cannot extend credit, the only way out of this dilemma would be to remove all of the payment orders (or selected ones) from the deficient bank from the day's clearing and recalculate every bank's net position without the payment orders from the deficient bank. This would be a drastic measure and would have been very difficult technically for the payment bureaus in Bosnia to do. This fact was not so obvious to our counterparts in Bosnia and Herzegovina, and we had to explain it several times. This became a very real and serious problem for the CBBH.

The temporary system that Thomas helped put in place to settle net inter-regional payments entailed putting the required amount of German mark bank notes in the trunk of a Mercedes and driving them from the payment bureau of one region to the payment bureau of another. In the beginning, this operation required special security arrangements, which were provided by NATO. The net amounts due between regions were settled once a week, or more often if the amounts got too large. If at the end of the week banks in the Republika Srpska collectively owed DM 4 million to the banks in the ZAP system (as a result of the net cross-region payments of their customers), the car would drive DM 4 million in bank notes from the Banja Luka SPP to the Mostar ZAP. The transfer of the cash at the border eliminated the temporary credit between the ZAP and the SPP. The operation really drove home what a payment settlement means. When we wire our desperate children the $800 they need at college before a check could reach them, the cash does not travel down the wire.

The operations of a currency board are, of course, straightforward with regard to its core functions. It needs to have an efficient procedure for banks to buy and sell cash and non-cash forms of its currency, for safeguarding its bank notes, and for investing the foreign exchange counterpart in a safe, liquid manner that will generate enough income to finance its operations. The most challenging aspect of establishing the operations of the CBBH was to ensure that a very unusual system of domestic non-cash payments would not inadvertently result in the extension of credit by the CBBH to banks as part of the daily payment settlement process and to link the three separate payment bureau operations in the country into one national system of payment. The interface between the CBBH and the payment bureaus that operated in the three regions of Bosnia and Herzegovina posed particular challenges for the operations of the Central Bank that proved to be more than hypothetical.

5 ADOPTING THE CENTRAL BANK LAW

Though the failure to adopt a central bank law was holding up almost $2 billion in U.S. foreign aid, no progress was made on the draft between our November mission and my return February 17–28, 1997. On the broader political front, new Federation and RS governments were put in place just before Christmas; and a new Council of Ministers of BiH, with equal participation of all three ethnic groups, was confirmed by the Parliamentary Assembly in early January. All three Joint Presidents represented hard-line nationalist parties, and cooperation at that level was grudging or non-existent.

Serge continued diligently and patiently to meet with his Board and to discuss the draft law without any real progress. Serge's style was to gently prod the Board members but never to force them. I don't believe that he ever forced issues to a vote before the law was formally adopted. His approach resulted in very slow process. But one thing we clearly learned was that if we did not have a reasonable degree of agreement or acceptance, our counterparts would simply not cooperate. It was not realistic to try to force a result until they were ready to accept it.

The sham merger of the ZAP and the ZPP into one organization is a good example of the failure of force. The applications of force that had been truly effective were NATO air strikes during the war. They helped bring about its end. At particularly exasperating moments, Alessandro could occasionally be heard to mutter: "Threaten NATO air strikes."

Upon our return in February, we learned that in the previous month the payments bureau in the RS (the SPP) had been made a bank, the State Bank of Serbia. We assumed (correctly) that the RS authorities intended to transfer the assets and liabilities of the NBRS (e.g., bank and government deposits) to the new State Bank when the NBRS was liquidated as required by the draft central bank law when it was replaced by the CBBH.

In light of this development, I doubted that the authorities in RS would be prepared to transfer the monetary liabilities of the NBRS to the CBBH. For political reasons, they would surely be reluctant to transfer government deposits to the CBBH; and the settlement balances of banks, which were small in any event, were probably needed to support the continued settlement of Yugo dinar payments. While we considered it important that the public remain free to transact in any mutually agreed currency, we argued that the government (state and Entity) should be expected to shift its financial operations to the new state currency over the next year or two. But it seemed prudent not to push too hard. Thus we proceeded with an approach that would only gradually draw the RS into use of the new currency as confidence built. In any event, unlike the NBBH, the NBRS did not have sufficient freely usable foreign currency assets (e.g., excluding its YUD assets) to back the transfer of all of its monetary liabilities to the CBBH. So it was better to go slow.

STEVE HANKE

One event deserves mention because of its consequences for the final version of the central bank law adopted some months later. Professor Steve Hanke visited Bosnia in mid-December to promote the currency board idea. Hanke was the world's most vigorous and persistent advocate of currency boards. He had studied the world's experience with currency boards during the colonial period and had published extensively on the subject. There was hardly a country he had not visited in his promotion of the currency board approach to monetary stability.

Following his visit, he published an article in the Winter 1996/97 issue of *Central Banking* in which he praised the adopting of a currency board by Bosnia but criticized some of the features we were trying to give it in our draft law. Serious people can debate most of the points he raised, so I would like to share his criticisms with you and our reasons for disagreeing. In the end, the seeds he planted took root and won out, though I am still not sure whether it was because the Serbs required the changes he proposed or whether the U.S. Treasury did. He wrote (in part):

> Article VII of the Dayton/Paris Treaty requires the Bank of Bosnia and Herzegovina to operate as a currency board for at least six years.... The Article VII mandate was a bold stroke. The IMF team that drafted the Article should be congratulated.... A currency board system is particularly well-suited to Bosnia....
>
> But will the Bosnian currency board work? To work well, particularly in an unstable country with a deplorable monetary history and divisive politics, the board should be strictly orthodox, one in which the monetary authorities have their hands completely tied. Unfortunately, the Central Bank of Bosnia and Herzegovina's draft law of 15 November 1996 deviates from this standard of orthodoxy. Some of the more significant "loopholes" are:...
>
> 3. The Central Bank may engage in open market operations. This capacity will allow the Bank to operate in the interbank market, but not as a lender of last resort, a function that is explicitly prohibited by the law. This limited open market capacity should be eliminated, because its use could potentially unleash disruptive speculation, as it did in Argentina in 1995.
> 4. The Central Bank may set reserve requirements for commercial banks. This capacity allows the possibility of discretionary monetary policy to enter the system through the back door, because changes in the reserve requirements would change the money multipliers and broad money aggregates. Bosnia should follow the lead of the orthodox currency boards and the Reserve Bank of New Zealand and eliminate a reserve requirement altogether.
> 5. Monetary liabilities (base money) must be fully covered by gross foreign exchange reserves. The word "gross" should be replaced with the word "net," because gross reserves may or may not be freely available to cover monetary liabilities fully.

I share Hanke's view that with clear, tough rules, banks and others will generally adjust as required. A bank that fails to make adequate provisions to satisfy its customers' needs and its own financial obligations will have to pay the price, which may include failure. Among other conditions, a currency board can only succeed if the authorities are willing to live by its tough rules (e.g., promptly closing a bank that is unable to meet its obligations). The rigorous enforcement of such a hard budget constraint provides very strong market discipline of the behavior of banks.

However, in the environment of Bosnia, where the banking system was in disastrous condition and would remain weak for years, I believed that the design of the currency board should protect the system from unnecessary shocks if it could do so within the strong discipline of the basic currency board rules. The major weakness and largest potential risk came from the payment system and the possibility that a bank would not be able to settle its end-of-day net payments at the payment bureau. We had built into the law several features to reduce these risks, features we believed would not reduce the rigor of the currency board arrangement. If they reduced unnecessary liquidity shocks to the system and/or enabled the system to better deal with such shocks, they would strengthen the system rather than weaken it. These, of course, were also the arguments made in favor of discretionary central banks, and Hanke was certainly correct to say that the powers of such central banks had historically been misused more often than not. The very limited tools we had put in the draft law did not, in our view, weaken the strong discipline of the basic currency board arrangement. But in light of Hanke's criticism, I would like to explain more fully these provisions (described in an earlier chapter) and our reasons for including them.

It is in the nature of banks that they lend or invest most of the money deposited with them. They must keep some cash for those few occasions when their customers withdraw more cash than they deposit and also keep some of their investments in securities that can be easily and quickly sold for cash. In addition, they must keep enough in their reserve accounts with the central bank to cover any net transfers of deposits from their bank to other banks each day. Without a lender of last resort (a traditional function of a central bank), banks must be able to manage their liquidity, including shocks to system-wide liquidity, without help from the central bank. A systemwide drain of liquidity from banks, as would result from seasonal increases in the public's need for cash, would normally be met by banks liquidating some of their foreign assets or by borrowing abroad and selling the foreign currency to the central bank for the needed domestic currency. An increase in the currency/deposit ratio of an economy reduces the money multiplier and would contract the money supply if banks were not able to increase base money by converting foreign assets into domestic currency. Banks should hold sufficient foreign assets in their portfolio to cover possible liquidity shocks (especially for the regular, and hence easily foreseeable, seasonal changes in the money multiplier). When one bank suffers a cash drain (rather than the system as a whole), it can normally replenish the lost cash by borrowing it from other banks with excess liquidity.

Last minute liquidity losses may create special problems for banks in a currency board system because the sale of liquid assets does not generally result in a payment on the same day. If a bank liquidates foreign assets it would generally receive payment as a credit to its reserve account at the central bank two business days later. This would not be good enough to cover an unexpected shortfall in a bank's reserve account at the CBBH in the face of net payments through the payment bureau at the end of day. As the CBBH would not be permitted to extend short-term clearing credits to banks, there would be the risk of one or more banks not having sufficient funds in their accounts to complete that day's net settlement of payment bureau payments. Such settlement failures could be very disruptive to the flow of payments and to the public's confidence in banks.

In Bosnia and Herzegovina, a major source of volatility in bank liquidity was likely to come from fluctuations in the size of the government's bank balances as a result of the mismatch in the timing of its tax and other receipts and its expenditures. If these balances were held with private banks, such fluctuations would not affect banks' balances with the CBBH and would not cause any particular stress for banks. However, choosing which banks to place money in can be difficult, and this difficulty gives the government the opportunity to continue interfering in the operations of the banking sector by depositing money in banks that cooperate with the government in extending loans to enterprises in which the government has an interest. In the case of Bosnia and Herzegovina, one must add the additional political dimension that each individual deposit will favor a particular bank owned by one of the three dominant ethnic groups in the country or operating in one of the three ethnic majority areas. Thus we recommended that government deposits be placed with the CBBH, even though this would result in wider swings in base money as a result of variations in the size of government deposit balances. This strategy constituted a further reason for providing the CBBH with some very limited tools for aggregate liquidity management (i.e., for stabilizing base money or for offsetting variations in the money multiplier).

Our draft law provided three tools for limited liquidity management, and Hanke objected to all three. He believed that these discretionary tools would reduce the discipline and credibility of the arrangement. We were persuaded, however, that the limits on the use of these tools adequately protected the currency board and that by facilitating the smooth functioning of the payment system, the credibility of the currency board arrangement would be enhanced rather than diminished. These three tools were described earlier and are summarized again here.

In addition to issuing currency, the Central Bank would be permitted to issue interest-bearing bills as a means of absorbing excess liquidity. The bills, like any other monetary liability of the CBBH, would have to be fully backed with foreign exchange assets. We anticipated that some bills would be issued at the establishment of the CBBH in order to absorb the liquidity that would be created by shifting existing enterprise deposits with the two regional central banks to commercial banks. The Central Bank would also be permitted to buy these bills back with national currency (limited open market operations—Hanke's point 3) when offered by banks. As both CBBH bank notes and bills would be fully backed with German mark assets, the exchange of one for the other would not change either the amount of DM assets held by the CBBH or the amount required for backing. We anticipated that such operations would be an important source of stability for daily interbank settlements by enabling banks to quickly replenish their settlement balances with the CBBH by selling CBBH bills back to the CBBH. This instrument could not be used as a long-term source of money creation because once all previously issued bills (which reduced liquidity when they were issued) were repurchased by the CBBH (or matured), there would be no further scope for additional liquidity injection from this instrument.

The CBBH would also be permitted to establish a uniform, interest-bearing reserve requirement (Hanke's point 4). We recommended the inclusion of this instrument for two reasons: First, in the absence of a lender of last resort, the use of required reserve balances with the CBBH for daily settlements was likely to be the single most important instrument of liquidity management by banks. Of course, without this requirement, banks would still be expected to maintain sufficient balances with the CBBH for settlement purposes. However, with very weak and inexperienced banks, no money and securities market likely for several years, and with no lender of last resort, we believed that potentially damaging mistakes were very likely. We believed that forcing banks to hold more liquidity than they might otherwise hold, thus reducing the risk of an end-of-day, system-wide settlement failure, would enhance the viability and hence credibility of the currency board arrangement. Second, in the event of a large liquidity shock (a sudden outflow of capital from Bosnia, or runs on banks that reduced the money multiplier), reducing the level of the requirement would provide a one-time instrument of monetary policy that could ease the stress of the liquidity shock. Once it is reduced to zero, its expansionary potential will have been exhausted. We recommended that the level of the requirement not be adjusted except under exceptional circumstances, but we believed that the existence of the instrument would enhance the credibility of the currency board arrangement.

The draft law defined the foreign exchange cover in gross rather than net terms (Hanke's point 5). Gross and net reserves would differ by any foreign borrowing that the CBBH might undertake. The law as we proposed it would limit such borrowing to no more than 50 percent of the CBBH's capital, thus tightly limiting the scope of this instrument. Defining the foreign exchange cover in gross terms would permit the CBBH to make up a small foreign exchange short fall (as might result, for example, from losses on its foreign exchange reserve investments or large capital expenditures) by borrowing abroad. No other instrument would permit the CBBH to remove a shortfall in foreign exchange cover. Without it, the restoration of the required cover would

Orthodox or flexible currency boards

Currency boards are adopted because of their simplicity, transparency, and certainty. They impose a strong discipline on the central bank against abuse or mistakes and on the government that might be tempted to misuse the central bank. Thus the introduction of elements of limited discretion might be seen as undermining the credibility of the currency board arrangement.

A counter argument is that if the rules of the currency board are so rigid that it cannot cope with shocks and stresses, it is likely to give way to alternative policies. In this light, limited flexibility might actually increase public confidence in the credibility of the central bank. Examples of such limited discretion that still limit and discipline what the bank can do are the ability to adjust a reserve requirement ratio within legally established limits and to sell and repurchase central bank securities that must also be fully backed with foreign currency.

have to wait for the accumulation of net income (profits) that could be transferred to capital (or to make up losses). We also believed that this provision enhanced the integrity of the currency board arrangement.

FEBRUARY 1997 MISSION

When I returned to Sarajevo from February 17 through 28, my team consisted of Chris Ryan (from my department at the Fund), Chaiha "Kim" Rhee, Leonard "Len" Fernelius, and Jean-Luc Couetoux.

There are several aspects of my work that make it particularly rewarding for me. These include: the unique intellectual challenge of resolving complex problems, usually in an institutional context very different from the one assumed when I studied economics in the university; the intensity of the uninterrupted focus we can give to our work in the field, where we are more or less isolated from other office responsibilities; the interesting and generally highly dedicated people we meet and work with as counterparts in the central banks we visit; and the wonderful colleagues and experts I work with on my mission teams. More than once I have heard the mission experience compared with combat in wartime. We are thrown together with strangers in a very demanding and intense environment. We work more or less around the clock toward narrow, well-defined objectives—often clarified as we go along. We experience together the exhilaration of breakthroughs and successes as well as the disappointments of setbacks and failures. Between these extremes, we work hard together, struggle with many frustrations, share many rewarding experiences, and bond.

My first IMF assignment as mission chief was to nearby Bulgaria in February 1992. Being mission chief is not like any other position in the mission. I was nervous about how I would do and consulted my colleague, Brock Short. Brock, a Canadian, had joined the IMF about the same time I had and had recently begun to lead missions himself. He gave me a number of useful suggestions, but one comment has always stuck with me. He said that the view ahead doesn't change much whether you are the fifth dog pulling the sled or the second, until you become the lead dog.

For that earlier mission I had not included an accountant from the Central Bank of Ireland, in part, because I had been told that the Deputy Governor of the Bulgarian National Bank, Emil Hersev, had not gotten along with the Irishman on earlier missions, and because I felt I lacked strength in accounting issues and chose not to take them up on my first mission. Nonetheless, during that mission, the Deputy Governor asked for a meeting on the draft chart of accounts being developed by the BNB. I was something close to terrified by the prospect of meeting with an official with such a man-eating reputation and discussing a subject that was not really my own. However, our meeting went well; and I remember returning to my hotel room, closing the door, sighing with relief and swelling with pride. I had survived! I had done okay, even well. I threw my arms into the air over my head and shouted, "YES, YES," and then I cried. It was one of the most purely happy moments of my life.

Bosnia produced many comparable moments, but a very important part of the experience for me was working with the wonderful people on my teams. Kim Rhee is at the top of that list. She had already worked with me in Bulgaria and Moldova and in setting up the Palestine Monetary Authority in the West Bank and Gaza Strip. She would play the key role in setting up the CBBH. Kim had been a division chief in our Bureau of Computing Services at the IMF and had retired some years earlier at a relatively early age after the death of her husband from a car accident. She had been the CEO of Data Resources with the job of downsizing it and preparing it for sale. In 1997 Kim was fifty-nine years old but looked and acted as if she were in her late thirties. On top of being

Kim Rhee (IMF), the author, and Leonard Fernelius
(retired Sr. Vice President of the Federal Reserve of Minneapolis)
in Pale—February 1997

bright, experienced, sensible, and hardworking (and a fabulous cook at the end of a long day), Kim was charmingly straightforward, winning and persistent. We joked that she was three Wonder Women in one. Our counterparts very quickly trusted her. She obtained their cooperation when no one else could. She was a delight to have on a mission. After several visits of several months each, she wound up staying for another two-and-a-half years in Bosnia as a resident expert under my supervision. Without her I simply would have failed to open the CBBH successfully on time.

Len Fernelius was another pillar of our team. He retired as Senior Vice President of the Federal Reserve Bank of Minneapolis in 1993, just in time to contribute to rebuilding the national payment systems of formerly centrally planned economies. While at the Fed he had, among many other things, chaired the Special Task Force on New EFT Formats, the Subcommittee on Payment System, and the Ad Hoc Committee on Services Pricing Administration. He had worked with me in Croatia and Moldova and for my IMF and World Bank colleagues in twenty other places on payment system issues and was much in demand as a payment expert. Len was quiet and businesslike but brought years of valuable experience and sound judgment to his tasks. He had a good sense of what was needed and what was possible at the day-to-day operational level as well as a broad perspective of the entire system. He said that he had not spent his life learning all this stuff just to play golf, and he wanted to share what he knew as long as he could still walk. He was challenging the IMF's age limits, but he could still out walk most of us.

Jean-Luc had been provided to us by the Bank of France, and he was to spend a year or so in Sarajevo helping the new central bank develop its accounting systems. He was, in fact, too young (early thirties) and had too limited an experience for what would be required of him in Bosnia. He made up for that as best he could by determination and hard work. Jean-Luc was likeable and worked to overcome his experience shortcomings to the point of endangering his health. During this mission and the next few

The author, Jean-Luc Couetoux (Bank of France), and Chris Ryan (IMF) in Sarajevo—February 1997

months as he remained in Sarajevo, he worked primarily with Ibrahim "Ibro" Smajlagic, the chief accountant at the NBBH, who was expected to be made the chief accountant of the new Central Bank. Ibro was also relatively young but knew the accounting system of the NBBH inside and out. Regrettably, he did not respect young Jean-Luc, struggling on a steep learning curve, and would not give him the time of day. Thus, Ibro lost the elements of good advice and help Jean-Luc would have been able to give. His rejection by Ibro was clearly demoralizing for Jean-Luc, and at times Kim and I worried about his emotional condition.

In addition to trying to move the draft central bank law to completion, our task on this visit was to lay the groundwork for the establishment of the new organization. We thus focused on its organizational structure, the information systems needed to serve that structure, and the accounting system. We also attempted to deepen our understanding of the payment bureaus and how they would need to be reformed in order to interface with the new central bank in a way that would protect the currency board arrangement. In our work, we were frustrated by the fact that until the central bank law was adopted, we had no clear mandate and no counterparts with whom to work. And Kasim was being unusually cagey and uncooperative. We received limited cooperation on that mission from the staff of the NBBH, who were, after all, to be given first shot at positions in the new Central Bank, which would be housed in the same building.

BANJA LUKA SPP

We had no doubt that reforming the payment bureau system was essential for the success of the new Central Bank and for the health of the banking system. An important part of that reform involved a restructuring of the way the payment bureaus worked. It was essential that the CBBH take control of the banks' reserve deposits. The ZPP had operational control of the banks' reserve and settlement accounts with the NBBH. We were insisting that that control be given over to the new Central Bank. This was a revolutionary idea for the bureaus, the beginning of the end of the payment bureaus actually. So we knew it would not be easy to gain the ZPP's cooperation. On this visit we began the discussion of these changes knowing that there would be many more before agreement would be reached.

Our understanding of how each of the three payment bureaus operated was still inadequate. In this connection, we made our first of many trips to Banja Luka and Mostar to meet with officials of the SPP and the ZAP. Because we spent much more time in Sarajevo, we had reached a better understanding of how the ZPP worked. In any event, its operations were more relevant for the start up of the CBBH because only the ZPP operated in a currency (BHD) that would be immediately converted into the new currency (*glasses*). The ZAP and the SPP were similar to the ZPP, but not identical.

For most of the four-hour drive, the trip to Banja Luka followed the same route we had taken the previous summer to Doboj, though we followed a different route for the second half of the drive. The heavy tank and other fortifications at the RS border continued to impress me. We could begin to forget that we were in a war zone while in Sarajevo, but not on these roads.

When we got to Banja Luka, we were stunned to learn that the Yugo dinar payments in Republika Srpska were still a fully integral part of the system of payments in the wider YUD area. A bank with its headquarters in RS received a statement each day from the SPP on its net position as a result of the payments and receipts of its customers throughout the YUD area. No distinction was made as to whether the payment was within RS or some other part of the YUD area, i.e., Yugoslavia. Each bank settled its daily net payments on its account with the NBRS, which was considered a branch of the National Bank of the Federal Republic of Yugoslavia (NBY) for this purpose. Banks in the RS abided by the regulations of the NBY, including the reserve requirement of the NBY (though its application in RS had already been suspended). With regard to "domestic" payments, the RS and SPP were part of Yugoslavia. I felt as if we had just learned a dirty little secret.

We also met with Ms. Petra Marković; the Deputy Governor; the staff of the NBRS; and the head of the Research Department, Simeun Vilendacić, who later became the head of the Banking Agency of the RS, which licenses and supervises banks in the RS. Petra was an attractive woman in her late forties or early fifties with a strong personality. Later in the year, after the NBRS had been closed, we were unable to make her the Director of the Main Unit of the CBBH in the RS because she had too many political enemies.

The most interesting meeting for me was with the Chairman and management of Agroprom Banka. The SPP had just been converted into the State Bank of the RS, and those present at this meeting expressed their anger at having the monopoly payment bureau—to which every one had to go to make YUD payments—suddenly become a competitor bank (to which everyone still had to go to make YUD payments).

We returned to Sarajevo for several days before driving to Mostar.

MOSTAR ZAP

The route to Mostar was new for us. We had grown used to the extensive destruction of houses and towns and the one lane, temporary bridges guarded by tanks and NATO soldiers along Bosnian roads. Mostar, however, was in the direction of the Dalmatian coast of Croatia and the terrain changed dramatically as the drive progressed. The first half was a modest climb through lush, green forests (on this February trip they were, of course, in winter mode) along a winding, two-lane road first on one side of the river then on the other. From there the scenery changed rapidly and dramatically. After passing through some sheer rock canyons, which rose high above the river, the river gorge broadened as other streams joined the one we followed and the mountains, then hills, turned arid and brown. We emerged into the dry, rocky terrain familiar along the Dalmatian coast. The sky was

Anka Musa (Bosnian Croat Vice Governor and former General Manager of the Mostar ZAP)

blue and the air was dry. And the war destruction reached new heights.

We arrived on time and our hosts were waiting. We met first with Anka Musa, the General Manager. Her entire professional career had been with the Mostar ZAP. Anka had been appointed the Deputy General Manager of the Federation ZPP as part of the U.S.-sponsored effort to build Federation-wide institutions. In principle the Mostar ZAP and the Sarajevo ZPP and their respective territories were merged into one institution. In reality not much had happened or changed. Anka had recently resigned as Deputy GM of the Federation ZPP because, in her view, she had not been allowed to participate fully in its operations. Information was kept from her. Anka was capable and tough, but with a slight grandmotherly touch to her. I was immediately fond of her, and she was to help us quite a bit in the coming years.

In the meeting that followed, we encountered the first hostile audience. It consisted of senior staff of the ZAP and a few commercial bank officials. The first element of hostility was their dissatisfaction with being "forced" into the Federation and the Federation ZPP. This had nothing to do with my mission, but we were a ready target. Secondly, they were angry that we had not visited them before. (We had been prevented by the unsettled security of the city and for purely logistical reasons.) When we did visit Mostar it was always for a much shorter period than our stays in Sarajevo. In fact, we were only there for the day. But as we moved beyond the initial venting, more substantive issues arose that we did not fully understand at that point.

I outlined for the group the general features of the currency board arrangement the new Central Bank would follow, the exchange of Bosnian dinars for the liability of the new Central Bank (*glasses*) that would replace existing arrangements with the national bank, and the future reform of the payment system of which they were a part. While the currency board arrangements were generally understood and welcomed, two aspects of my remarks provoked strong reactions.

When I described the monetary and central banking activities of the Croat ethnic majority area (i.e., the area served by the Bosnian ZAP) and the Serb ethnic majority area (i.e., the RS or the area served by the SPP), I suggested that the ZAP's relationship with its "parent" in Zagreb (the capital of Croatia) was similar to that of the SPP's relationship with its parent in Belgrade (the capital of Yugoslavia). My point was that the only truly domestic currency, the Bosnian dinar issued by the NBBH, made the monetary arrangements of the Muslim area different from those of the ZAP and SPP areas, both of which used the currencies of their neighbor (the Croat kuna and the Yugoslav dinar).

The Bosnian Croats quickly and strongly objected to my comparing their situation with that of the RS. The NBRS in Banja Luka was indeed a branch of the National Bank of Yugoslavia. The SPP system of payments was fully integrated into the Yugoslav-wide system. The Bosnian Croats, it seems, were bitter that they had not enjoyed the same support from their "parent" in Zagreb and doubly resented my suggesting that they had. There was no monetary relationship between the National Bank of Croatia (as the Croatian National Bank was then called) and the Mostar ZAP. The Mostar ZAP had no account with the NBC and no arrangement for currency shipments or for clearing payments between residents of the Croat Majority Area of Bosnia and Croatia. They felt abandoned by their "parent" and struggled through the war to maintain a monetary system alone. How dare I suggest that they had enjoyed Zagreb's help and comfort when they had not.

The second point, which provoked even stronger reaction, had to do with our intention to redeem Bosnian dinars one for one for German marks (until *glasses* could be issued by the new Central Bank against those German marks at the same rate). The Croats thought that this aspect of winding up the existing central banks (the NBBH and the NBRS) was unfair to the ZAP and the Croat Majority area. While it had no central bank, its ZAP had performed some central bank functions. Forgive my repeating the point if it remains clear in your mind, but unlike the ZPP and the SPP, which operated on the basis of deposits with their central banks (NBBH and the NBRS), the Mostar ZAP had no relationship with a central bank. It had severed its relationship with the NBBH during the war and had never established one with the National Bank of Croatia. It thus took on limited central bank functions itself. When banks in its area made deposits with it, the funds became an asset of the Mostar ZAP; and the banks' deposits were liabilities of the ZAP. This was not the case for the ZPP and the SPP, which were only doing the bookkeeping for their banks and central banks.

A key question was whether ZAP activities were increasing or regulating the kuna money supply in their area. This would be the case if the ZAP had loaned some of the cash deposited with it. We did not have a clear understanding of the asset side of the ZAP's books, nor did we understand why the Bosnian Croats thought the redemption of Bosnian dinars at the rate of one to one would be unfair to them. Once again we were suffering from the necessity of dealing through interpreters in trying to understand complex and alien systems. We would hear more of this in the future.

JAIME

Upon our return to Sarajevo I met briefly with Jaime, a former IMF colleague then working for David Lipton, an Assistant Secretary of the U.S. Treasury. Jaime had been sent by Lipton to try to break the deadlock on the central bank law. The disputes over the central bank law were dragging on with no signs of real progress. I attributed this to a lack of political will to implement this important part of the Dayton agreement.

Jaime expressed the view that the failure to achieve an agreement on the law was because we had proposed too liberal a version of a currency board arrangement. I had not encountered objections to, or even serious discussion of, those aspects of the law that defined the exact nature of the kind of currency board the new Central Bank would be. Our counterparts didn't really seem concerned over just how "orthodox" the currency board arrangement should be. The unresolved issues concerned the makeup and voting strength of members of the board, the location and powers of the Central Bank's branches, and the differentiation of the design of the bank notes between the two Entities. Until Jaime's suggestion that these issues might be behind the Bosnian Serbs' reluctance to come to an agreement, the question of how orthodox the law should be had only been raised by Steve Hanke.

A pure currency board only issues bank notes against foreign currency. We recommended that in addition to issuing bank notes, the CBBH should also accept deposits from banks and from the government. In short, we recommended that it be a central bank, limited by currency board rules. This is the case for most currency boards that exist today. We viewed the use of bank deposits with the CBBH for the settlement of interbank payments as facilitating the unification of the financial system in the war-torn and fragmented country and contributing to a more efficient system of payments. However, involving the CBBH in the settlement of non-cash payments, by allowing it to accept deposits from banks (even though they were fully backed with German marks), opened it to the risk that it might be drawn indirectly into extending credit as a part of the settlement process. Such credit would increase the Central Bank's monetary liabilities without increasing its foreign exchange assets and would thus violate currency board rules.

I discussed these risks and our proposals for dealing with them in an earlier chapter, but it was so essential to the ongoing debate that it is worth another somewhat different look. The implications of the strict rules of a currency board for liquidity management by banks is best appreciated by examining the daily settlements of domestic non-cash payments processed through the payment bureaus in Bosnia and Herzegovina (the ZPP, ZAP, and SPP). This is the context in which the problems of dealing with liquidity shocks in the real world of daily payment operations in Bosnia and Herzegovina can be seen most clearly.

An individual bank has a potential problem if it experiences a net loss of reserves during the day as a result of its payments and its customers' payments that exceed its excess reserves (reserves in excess of the required level) with the central bank. In order to settle its net clearing-house payments that day (or to preserve required reserves), it can borrow from other banks, sell liquid domestic assets, sell foreign exchange (if it can anticipate the problem two days in advance), or borrow from the central bank. If the banking system in aggregate needs liquidity, then the only options are for banks to sell foreign exchange or borrow from the central bank. Under currency board rules the CBBH is not permitted to extend credit to banks or anyone else. The lack of a lender of last resort has led banks to hold liquid foreign exchange assets and excess reserves with the CBBH at higher levels than they would under a full-fledged central bank. This adds to the cost of banking. The consequence of having no lender of last resort would obtain whether banks were able to settle their payments with their deposits at the Central Bank or not.

Deciding just how strict the currency board should be was one of the most important substantive issues that the authorities faced. I took the position that the public's confidence in the Central Bank's adherence to the currency board arrangement required by the Dayton agreement would be strengthened by giving the Central Bank limited tools of liquidity management, while rigidly binding it to the requirement that it freely convert its monetary liabilities for foreign exchange and that it always have more than enough foreign exchange with which to do so. I also felt that its credibility required a total prohibition against extending credit of any kind for any purpose. I reasoned that giving the Central Bank the tools to deal with one of the greatest weaknesses of a currency board arrangement would strengthen the credibility of its commitment to currency board rules, as long as it could not extend credit to anyone and maintained full foreign exchange backing. Specifically, as discussed in greater detail earlier, the draft law that we proposed in November provided for the CBBH to issue bills (which would be part of its monetary liabilities that must be backed by foreign exchange), to conduct open market operations in those bills, to impose a reserve requirement uniformly on all bank deposits, and to borrow abroad up to 50 percent of its capital, while forbidding it to extend credit.

Echoing the arguments of Steve Hanke, Jaime disagreed with these departures from orthodoxy. I grew concerned that he would plant distrust of our draft with the Serbs where, as far as I could tell, none existed.

INTERREGIONAL PAYMENT BUREAUS

In the payment area we also focused some of our practical attention on the enhancement of the interregional system of payment clearing and settlement that Thomas Schiller had set up. The first payoff of the new Central Bank would come from more efficient interregional payments in the new currency (*glasses*). We were keen to realize this advantage from the first day of operation of the CBBH. During this February visit we proposed the design of a payment order for transferring bank balances of *glasses* within or across the three payment bureaus in an efficient way and for the settlement of net amounts between banks each day using the new reserve/settlement accounts with the CBBH. At our suggestion, Governor Robert requested each of the three payment bureaus to send the head of its computer departments for a technical discussion of the requirements for countrywide transfers of the new money using a common payment order and electronic communications. This method would improve on and replace Thomas's separate, unintegrated system with periodic fax/Mercedes settlements.

We chaired the first such meeting of the working group at the end of our visit, and it was a truly touching event. The ZAP, ZPP, and SPP had been one organization before the war and its senior employees and management had worked together for years. The working group brought together some old friends and colleagues for the first time in five years. Grown men embraced with tears in their eyes. They couldn't stop talking about how happy they were to be working together again. At the sight of it, tears filled our eyes as well. The Central Bank was contributing to the healing of the country. Commerce and economic interest was winning out over politics and bigotry. But the process was slow.

We recommended that a law should be passed at the state level that would support and govern such payments. This law was designed to overturn a restriction on such payments now in the RS internal payments law and to govern only payments in the State currency (*glasses*). I also proposed that this law permit banks to make payments (a change already adopted by the RS), which would end the payment bureaus' monopoly. All members of the CBBH Board supported these proposals, but in the end we were required to seek separate Entity payment laws.

I returned to Washington, and Jaime made several more trips to Bosnia on behalf of the U.S. Treasury. Serge continued to work in his usual low-keyed, non-confrontational way with his Board toward a resolution of the differences of view. Kim and Jean-Luc stayed on, making several visits of about a month each.

THE OUTCOME

In March, I received a new draft of the central bank law from Serge that contained some troubling changes. We prepared and sent comments.

Suddenly in mid-May it was clear that there was significant movement toward a solution; but I was not directly involved. Assistant Treasury Secretary David Lipton called me several times with questions about positions being proposed by Jaime in the field. I was growing uncomfortable.

The Croat Bosnians in Spring 1997: From left to right: Zlatko Barš (Director, Federation Banking Agency), Jure Pelivan (Croat Board member of CBBH and former Governor of NBBH), Anka Musa (Chairman, Mostar ZAP), Alessandro Zanello (IMF, resident representative), Kim Rhee (IMF, payments advisor), Serge Robert (Governor CBBH), and Dragan Kovačević (Vice Governor CBBH)

LAST MINUTE CHANGES

I received another draft in late May that continued to contain features I did not like. While thinking about our comments, we suddenly received an announcement that the draft had been approved by the Board and presented to the Joint Presidency for endorsement. I was shocked and furious. I spent Saturday carefully reviewing the draft and sent the following letter to Serge:

May 31, 1997

Dear Governor Robert:

We received yesterday the final draft text of the Law on the Central Bank of Bosnia and Herzegovina that you sent to the Joint Presidency May 29, 1997. It represents a substantial achievement of which you and the other members of the Board may be proud. Regrettably some important problems with the draft that we reviewed in March remain, and more regrettably still some new serious flaws have been introduced of which we were not aware and on which we have not been consulted. In the interests of time I am sharing with you my comments (Mr. Asser will return to Washington Monday) on the remaining weaknesses and/or inconsistencies in this draft that I hope the Board will consider addressing. I take them up in the order in which they appear in the draft.

1. Article 2.3.d. gives the Bank the power to issue regulations with regard to monetary policy. By citing explicitly Article 2.3.a. and omitting subsections b and c, it denies the Bank the power to issue regulations in the payments area (this is less clear to me with regard to reserve management because that is an internal matter for the Bank, which it cannot avoid regulating internally). This limitation contradicts the provisions of Article 58, which gives a more limited power to regulate interbank payments. Article 58 has been changed from our recommendation or we erred in its formulation, but it now would seem necessary to adopt a separate internal payments law for Convertible Marka [the term eventually adopted for *glasses*], before payments could be made in Marka bank deposits. We had hoped to avoid a new law by providing clear authority to the CBBH to issue regulations with regard to payments of Marka.

2. Article 2.4 divides the responsibilities of the Board in a way that simply may not be permitted in law and directly contradicts the powers of the Board correctly given in Article 7. For example, Article 2.4. takes away from the Board the power to set reserve requirements while Article 7.b. correctly gives that power to the Board, which is more explicitly and fully treated in Article 36 (incorrectly given as Article 37 in the table of contents). I assume that the (understandable) goal of this provision is to establish clearly that the activities of the Bank (as given in Art. 2.3.) are to be executed in the various offices of the Bank (head office and other units). This is already clearly and adequately stated in Article 2.3, but if the Board wants to repeat that point, my strong preference would be to state this (normally obvious) point in Article 5 (I suggest language for this purpose in paragraph 4 below) and to delete all of Art. 2.4 (including Art. 2.3.f. which seems to have been broken away from Art. 2.3.a. in order to differentiate who makes policy from who implements it). However, if you consider it easier to obtain the Board's agreement by keeping a statement of the specific tasks of the branches in Art. 2.4., then you might consider replacing Art. 2.4. with:

"Article 4.

a. The execution of the Central Bank's policies and activities provided for in paragraph 3 will be carried out by the head office, main units, and other branches of the Central Bank;

b. Other basic tasks of the head office and main units of the Central Bank shall be. . . ."

3. It is completely inappropriate for the Central Bank to perform foreign exchange operations for banks (e.g. exchanging dollars or YUD for DM). This is what would be required by Art. 2.4.b.I. If it can't be dropped altogether, I suggest the following language:

"I. to undertake the sales or purchases of the Marka against DM prescribed by Article 33."

I hope that it is clear that the Board may delegate this activity to others as well. I assume, for example, that the payment bureaus with their vaults and security procedures should continue as agents of the Central Bank in exchanging Marka for DM with the banks and public.

4. The activities of the branches should be moved to Article 5. Art. 5.1., which provides for "three Vice Governors" directly contradicts Art. 17, which provides for "such Vice Governors as the Governor shall appoint. . . ." Art. 5.2, which provides for "a head office and main units," contradicts Art. 1.3, which in addition to offices abroad provides for "representative offices." In addition to correcting the contradictions, I suggest adding (in place of Article 2.4):

"3. The head office and other units of the Central Bank shall maintain current accounts for banks and official entities, buy and sell Marka for DM, collect data related to economic and financial activities, and undertake other activities that might be assigned to them by the Board, in the region in which they are located."

5. In Article 25 it is not possible (as we noted in our March comments) for the allocation of net profits to "decrease" capital and as a matter of policy, authorized capital, once increased by previous allocations of net profit, should not be reduced (it is the entire purpose of Article 29 to prevent such a reduction and the current language seems to deprive Art. 29 of any functional meaning). I assume the failure to remove "decrease" is simply an oversight.

6. In Article 27.c., allowing the Board to create new special reserves to which profits may be allocated is potentially risky without the approval of the Joint Presidency. The requirement of unanimity, at least, provides some protection against abuse.

7. The new Article 31 has adopted a net foreign exchange reserve backing requirement in place of the gross foreign exchange reserve requirement around which the IMF draft was built. We had proposed gross reserves in order to allow the possibility that the Central Bank might borrow abroad to cover foreign exchange reserve backing shortfalls but provided a tight limit on the amount of such borrowing in Article 34.3. In switching to a net reserve approach, the limitation on foreign borrowing in 34 no longer serves any purpose and should be

dropped. More importantly, the change to net reserves was done incorrectly with potentially disastrous consequences and thus it must be corrected. This is aside from the wisdom of the change, which leaves the Central Bank with no means (except future profits) to correct a violation of the 100 percent backing called for in Article 31 as could result from a decline in the DM value of dollar and gold holdings of the CBBH. The liabilities that must be deducted from foreign exchange assets include (A) "any credit balances . . . held on the books of the Central Bank in the accounts of foreign central banks or other foreign financial institutions;" They also include (B) "any Convertible Marka held by the IMF." While it is unclear what is meant by this, it presumably refers to the same thing covered by (A) that precedes it, i.e., balances in the IMF #1 account with the Central Bank, and is thus redundant. The real problem is that these liabilities are being double counted. They appear as monetary liabilities that must be covered by net foreign exchange reserves and in addition they are deducted from gross foreign exchange. This is a non-workable mistake. In addition to the shambles it makes of an IMF purchase, take the simpler example of a deposit that the World Bank might make with the CBBH. The WB would pay, say, DM 100 and receive a Marka 100 credit balance with the CBBH. This should increase monetary liabilities and foreign exchange assets by the same amount and all would be well. But in the current draft, monetary liabilities would go up by 100 and NET foreign exchange assets would remain unchanged after netting out the liabilities to the WB from the increased gross reserves.

8. I have been arguing for some time that it was a bad idea for the Central Bank to buy and sell DM without a small spread. However, it is a far more serious matter for the Central Bank law to regulate the price at which other financial institutions must deal in DM and it is inappropriate, as well as very bad policy, for the Central Bank Law to obligate banks and others to engage in these exchanges at the fixed rate. How will the Central Bank supervise and enforce this requirement on financial institutions? To my mind this requirement will put the Marka at a disadvantage as banks will find ways of avoiding the losses from dealing in Marka that the Law would now impose and the public will get poorer service when dealing in Marka.

9. The limitation of the reserve requirement to Marka also seems designed to put it at a competitive disadvantage. Will DM, YUD, dollar, and kuna deposits with banks be free of reserve requirements? Remuneration of Marka reserve requirements became a particularly important instrument for minimizing the damage of this provision. Thus I strongly urge that Article 36.3. be made more flexible by requiring remuneration at market rates above 5 percent but permitting the Board to lower the unremunerated part if it chooses to.

10. Article 50 imposes an inappropriate (unfortunately contained in the IMF

draft as well) limitation on investments of foreign exchange assets. The CBBH should be able to hold any of the assets described in Article 31.2.b.

11. The draft only provides for the publication of an annual financial statement. This is not the practice of other currency boards (or central banks for that matter). Transparency and public confidence that the Central Bank is operating according to the rules are served by much more frequent publication of proforma financial statements—the norm is monthly and I recommend that that requirement be added to the law.

We look forward to seeing you soon.

Sincerely,
Warren Coats
Advisor,
Monetary and Exchange Affairs Department
International Monetary Fund

NET MONETARY LIABILITIES

Serge was not pleased with my letter, and Scott Brown was disturbed by it. It had been very difficult getting the draft to this stage, and it would not be easy to change anything at this point. As difficult as it was for me to swallow, I accepted in my discussions with Scott that the only thing that really had to be changed was the mess that had been made of the switch from gross to net foreign assets in the requirement to cover monetary liabilities (see point 7 in the letter above). Jaime called from the U.S. Treasury to discuss what might be done. John Dalton, Tobias Asser, and I worked on alternative formulations that would coherently reflect the net approach that the authorities (or was it really Jaime?) apparently wanted, looking for the approach that would involve the smallest change in wording. We apparently found it at the same time as David Lipton and Jaime, because when I called Jaime he indicated that they also had the same idea.

All that was needed was the addition of one word to the definition of monetary liabilities. The provisions could be made coherent by defining the monetary liabilities that needed to be backed by "net foreign assets" also on a net basis. In our draft, and in the revised May 29 draft, all deposit liabilities of the CBBH were included in the definition of monetary liabilities needing cover. In the phrase, "Credit balances of all accounts . . . [of] account holders," we suggested inserting the word "resident" so that it would read "[of] resident account holders." Thus, for example, a deposit with the CBBH by the World Bank would not increase the liabilities that the CBBH needed to back with foreign exchange. But because the foreign currency asset counterpart of such a deposit must also be deducted from foreign currency assets to obtain "net foreign assets" such a deposit would not add to those assets either.

In one of the more interesting historical footnotes on the establishment of the CBBH, Scott arranged for the official copy of the draft to be changed without a new decision by the CBBH or the Joint Presidency, by claiming that he was correcting a clerical typing error.

CURRENCY NAME AND NOTE DESIGN

Just before the draft on the central bank law was agreed and submitted to the Joint Presidency, the name of the new currency was chosen. Each member of the Board had made interesting and worthy suggestions for a name for the new currency between November 1996 and May 1997. My Swedish friend Einar Du Rietz even provided me with a list of currency names that had some historical roots in the area (which almost disqualified them by definition). But before there was a political will and commitment to move forward, no name would be acceptable to all three groups. My favorite example of this was the name proposed by Kasim Omićević late in the game, when we thought it was getting more serious. In the spirit of the euro, Kasim suggested Baher. Baher was an invention with no history to tarnish it for one group or the other and was drawn from the name of the country. Manojlo Ćorić vetoed the name because, as he explained, he came from a region of the country in which the "h" was not pronounced. Clearly the time was still not quite right to move forward.

When that time was reached in May, all of the really good names had already been rejected. At that point David Lipton of the U.S. Treasury suggested the pedestrian, but descriptive name Convertible Marka (KM), which was immediately accepted.

The law made KM legal tender, while explicitly protecting the right of private persons and companies to transact in any mutually acceptable currency. The law required public officials to:

undertake all efforts to promote the use of the Convertible Marka in the payments of all revenues and expenditures of the budgets, public agencies, and public enterprises at all levels of government. During that process, other currencies in use prior to the entry into force of this Law will continue to be used. Following the introduction of the Convertible Marka by the Central Bank, the Presidency of Bosnia and Herzegovina will review these efforts every three months on the basis of an analysis submitted by the International Monetary Fund of the efforts made by the authorities to promote the use of the Convertible Marka. (Article 38.5.)

The law also provided that "as an interim measure until a permanent solution for the design of the notes has been agreed upon," the CBBH would issue "Coupons."

The Coupons will have common design elements as well as distinct design elements for the Federation of Bosnia and Herzegovina and the Republika Srpska.... Both versions of the Coupon will have equal status as legal tender throughout the territory of Bosnia and Herzegovina. (Article 42.3.)

The design for each Entity had to be acceptable to the other, and no agreement was reached until the Office of the High Representative reached a decision on the design and presented it to the Joint Presidency in February 1998.

LIQUIDITY MANAGEMENT INSTRUMENTS

The law that was adopted removed all of the limited discretionary elements of liquidity management that were in our draft, except for the reserve requirement; and it severely limited the Central Bank's scope for adjusting the reserve requirement. The CBBH could not issue its own bills (other than bank notes) and could not engage in open market operations in these (or any other) bills. And, as had also been provided in the IMF draft of the law, the CBBH could "not under any circumstances, grant any credit." (Article 67.1.a)

While the very limited authority to borrow abroad remained in the law, it could not serve the purpose we had seen for it (namely, to cover shortfalls in the foreign exchange backing of monetary liabilities). The law changed the backing requirement from the gross foreign exchange assets that we had recommended, to a net concept. In effect, the monetary liabilities of the CBBH had to be covered by net foreign exchange assets of equivalent value. Thus, any increase in gross foreign exchange assets as a result of borrowing would leave net foreign exchange assets unchanged; and thus such borrowing could not remove a shortfall in the required backing of the CBBH's monetary liabilities.

As a practical matter, the law left three ways in which the banking system could deal with a potential liquidity shortfall at the time of the end-of-day net settlement of domestic non-cash payments. The first two were for banks (1) to hold reserves in excess of the required level (excess reserves) and (2) to sell German mark bank notes on hand in their vaults to the Central Bank. Both of these were costly in terms of forgone interest earnings. The third was to utilize required reserves, if the requirement permitted averaging. To maximize the value of the reserve requirement for this liquidity management purpose, the IMF draft law had granted the CBBH the power to establish by regulation a uniform requirement on all deposits that would be met on an average basis and that would be substantially remunerated. The first three of five provisions on required reserves in our draft law (Article 38) were:

1. In the conduct of its monetary policy, the Central Bank may require by regulation that banks shall maintain deposits with the Central Bank at prescribed minimum levels that relate to the size of their deposits, borrowed funds and such other liabilities as the Central Bank may determine by regulation (required reserves). Reserve requirements shall be applied uniformly to all banks.

2. Required reserves shall be maintained by way of such cash holdings or by way of such money deposits with the Central Bank, and shall be calculated as average daily reserves over such time periods as the Central Bank may from time to time prescribe by regulation.

3. The banks shall be paid interest at market related rates by the Central Bank on the amounts by which their required reserves exceed the equivalent of three percent of the aggregate amounts of their respective liabilities.

We had in mind a one-month settlement period for a required ratio of 10 percent of all deposits in order to give considerable scope to liquidity management by banks. We intended for the details of the regulation to be adopted by the CBBH Board in the form of a regulation.

During the debates over the draft law, there appeared to be some danger that the reserve requirement would be lost along with the other liquidity management tools (though the source of this danger was never clear to me, I suspected Jaime). In the end, the reserve requirement was saved but in a greatly restricted form spelled out quite fully and rigidly in the law. The law provided for a ten-day settlement period, a limited range for the requirement ratio, applicable only to KM deposits, which for some time were bound to be rather small. This law also potentially disadvantaged KM deposits since other deposits were not subject to such a requirement, and remuneration of required reserves was more limited than we had proposed. The law provided in the first three of five sections in Article 36:

Minimum required reserves: best practice

Minimum required reserves, consisting of vault cash and current account deposits with the central bank are a monetary policy instrument for limiting and stabilizing the money multiplier by limiting the amount of bank deposits that banks can lend. When properly designed they can contribute to bank liquidity management as well. They perform these functions best when they

a. apply to the same deposit liabilities included in the deposit component of broad money;

b. apply to all foreign currency deposits of the same type;

c. are satisfied by domestic currency vault cash and current account deposits with the central bank;

d. are satisfied on an average basis over the maintenance period (two weeks to one month); and

e. are remunerated at the market rate of interest.

1. The Governing Board of the Central Bank will require by regulation that banks shall maintain deposits with the Central Bank, through its head office or main units, at prescribed minimum levels of between 10 and 15 percent of their deposits and borrowed funds denominated in Convertible Marka. Reserve requirements shall be applied uniformly to all banks.

2. Required reserves shall be maintained by way of cash holdings or by way of deposits with the Central Bank, through its head office and main units, and shall be calculated as average daily reserves over ten-day periods.

3. The banks shall be paid interest at market related rates by the Central Bank on the amounts by which their required reserves exceed the equivalent of 5 percent of the aggregate amounts of their respective liabilities.

EXCHANGE RATE SPREAD

The central function of a currency board is its obligation to convert domestic currency to a foreign one at a fixed exchange rate. The law established this obligation in two Articles:

> The official exchange rate for the currency of Bosnia and Herzegovina shall be one Convertible Marka per Deutsche mark (Article 32).

> The Central Bank shall without restriction purchase and sell Convertible Marka on demand for Deutsche marks within the territories of Bosnia and Herzegovina at the exchange rate indicated in Article 32 of this Law (Article 33.1).

In order to provide a financial incentive to conduct normal foreign exchange business outside the CBBH, our draft law had permitted the Central Bank to transact at rates within one quarter of one percent of the official rate and to limit its transactions to banks or other financial institutions. It would also have been permitted to limit the fees and commissions charged by banks for buying and selling KM against DM with the public.

In order to maximize public acceptance of KM, the law as finally adopted removed these spreads for the CBBH and for banks altogether and required the participation of banks:

> Commercial banks and other financial institutions in Bosnia and Herzegovina shall purchase and sell without restriction, fees, commissions or other charges Convertible Marka for Deutsche marks on demand, at the exchange rate indicated in Article 32 of this Law (Article 33.2).

Until these provisions could be amended along the lines of our original proposal (which was finally done in late 2001), we recommended that the CBBH remunerate banks for the subsidy to the public implicit in the absences of spreads or fees in such dealings. Once the CBBH started operations, these provisions created problems that were overcome by stretching the meaning of the law.

BRANCHES

The law preserved the essence of our draft's treatment of branches of the CBBH. However, the sensitivity of, and struggle over, this issue can be clearly seen in the language on this subject in the law as finally adopted.

Our draft stated:

> The Central Bank shall have its head office in Sarajevo. The Central Bank shall establish and maintain branch offices in the Federation of Bosnia and Herzegovina and the Republika Srpska; these branch offices shall have no legal status or authority independent from the Central Bank.... (Article 1.3.)

The law as adopted stated:

> The Central Bank shall have its head office in Sarajevo. However, it will decentralize its activities in other locations of the common institutions of Bosnia and Herzegovina. The Central Bank shall establish and maintain a head office and main units in the Federation of Bosnia and Herzegovina and the Republika Srpska; these main units shall be established in the Federation, and one in the Republika Srpska. They will perform their duties as decided by the Governing Board and the Governor, and under this law they may operate through accounts opened with the appropriate authorities in the payment system.... (Article 1.3.)
>
> > The main unit in the Republika Srpska shall be called:
> > Main Bank of the Republika Srpska
> > Of the Central Bank of BiH (Article 74.I.)

When I first read the above name of the branch in RS, I assumed that it was a typo. But it was not. A translator's note accompanying the English text stated: "[Note: in local language, this name is: Glavna Bank Republike Srpske Centralne Banke BiH]." The translator apparently had trouble believing it as well. When I later organized our technical assistance program for Kosovo and still later for the Federal Republic of Yugoslavia (FRY), I learned that this was language from the central bank of FRY law and that the distinction between a main unit and a mere branch had historically been very significant.

The Serbs, especially, seemed determined to preserve as much distinction between their Main Unit and the rest of the CBBH as possible. We came to suspect that the name of the CBBH would be lost in the RS. In fact, however, when the Main Bank of the Republika Srpska opened in Pale (it has since been moved to Banja Luka), Central Bank of Bosnia and Herzegovina was spelled out in full on the front of the building housing the branch office. Ljubiša Vladušić, the enlightened and very effective Bosnian Serb Vice Governor of the CBBH, had quietly taken this decision. He proudly pointed it out to me when I saw it for the first time a year later.

Ljubiša Vladušić
(Bosnian Serb Vice Governor
of the CBBH)

Throughout the law there were references to "tasks of the head office of the Central Bank and of the main units." One of many examples could be seen in the reserve requirement provisions quoted above.

An argument put forth by all sides (but more strongly by the Bosnian Serbs) with which we had considerable sympathy, maintained that in order to gain public acceptance of the new Central Bank and its currency, each group would need to see them as (to some extent) their own.

Thus the version of the central bank law (and hence of the currency board arrangement) that was finally adopted differed in some respects from the version we had proposed in the published report of our November mission. While I was unhappy about some of the changes, none of them compromised the basic principles of a currency board arrangement agreed to in Dayton. The CBBH that was adopted was the closest to the pure form of currency board of any existing central bank. The few that were even purer were small island monetary authorities like the Cayman Islands Monetary Authority, which is not even a central bank.

6 PREPARATIONS FOR THE CENTRAL BANK'S START UP

THE JUNE 1997 MISSION

I returned to Bosnia with a team of experts from June 12–24, 1997. With the passage of the new law imminent when we arrived, we knew that we had little time left to prepare for the CBBH's opening.

Over the past year, our considerable technical assistance toward establishing the CBBH had been hampered by the politically motivated lack of cooperation of one or another of the three ethnic groups into which the country was divided. When the Central Bank Law was finally adopted on June 20, 1997, during our visit, our counterparts consisted of the Governor (selected by the Fund) and the other three members of the CBBH Board, and the staff of the existing two central banks and the three payment bureaus operating in the three ethnic majority areas of the country. Many of these counterparts had not always been permitted to cooperate with us. We hoped that things would now change.

The CBBH itself had no staff, and it was not yet clear what staff would be needed or who they would be. Preference would be given, of course, to the existing staff of the NBBH. This would create a problem down the line for the ethnic mix of the staff of the new institution, but it was not practical to move forward any other way within the time limits we faced. We hoped to borrow administrative and accounting systems from the NBBH as well, to the extent possible. Kasim, however, was clearly making it difficult for his NBBH staff to work with us, even if they had anticipated being employed by the new institution. Thus we hardly had any official counterparts at all in developing the establishment plan and preparing for the opening of the new institution. Our two key counterparts were Enver and Ibro, and Ibro's cooperation was very limited.

To simplify enormously, three things needed to be done by August 11. (1) A new institution needed to be organized and staffed with sufficient structure and procedures to perform its initially limited operational tasks. (2) A new currency needed to be introduced and exchanged for BH dinar (BHD), which needed to be retired. (3) The settlement of domestic non-cash payments needed to be transformed and taken over by the new institution. We were nothing, if not ambitious.

There were several factors that made this extraordinary undertaking somewhat easier than it might have been. The primary one was the fact that only the BHD was being directly converted into the new currency (KM) and was thus going out of existence. So only the BHD monetary liabilities of the NBBH were being taken over by the CBBH. The kuna and YUD were currencies of foreign countries (Croatia and FRY) and would need to be converted into KM in the marketplace (or into DM and then through the currency board mechanism). While establishing the CBBH would also entail opening branches (Main Units) in Mostar and in the RS (in addition to the one in Sarajevo), these branches would not need to be operational on the first day, since there would be no KM deposits or payments in their areas initially.

Thus for all practical purposes, the three main events (open CBBH, convert BHD to KM, and reform domestic payment settlements) that needed to take place on August 11 pertained only to the area served by the NBBH and the ZPP. In addition to these factors, because there was no agreement yet on bank note design, the new currency would be initially introduced in non-cash form until bank notes could be printed and introduced at a later time. Thus all BHD account balances and prices would be converted to KM, a relatively simple operation, and BHD bank notes would continue to circulate for some months.

This visit concentrated on the preparations needed for the above events. These included the preparations of the operational procedures within the CBBH for its oversight of banks' reserve accounts (including their compliance with the reserve requirement and their daily settlement of net payments through the ZPP) and for its management of its foreign exchange reserves. Thus, in addition to Chris, Kim, Jean-Luc, and Len, I also brought Benjamin Geva, a payments law professor at York University, Canada, and Hugh O'Donnell, a foreign exchange reserve management expert from the Central Bank of Ireland.

Ben and Hugh were like night and day. Ben was a world-renowned expert on payment law. He was widely respected in his field. His participation in my mission gave him the opportunity to turn his views on what should be in a payment law (most countries don't have such a law) into an actual law. He was about to father a law, and he was beside himself with excitement. Having academics on my missions always renewed my appreciation (by observing their excitement) of the unique opportunities our work at the IMF gives us to effect real world policies. Unlike most students in universities, our counterparts' careers and their countries' well being depended on mastering what we were saying. They made very exciting students to work with.

Ben was also the nearest thing to a social child I have ever had on my missions. His legal skills were beyond question. From the public presentations he made of his proposals, it was also clear that he must have been an outstanding university lecturer. However, in one-on-one meetings with our counterparts, he struggled to find effective ways of expressing himself. He didn't have a very good sense of how to appropriately relate to them. Like all expectant fathers, he would do anything necessary to succeed; and he worried a lot. He worried A LOT. He would later suggest that I write to the Federation Finance Minister to insist that "Ben's" draft law be commented on by a particular date. He asked over and over if we had checked on this or that, and if such and such had been done. We called him High Maintenance Ben, but no one's heart was bigger. No one was more eager to work hard. When payment law was involved, I wanted him on the team and I knew he would do whatever was necessary to be available. I subsequently brought him with me to Kosovo and then to Belgrade. Still later he worked for us in Afghanistan.

Hugh, on the other hand, was tranquil, careful, soft-spoken, and cautious about presuming anything. He also smoked almost as much as our Bosnian counterparts and had a typical Irishman's love of drink, always after the day's work was done, of course. Hugh also was a playwright whose work had actually been performed in Dublin. He was always a pleasure to have on missions and in the evening brought interesting and different perspectives to our work, focusing on the personalities and subtleties of our counterparts.

PAYMENT SYSTEM REFORMS

During the year I had been working on Bosnia, my understanding of how the payment bureau system worked changed some every time I discussed it. Our June 1997 visit was no different. This always left me a bit uncomfortable with any proposals I wanted to make.

The entire system needed to be reformed, and we began initial discussions of what a future system might look like. However, our much more limited, immediate goals were to replace the BHD with the KM, to establish the future Central Bank's operational control over the deposits banks would have with it, and to protect the currency board arrangement against credits to banks that might be forced on it by the payment system.

Because bank notes would not be introduced until some months after the target opening of the CBBH, the conversion of BHD to KM would initially be limited to the conversion of deposits at banks and prices of goods and services, a relatively easy task. Central Bank control over banks' deposits with it was more complicated and controversial and proved much more difficult to achieve.

We discussed with our counterparts the steps needed to adapt the existing systems of payment to achieve these goals by August 11. These included:

- conversion of BD deposits to KM at the rate of 100 to 1;
- the adoption by the Parliaments of the two Entities of laws that introduced payments in KM;

- the adoption by the CBBH Board of the terms and conditions for bank reserve accounts and for the current and time deposits of the State Government;
- opening banks' reserve accounts for each bank (before the transfer to the CBBH of existing balances with the NBBH);
- certain accounting adjustments at the ZPP, including the consolidation of the required reserve accounts and settlement accounts into a single reserve account;
- adoption by the Board of the CBBH of: agency agreements with the SPP, ZPP, and ZAP to perform services (cash handling and storage, and providing interbank settlement information), the reserve requirement regulation, bank reporting requirements, and the procedures for settling net interbank payments on banks' reserve accounts; and
- establishment of the telecommunications links needed to transmit payment orders and information between payment bureaus and branch offices of the CBBH and between the CBBH branches and its head office.

Our real worry was our ability to protect the currency board arrangement. The CBBH could not extend credit of any kind. In particular, it could not extend credit to a bank that did not have sufficient funds in its reserve account with the CBBH to settle its net obligations at the end of the day. As explained earlier, it is a feature of a net settlement (clearinghouse) system, as were operated by the three payment bureaus, that a credit is extended if some banks are credited when at least one other cannot settle because of a negative balance. In other words, settlement of the net amounts must be all or nothing (all banks or no banks), if no credit is to be extended by the central bank.

The systems and procedures in place at that time, worked satisfactorily to ensure that the payment bureau would not process a payment order from a depositor for more than he had in his Giro account with the payment bureau and thus with his bank. This was a great strength of the system over the use of checks more common in the United States. The weak point (because of the nature of banks) was that even if all issuers of payment orders had sufficient funds in their accounts, there was no assurance that their banks would have enough in their Giro account at the payment bureau (and hence in their reserve accounts with the Central Bank) to cover all customer payments that might be made each day. The technology in place did not permit the payment bureau to check the associated bank's Giro balance before accepting and processing a payment order from a bank's customer. This could only be done at the end of the day on a net basis.

The procedures and obsolete computer operations in the Federation Payment Bureau's offices effectively forced banks to manage their reserve positions by maintaining large excess balances in the Central Bank and in some cases caused overnight overdrafts. When a bank did not have sufficient funds in its reserve account, it was permitted to borrow the needed funds from its required reserves (a separate blocked account).

I asked Len to give special attention to the need to protect the currency board arrangement. This protection against bank overdrafts needed to take into account the merging of payment settlements into one central bank for all three payment bureau areas. In the system that we proposed and that was accepted by the three bureaus, each bank would have one reserve account with the CBBH for the consolidated activity of all of its branches. This reserve account would be managed by the bank's head office and would be maintained with and monitored by the branch of the CBBH in the payment bureau area in which the bank's head office was located. Each day the relevant payment bureau would submit a payment order (on behalf of each bank's head office in its area) authorizing the local branch of the CBBH to debit and credit the banks' reserve accounts for the net amounts due to and from each bank in its area. The balances of all reserve accounts would be consolidated at the main office of the CBBH in Sarajevo.[1]

Since it would not be possible to ensure that net payments of a bank's clients would not exceed the bank's reserve account balance at the CBBH, we proposed several additional changes in the current settlement procedures of the payment bureaus to ensure that the CBBH would not extend credit to banks:

1. Payments to payees could not be final until final settlements among banks were confirmed (though the payee's bank might choose to accept the risk of

providing the funds earlier). This required a change in the law and regulations. Ben prepared a draft of such a law and regulation.

2. Net amounts due had to be computed and advised to banks at least one hour before final settlement on the books of the CBBH in order to give banks time to increase their reserve account balances if needed (by borrowing from other banks, selling assets to other banks, or selling German marks to the CBBH).

3. In the event that a bank failed to acquire the needed balances with the CBBH, the payment bureau had to be technically prepared to unwind and recompute the net settlements of all other banks before settlement at the CBBH could take place.

These changes were not achieved without a battle. At that time, banks in the Bosniac area had two deposits with the NBBH. Their required reserves were held in a blocked account called the 201 account. The other account, called the 620 account, was used for interbank and other payments by banks, such as the end-of-day net settlement of all payments through the ZPP. While these deposits were liabilities of the NBBH and it held the asset counterpart, they were fully controlled operationally by the ZPP. The story was complicated by the fact that, while ZPP management understood this fact abstractly, it acted as if and felt as if the "money" was with the ZPP.

To us, Central Bank operational control over these accounts meant that the instruction to debit or credit those accounts had to come to and be executed by the Central Bank. Legally, if the Central Bank did not record the debit or credit in its accounts, it didn't happen (even if the ZPP recorded it to its shadow accounts). The ZPP's processing of payment orders during the day should be considered message clearing rather than settlement. At the end of the day the ZPP would send the net results to the Central Bank to be settled. At the end of the day and overnight, all accounts at the ZPP would have zero balances. As explained earlier, every bank participating in the net settlement would need to have sufficient balances to cover any net debit that might be required of it before any of the net settlement could be executed. It had to be all or nothing.

We held several meetings with the ZPP management. The chairman, Maruf Burnazović, was a likeable man and genuinely wished to be cooperative, I think. He seemed prepared to listen to our proposals and the reasons for them and to give them serious consideration. The Deputy Chairman, Avdo Ajanovic, was a different cup of tea. He seemed to have been brought in whenever the ZPP wanted to stonewall us. He would present long histories of the payment bureau system and why they were proud of its achievements and yada yada yada. We heard the same stories over and over. When he attempted to address the issue on the table, which was rarely, he only confused us all. I think that he even confused his colleagues. Increasingly as time went on, Maruf would urge him to be brief or come to the point, and on occasion, even to be quiet. My interpreter turned to me once and whispered that she could not really understand his old Soviet speak herself. "Must I really interpret this?" she asked.

We were torn between what we knew was needed to protect the CBBH and concern that we still did not fully understand the details of the current operation. We pleaded for more meetings with the technical staff. These were generally more informative and apolitical. But the technical staff did not always feel free to express themselves and had to struggle to understand our perspective as we struggled to understand theirs. Over the many hours spent across the table from our counterparts, a kind of bonding occurred, but not with Avdo. I always shuddered at the sight of him.

It is still difficult for me to fully understand why this was such a big deal for the ZPP. It was in many respects what they were doing, even if they thought of it differently. But they strongly objected. In order to gain their general cooperation, without which the launching of the CBBH would not have been possible, we finally gave in on some cosmetic features of the arrangement we wanted. We provided for the notional "transfer" of reserve account balances from the CBBH to ZPP each morning and their return each evening for the net settlement at the CBBH. It was to be as if reserve account balances (or a designated amount of them) were with ZPP during the day and the Central Bank overnight. The important thing was that they accepted the essential premise that the settlement would not have occurred until the CBBH posted the settlement amounts to the reserve accounts with it.

We actually had two further reforms in mind. The first was to consolidate the required reserve and settlement accounts (201 and 620) into a single reserve account. This would be combined with a revision of the reserve requirement that would allow it to be satisfied on an average rather than a continuous basis. The ZPP had no problem "transferring" the 201 account fully to the CBBH, but they were not willing to consolidate the two, which would mean also "transferring" the 620 balances to the CBBH, until we had worked out the arrangement described in the preceding paragraph. The second reform, which was more revolutionary and dangerous for the ZPP, was to permit banks to send the payment instructions for the use of their reserve accounts at the Central Bank directly to the Central Bank (rather than through the ZPP). This would lay the groundwork for the subsequent full takeover of control of interbank (or so-called large value) payments by the Central Bank. It clearly foreshadowed the dramatic reform if not the demise of the payment bureaus.

Near the end of the mission, Len came to the mission's evening meeting with new information on the system. The mission members met every evening in my room before dinner to share information on the meetings they each had attended during the day (as we generally had separate meetings). Ibro had stated, Len said, that the 620 account balance for each bank with the ZPP was the sum of the customers' Giro account balances for that bank and the bank's balance for its own account (a 500 account series). As a result, he argued, the customer account balances had to be deducted from the balance in the bank's 620 accounts in order to measure base money,[2] "because the customers' balances were already counted in the 620 balances." On the basis of this information, Len and I began to discuss the possibility of requiring banks to limit their customers' balances with the payment bureau to what they needed for immediate payments that day so that the reserve account balance with the CBBH (the old 620 plus the reserve requirement account 201) would be enough to cover both the bank's and its customers' net payments for the day.

We concluded that it would be difficult to enforce the system we had proposed, even with its changes. What if the CBBH was unable to settle the day's net payments for a number of days running? The ZPP was very likely to continue processing payments in the following days as if the previous day's payments had been settled. What could force the two systems (the Central Bank system and the payment bureau mirror of it) to stay together?

We decided to introduce a pay-in-advance approach. If the banks had to limit the sum of their reserve account balances for their own use and the Giro balances of their customers to what was in their reserve accounts with the CBBH, the system would be safe. Under these conditions, monitoring payment orders to stay within the balances of each customer's Giro account would be sufficient. Each morning, banks would need to ensure that their opening Giro balance (by transferring funds from the CBBH reserve account to their Giro account at the payment bureau) was equal to or greater than the sum of their customers' Giro account balances available for payments that day. They would then fund their customers' Giro account balances by debiting their own. Such a system of prefunding Giro accounts each morning, if rigorously adhered to, would prevent reserve account overdrafts when the system computed its net settlements each evening. It would cause banks to hold larger excess reserves and thus would be inefficient, but in the short run it would fully protect the CBBH against settlement overdrafts.

We quickly revised the scheme we had been developing to incorporate this additional feature. I discussed it with Enver and Ibro and they agreed that it should work.

CENTRAL BANK LAW ADOPTED

The Central Bank Law was passed by the State Parliamentary Assembly on June 20, 1997, near the end of our visit. The law went into force on June 28, 1997, and required that the CBBH begin operations within 45 days. I marked the days in my calendar until the Central Bank's mandated opening. The last legally possible day was August 12. In order to execute the transfer of bank reserve accounts to the CBBH on a weekend, when banks are normally closed, I recommended, and Serge agreed, that the CBBH would begin operations on Monday, August 11, 1997.

We were under enormous pressure. In addition to the payment system issues discussed above, we focused on the requirements for the CBBH to be in "full" operation by August 11, 1997, the first day of business after the transfer of all monetary liabilities and assets from the

NBBH to the CBBH. On that day the CBBH would own, and must manage, foreign exchange reserves expected to amount to about DM 230 million. And as discussed above, it would be necessary for it to be able to settle all net payments of KM each day using banks' reserve accounts with the CBBH.

These required challenging legal and operational changes in the three payment bureaus operating in the country, as well as putting the key staff and systems in place at the CBBH. While the old Bosnian dinars would continue to circulate until they were redeemed for the new, yet-to-be-designed-or-printed Convertible Markas (KM), all bank deposits and assets denominated in BHD would need to be redenominated as KM (at the rate of KM = 100 BHD over the weekend of August 9–10). We recommended that the CBBH issue an Interpretation of General Application under Article 7(b) of the Central Bank Law to facilitate the introduction of the KM and the conversion of BHD public and private obligations and debts to KM. We also began planning for the physical introduction of the KM that was to take place three or four months after the conversion of (cashless) obligations and debts.

Potential overdrafts from settling net payments through the ZPP were only one of our concerns for the integrity of the new Central Bank and its currency board rules. Serge Robert expressed his serious concern with regard to the security of Bosnian dinar (BHD) currency notes in the vaults of the NBBH. There was also a few million dollars equivalent of German mark bank notes in the vault. Security of the vaults was very poor. If additional (unissued) notes got into circulation, their redemption for the new currency to be issued by the CBBH could cause the total redeemed to exceed the foreign exchange backing provided by the NBBH to the CBBH. We made a number of recommendations for improving security immediately. For one, we recommended that the transfer of monetary liabilities and foreign exchange assets from the NBBH to the CBBH clearly establish the NBBH's continued obligation to cover BHD currency with DM in the event that BHD redemptions exceeded what had been recorded as issued. I also urged Serge to appoint the chief security officer as soon as possible.

The physical improvement of the vault security systems (and other physical investments in the headquarters building occupied by the

CBBH) was complicated by the fact that the legal title to the building was unclear and was not likely to be resolved for some months. This ambiguity resulted not only because of Yugoslavia's system of public and social property (worker ownership), but also because of the need to establish whether public property now belonged to the new state or to the Entity level of government. The CBBH would be a state (i.e., national government) institution. Though the NBBH now served only the Bosniac part of the Federation, before the war it had been the central bank for all of Bosnia and Herzegovina. We provided the authorities with the text of an agreement that we thought would help protect the claim of the CBBH to any future investments in the building, and I met with World Bank and USAID staff in an effort to ensure that title of future grants and equipment would go to the CBBH rather than to the NBBH.

We also needed to define the roles of the Main Units in Mostar and Pale (later Banja Luka) and their relationship to the CBBH headquarters in Sarajevo and to the payment bureaus in their respective areas. The system needed to be efficiently integrated, but it also needed to satisfy the strongly held views of the three ethnic groups. Though believing that the Main Units needed some degree of self-identity, we opposed the emergence of a separate identity for the Main Units that would detract from the single nationwide central bank. But we accepted the need for each region to feel a sense of ownership of the whole undertaking for it to be successful.

We proposed that the Main Units have a face-to-face relationship with the banks headquartered in their areas and with the payment bureaus operating in their areas. Each bank—that is to say the main office of each bank on behalf of all of its branch offices—would open its reserve account with the CBBH at the Main Unit serving the area in which the bank was located. Payment orders to debit that account, whether coming directly from the bank or indirectly through the local payment bureau, would be presented to the appropriate Main Unit. Payment orders to credit these accounts—because of a deposit of cash with or sale of DM to the CBBH by the bank, or a transfer from another bank— would also be presented to the Main Unit of the bank. If a credit were the result of a transfer from a bank operating under a different Main Unit, the payment order would be forwarded from the other Main Unit.

Thus the task of monitoring each bank's compliance with the reserve requirement and of transferring funds to each bank's Giro account with its payment bureau each morning and of confirming the daily net settlement of payments each evening would be carried out by the Main Units with respect to their banks.

The CBBH had one consolidated set of books but it was made up of separate accounts maintained by each Main Unit. These arrangements made it necessary for us to design the procedures for undertaking transfers between reserve accounts maintained in different Main Units. With respect to the settlement of payments through the payment bureaus, these arrangements gave rise to a difference in the amounts of daily settlements within each Main Unit and between them, which almost fully reflected the existing difference between daily net settlements within the SPP, ZAP, and ZPP and the interregional payments between them. Thus we began designing the procedures and instructions for much more complex settlements. The new system would use interregional settlements on the books of the CBBH to replace the periodic cash settlement from the trunk of the Mercedes now driving German marks between Mostar, Banja Luka, and Sarajevo.

ANOTHER ROAD SHOW

The issues were different in the RS, which had a more modern payment law. Its Internal Payments Law and the Foreign Exchange Law required that all domestic payments must be made in Yugoslav dinar. Thus it would be necessary at a minimum to amend these laws to allow the use of KM. We recommended, however, that the changes needed in the RS be achieved by adopting in the RS essentially the same new payment law we proposed for the Federation in order to clearly establish the relationship between depositors and banks and between banks and the Central Bank (even if they used payment bureaus as third party processors).

In an effort to address the above (and other) technical aspects of introducing KM into the three payment systems, we held two meetings during this visit with members of the Inter Entity Payments Technical Planning Committee. This was the formal name given to the technical working group on payments, a group we had convened during the previous mission. The purposes of these meetings were to explain the strategy for starting up the CBBH and introducing its new currency in more detail, to test it with this group and refine it as necessary, and to jump-start the work needed to implement it. The first meeting was held during the beginning of our visit in Sarajevo. Little progress was made due to the attendance of too many people. The large attendance and the fact that things were getting real, caused the discussions to be more political than they had been before. When attendance was limited to the technical staff, posturing was minimal and meetings had a more problem-solving atmosphere.

Later during this visit, we held another meeting of the Inter Entity Payments Technical Planning Committee, this time in Mostar. Anka Musa hosted the meeting in the headquarters of the Mostar ZAP, of which she was chairman. Enver Backović, a Vice Governor of the NBBH, accompanied us. He was expected to become the Bosniac Vice Governor of the CBBH. Enver had not been very keen to come, but did not show the same nervousness as this former Muslim war hero had subtly revealed when we traveled together for the first time to the Serbian held territory of Duboj almost one year earlier.

We arrived at the Mostar ZAP after what should have been a two-hour drive from Sarajevo, about forty-five minutes late. The Committee members and Anka were waiting for us. All three regions were represented. I explained the general features of the plans to redeem BD for KM (once they were available) and to convert account BDs. I also discussed the role of the CBBH's Main Units in Mostar and the RS. I was prepared to discuss the drafts of Regulations and Instructions for the new payment arrangements with the CBBH that had been faxed to them the night before. However, I was immediately blasted by the Croat contingent for not having given them enough time to seriously consider the drafts. This was a legitimate complaint since we had only finished preparing them the day before. We were all operating under very demanding deadlines and this was the best we could do as we struggled to fashion the details of this complex system.

However, I was quite unprepared for the attack that was unleashed on the BD conversion plans. We were told strongly that it was unfair to redeem Bosnian dinar at the planned rate. I explained again that the

BD was the only currency issued by one of the monetary authorities in Bosnia and Herzegovina and that other currencies could be exchanged for the future KM by converting them at market rates into German marks. I maintained that it was necessary to limit the currency the CBBH could receive to German marks (once BD were redeemed) in order to protect the integrity of the currency board arrangement, something they all supported. The CBBH would have enough German marks to redeem all BD at the 100 to one rate. So what was the problem? My explanation did not at all satisfy them. Somehow the arrangement was unfair to the Croat population in some way. We listened carefully to our interpreters, who didn't seem to understand the complaints either. We were all quite confused.

Eventually Enver indicated that he knew what was behind the complaints. It seems that when BD were issued in exchange for the previous rapidly inflating currency (the previous Yugoslav dinar), the Mostar ZAP, which at that time still used the NBBH as its central bank, sent a shipment of currency to Sarajevo (or perhaps it was a debit to its settlement account with the NBBH) to pay for new Bosnian dinars. However, it never got the shipment of BD. The Mostar ZAP had been robbed by the NBBH as far as it was concerned. Enver explained (though I must admit, I was so confused that I am still not sure that I have the details right) that the shipment of new BD bank notes was lost in transit. It vanished on the road between Sarajevo and Mostar. According to Enver the currency became the property of the Mostar ZAP when it left the premises of the NBBH in Sarajevo. According to the Mostar ZAP, they paid for something they never got. Then, of course, along came the Croat/Bosniac war.

I still didn't see what this had to do with the fairness or lack thereof the BD/DM redemption that I had outlined. I assumed that the occasion of our visit was being used to raise this old sour point. I was sure that having Enver, a former enemy, at the table added fuel to the fire. If there is any clarity to my explanation now, there was none then. I argued that if there was an unresolved dispute between the Mostar ZAP and the NBBH, "normal" legal channels should be used to press their claim. However, it seemed to me that it had nothing really to do with the plans I had just presented for establishing the CBBH and its currency. Now that I think I understand their complaint better, I still have no better advice to offer.

As generally happened in these meetings, after a period of venting, the tone mellowed and more serious work ensued. The fact was that the whole operation of starting the CBBH and issuing its currency was almost completely a Sarajevo-area (that is ZPP-area) operation because that was the only area being serviced by the NBBH after the war. It also had the only currency and deposit liabilities to redeem. Thus as a practical matter we had a bit more time to work out the operational details of settling interregional payments with banks' accounts with the new CBBH.

Following our meeting, which lasted about four hours, we and the other visitors were invited to a luncheon at a local restaurant. The restaurant, which we were to visit several times again in the future, had an excellent fish menu. We all sat around a long table. We numbered about thirty, counting some local bankers. Croatia produces some nice white wines, and our Croatian hosts were eager to entertain us with some of their finest. The mood and conversation warmed. As time passed, the volume of the conversation rose as the participants become less inhibited and more enthusiastic. Then Avdo from Sarajevo's ZPP—who talks too much, and mainly nonsense, when he is sober—let loose with a nasty tirade against something or other (our hosts most likely—the interpreters were refusing to interpret). Everyone else stopped in the midst of their conversations. Avdo continued to be the only voice breaking the sudden silence. After a few very embarrassing minutes (which seemed a very long time under such circumstances) Avdo ran out of steam and sat down and remained silent for the rest of the event. But that broke the spell. The meal was rapidly concluded; the camaraderie of the earlier hours was lost.

We got back into our cars and drove back to Sarajevo, while the Serbian group returned to Banja Luka and Pale.

DINNER AT KIM'S

As Kim and Jean-Luc were semi-resident in Sarajevo at this point, both had rented apartments for several months. On the Friday evening, near the end of the mission, we gathered at Kim's apartment for one of her fabulous dinner parties for the mission members. They were fabulous because Kim is an excellent cook, her hospitality is warm, the conversation was always interesting, and she did it all within minutes of returning from the office, often with the guests in tow. This last incredible trick was made possible by the nature of most oriental cuisine (e.g., stir-fry) and Kim's willingness to get up at five in the morning to chop all of the ingredients.

Upon our arrival, Kim produced a new regional brandy for our assessment. I sipped and sat quietly on the sofa while others talked. I was talked out. Hugh and Kim where talking in the kitchen so intensely that she actually overcooked one of her hors d'oeuvres. With a directness that he reserved only for such occasions, Hugh was asking whether Kim found that her feminine sexuality didn't provide her with particular advantages on occasion, and was she conscious of deliberately exploiting this advantage. It was something like that, as I was only half listening, but with growing amazement. In fact, she did in a fully professional, but effective way, fully exploit her femininity. I assume that in whatever way we can we each exploit whatever tools we have in order to be effective.

The IMF is a multinational, multiethnic organization *par excellence,* and genuine sexism or other cultural insensitivity is not tolerated. But thank God we were free of the ridged and stifling rules of the American corporate workplace, in which Hugh's conversation would have been unthinkable. Here in Sarajevo, Kim's voice simply got louder and more irritated (the long hard day!) and she burned the dumplings. I rose and wandered into the kitchen and began to insert some (hopefully) calming comments. But Kim really needed no one's help and Hugh's questions where meant deliberately to be provocative in the way a playwright explores his or her subjects.

Following dinner, at which we enjoyed one of Croatia's better white wines and one of Montenegro's better reds, the team moved back into the living room. Kim, Hugh, Ben, and Jean-Luc (I had ordered him to come), were sitting on the floor while Len, Chris, and I sat on the sofa and a chair. The now mellow conversation moved to the ethnic and family backgrounds of the team members and then to song. Kim led off with a song in Korean, Hugh sang a long one in Gaelic, Ben in Hebrew,

Chris in Australian English, and Jean-Luc in French. Len and I abstained (a shy American Anglo-Saxon in my case—Len was a second generation American Swede). It was a beautiful and warm experience. And we needed it. It was one of the many rewards my work has brought me.

JOHN DALTON'S VISIT

The accounting system is the heart of a financial institution. We were not merely installing a new chart of accounts and matching procedures, but new accounting standards and a new way of conceptualizing the operations of the Central Bank, especially its relationship with the payment system. All of these together posed a very formidable challenge. Jean-Luc was giving it his all, but every new issue outside his limited personal experience required considerable study on his part. The fact that Ibro continued to generally ignore him was the straw that broke the camel's back. Jean-Luc was sinking and needed help.

I sent for my IMF colleague John Dalton. John was a former manager of a branch of the Reserve Bank of Australia and a first-rate accountant, auditor, and manager. He was still only in his forties. He was easygoing, quick, and didn't know what "no" meant. John saved the accounting project and more or less finished off Jean-Luc's self-esteem in the process. John resolved most of the accounting issues that had dangled for months, oversaw installing the new chart of accounts on the NBBH's computer, wrote accounting instructions for the key transactions with the CBBH for the banks and the ZPP, working out the operational steps and instructions in the process. He did this in about ten days; and poor Jean-Luc, who had truly worked himself almost into the grave, was completely undone by John's easy success and his own hard-fought failure. He slipped into a depression that Kim and I feared could be dangerous.

While the difference in performance was huge, John was an unusually talented guy and also had years of the right kind of experience to draw on for what was needed. Jean-Luc had put in an enormous amount of hard work and made real contributions but against odds that were too great. I blamed the Bank of France for having sent someone too young and inadequately prepared to such a daunting task. As Kim and I watched him suffer, it broke our hearts. By mutual agreement, we cut his one-year resident assignment short and after the CBBH had opened, sent him home early. But in the end, he had grown and been strengthened by the experience.

7 THE OPENING

MY ARRIVAL IN SARAJEVO

The work plan for the 52 days from June 20 to August 11, 1997 (one day before the deadline in order to take advantage of the weekend), recommended by my June mission, called for the appointment of key CBBH officers the week of June 30 and the approval by its governing Board of the CBBH's organizational structure, staff levels, and salary scale the week of July 7, followed by the rapid staffing of all core positions. These staff members would then prepare for the operational start up of the Bank. The start up would involve the weekend transfer of the monetary liabilities of the NBBH to the CBBH along with a comparable value of foreign exchange assets, opening foreign currency accounts, establishing authorized signatories to operate these accounts, and the transfer of payment settlements in Bosnian dinar from the ZPP to the CBBH in KM.

Kim and Jean-Luc had been in semi-residence in Sarajevo for several months. Following my June mission, and John Dalton's visit in July, Bertil Perssen, a retired organization and management expert from the Riksbank in Sweden also visited in July. I assumed that it would not be necessary for me to return to help with the opening, but, of course, I

113

knew that it was a possibility. Nonetheless, I planned a vacation (AT HOME!) for the first three weeks of August.

Because of the political bickering by the Board, none of the above actions had been taken when Kim called from Sarajevo on Thursday, July 31, to say that the Governor wanted me to come after all. One part of me wanted to be there for the opening, whether I was really needed or not. I had worked very hard along with Chris, Kim, and many others over the previous year and a half to make this day happen; and being present for the opening would be a bit of a payback. But until Kim's call, I was not really convinced that I had much to add to the preparations at that point, and I did have many plans for my three weeks at home and the rest that I badly needed. I was also deep into preparations for an early September mission to Croatia.

The lack of action by the Board had put an unrealistic burden on our technical assistance. But the months of isolated preparations by the IMF, unassisted by counterparts, made it possible to even consider opening on time. I booked a flight for Wednesday evening, August 6, that would put me in Sarajevo the afternoon of August 7 and one leaving Sarajevo on Thursday, August 14. At Alessandro's urging I stretched my schedule a bit at both ends and flew out of Washington on Tuesday (with the return rescheduled for Friday). The number of flights and departure cities for Sarajevo was rapidly increasing. Zagreb, which continued to be the departure point for NATO and UN flights, was no longer the only choice for regular airline flights, which now also included Rome, Ljubjliana, Vienna, and Zurich. I was on United's nonstop flight from Washington to Zurich. I was on the ground in Sarajevo and in the terminal by 2:30 p.m. where I was met by Devna, Alessandro's secretary, and Ivica, his driver.

Ivica "Ivi" Perović had been born in Bosnia but had grown up in Chicago when his family moved there in the seventies. He had obtained a degree in chemical engineering and returned to Bosnia only to be engulfed in the Balkan wars. There were no jobs in chemical engineering in 1997, and the salary of a driver for the IMF resident representative was relatively very attractive. Ivi was a very handsome, cheerful young man, with a broad uncomplicated smile. I assume that he was simply born to be happy. On each return to Sarajevo as I climbed the steps in the Central Bank building to the third floor IMF office, Ivi was usually one of the first to greet me with his bright smile and surprised, "Oooh, Mr. Cooooats, yourrr back."

From the outside, the Sarajevo airport looked pretty much as it had when I arrived the first time. On this return (I had been there only six weeks earlier) the terminal seemed "almost" normal. This was especially so in the departure area, I noticed when I returned to leave nine days later, which then seemed to have most of the features one finds in airports more or less in final locations (quite different than the layout six weeks earlier). My luggage was now off-loaded from the baggage wagons onto one of five conveyer belts with metal rollers down which the bags could be pushed in order to spread them out for easier access. The five belts radiated out from a single unloading point in an arrangement I had never seen before. Six weeks earlier they were still using the single, short unloading platform around which only a few people could crowd at a time.

"Hi, Mr. Coats, how was your flight?" asked Devna as I walked out of the "baggage claim area" and past customs. Her smiling face was always a welcome sight. On the drive into the city, the gutted tanks that had littered the road when I arrived the first time had been removed months earlier.

By 3:30 p.m. I had checked into the Hotel Bosna and walked the short distance to the National Bank of Bosnia and Herzegovina, whose building would become the Central Bank of Bosnia and Herzegovina a few days later and which was the hub of all of our activities. Alessandro's resident representative office was there as well. The guard at the entrance recognized me, or at least the words "IMF" and waved me by. As I reached the second floor landing, the floor on which are found the Governor's and Vice Governors' offices and the boardroom, I saw Kim walking in the direction of the Governor's office.

"Kim, Kim!" I called out.

"Oh, you are here," she said. "Good. I am on my way to meet the Governor." There was never an occasion when seeing Kim—a lovely, smart, warm, and gregarious woman—was not welcome, but first sightings are always particularly poignant. I had been on my way to Alessandro's office and then to find Kim and Jean-Luc for a briefing. I needed to be up to speed as quickly as possible, but I followed her into Serge's office.

Serge greeted us with his bright, friendly, French smile, and started something like "You know . . . you know what they are saying now . . . I can't stand it any more. Oh well, what can you do? Welcome back, Warren." I no longer remember which of our local friends was being difficult at that moment, as they seemed to take turns faithfully.

What I learned was not generally very comforting. While things outside the control of the Governing Board had progressed, the Board itself had adopted few of the measures that our June mission report had recommended. As usual, Board members continued to argue over the role and exact composition of the CBBH branches (referred to as Main Units—language that I had refused to use in our June mission report). The Board had only finally agreed to the organizational structure of the CBBH and its Branches a few days earlier. They had not adopted any of the Instructions and Regulations needed to open the Bank, and they would not meet again until two days after the opening. I did not (and still do not) understand why the Board was not meeting every day until its necessary work was done.

I asked what we knew now about the details of the actual transfer of monetary liabilities and assets from the NBBH to the CBBH that was to take place in two or three days and what arrangements had been made for the transfer of physical assets of the NBBH that might be needed by the CBBH (building, vault, cars, supplies, etc.).

"Very little," replied Serge. Kasim, who was in his final days as Governor of the NBBH was revealing nothing, saying that everything would be clear at the meeting of the Transition Committee on Friday—THE LAST DAY OF THE NBBH'S OPERATION AS A MONETARY INSTITUTION!

As a legal matter, the CBBH came into existence on June 28, eight days after the adoption of the law. Though it was not expected to take over monetary operations from the NBBH until August 11, our June mission report had assumed that it could and would formally hire staff and begin administrative operations promptly after June 28. As indicated above, this also had not happened. I suspected that this failure had something to do with the poor relations between Serge and Kasim, and/or the general uncooperativeness of the Board.

I proposed to the Governor that, as the law required, the CBBH would start its operations no later than August 12 and that he should sign all of the Instructions and Regulations needed to start and refer them to the Board for ratification when it got around to them. How else could he observe the law and open on time? He agreed, and a way forward, around the troublesome Board, had been found.

Several weeks earlier, after much insistence by Kim, ten staff members of the NBBH finally had been selected and assigned to work with her and Jean-Luc in preparing for the opening. At this point, the CBBH had a Governing Board; and two of its three Vice Governors had been formally appointed. A third Vice Governor had been appointed and had already resigned as the result of a dispute among his Croat sponsors, though a replacement had been identified, Dragan Kovačević. None of the Vice Governors were actively on the job, except for Enver, who remained the Vice Governor of the NBBH for foreign exchange operations until August 8.

I assume that it is clear why there were three Vice Governors. The members of the Transition Team had identified 40 staff of the NBBH who would be offered positions in the CBBH on Friday (August 8). Just to keep it fresh in your mind, August 8 was the last regular working day before the start up of the new Central Bank. Opening on time seemed impossible.

In addition, Jure Pelivan, the Croat member of the Board, had become more and more vocal in his opposition to opening until certain other issues were settled. These included defining the area covered by the Mostar Main Unit and closing the NBBH. The CBBH could have defined the area served by the Mostar Main Unit any way it wanted. However, it only made sense to do so in ways that would technically allow banks covered by it to communicate with it and to have their payment orders processed by the ZAP. However, the political subdivisions, which also defined the area of ZAP operation, were being reviewed at the political level and were to be adjusted. Thus it was not practical to define the area covered by the Main Unit until the higher level political decisions were made about which areas municipalities were to be in.

The NBBH question, as usual, was more complicated. Jure complained that though the NBBH was planning to transfer its monetary liabilities, it should be transferring all of its deposits. However, it didn't have enough foreign exchange backing to do so. Thus the currency board would be unsound. In addition to this point, he argued that the CBBH should not open without the capital required in the law. We frankly didn't know what Jure was talking about. He had a way of expressing himself that was very confusing to us. I remember a Board meeting at which Manojlo turned to Jure after a long intervention on Jure's part and said disgustedly, "Jure, I don't understand anything you have said." Manojlo had the advantage of hearing Jure's comments in their mother tongue. We were to learn, however, that when properly understood, Jure had a very valid point. Looking back I think that we had simply misunderstood him all along,

Despite all, Kim and Alessandro insisted that the Bank could and should open. The Federation Payment Bureau had worked hard to prepare for the opening, and the payment system should be ready in the area using the Bosnia and Herzegovina Dinars (BHD). While the CBBH was to be the new central bank for all three regions, in fact its initial opening only had relevance for the Muslim area served by the NBBH. The Croat and Serb areas had no bank notes to be redeemed, nor deposits to be converted. As the public opened KM deposits in banks in those areas, those banks would need to open KM reserve accounts with the CBBH; and the ZAP and SPP would need to be able to process KM payments. Since there was no agreement on bank note design yet, the CBBH would also open without bank notes. The public would continue to use whatever bank notes they had before (DM, BM, YUD, and kuna). These unfortunate facts fortunately made it simpler to start up the CBBH.

If the issues were purely technical, it surely would have been wiser to delay the opening a month or two, so that public understanding and participation would be broader, and the CBBH could be more fully staffed and prepared. However, we had so often encountered arguments that were designed only to delay progress that we concluded such delaying tactics were at work here too. We thought that Jure was complaining and the Board was stalling just to slow progress. Thus we concluded that we should take the handle the law gave us and open even if things were rushed and not fully prepared (as long as we would not freeze up the payment system in the process).

I ran into Alessandro soon after my meeting with Serge and spent most of the rest of the afternoon in the office used by Kim and Jean-

Luc and an interpreter/secretary. We reviewed the status of the work plan laid out in our June mission report and discussed priorities before the opening. We were assuming that the Bank would open as scheduled, but still had one or two more days during which it could be called off. We took a short dinner break at Kogos next door—spaghetti—and returned to the office until 10:00 p.m. when jet lag and fatigue (I had not slept much on the overnight flight from Washington) overtook me and I returned to my little room at the Hotel Bosna.

THE BANK BRIEFING

The next morning I had breakfast in the hotel dinning room. The hotel provided a very modest buffet of bread, cold meats (for the Germans), scrambled eggs over a warmer, cold cereal, some fresh fruit, and, of course, orange juice and coffee. How much can you really eat at breakfast anyway? I arrived at the office before 7:30 a.m. and Jean-Luc was already there. He was in the office ahead of me almost every morning. After working on some documents, which included last minute adjustments to the reserve requirement regulation, I visited Enver to discuss the 10:00 a.m. meeting with bank representatives to review the weekend activities and Monday's start up of the CBBH.

Enver explained that he, Kim, and the Governor had met with the banks the week before and that the Governor had given a general overview of what was happening. In addition, the banks had received drafts of the Instructions that would be formally issued to them today. Today's meeting would be following up on the earlier ones and would answer any last minute questions. I discussed the prefunding scheme that we were introducing and asked whether he thought banks would have trouble with it. "We shall see what they say at the meeting," he said.

Kim was in the IMF resident representative's office putting together the first four Instructions for the next week, which had been formally signed by Enver. In addition, I obtained Serge's signature on the reserve requirement regulation. At 10:00 a.m. we walked up one floor from Enver's office to the large meeting room in which the bankers had assembled. I had expected about fifty people (the number of banks in the Bosnian region), but there were three times that number. Enver opened the meeting and turned it over to me.

I explained that the Central Bank Law and the general rules of a currency board arrangement did not permit the CBBH to extend credit. Thus they could not provide lender of last resort services to ensure the completion of the daily net settlement of domestic payments. The operations of the payment system needed to take that into account. Several mechanisms were being provided. The reserve requirement had been reformulated so that in the future it could be met on average rather than continuously. Banks' separately required reserve and clearing accounts were being combined into one account so that banks would have automatic access to these amounts. Reserve averaging would be the first line of defense in protecting bank liquidity and the functioning of the payment system without central bank credit.

Two other important changes would help protect the currency board arrangement. One was the control that the CBBH would have over the daily settlements, which would not be final until the CBBH had posted the net payments to banks' reserve accounts on its books. The other was the requirement that each bank's Giro account at the payment bureau, and the Giro accounts of its clients, must be prefunded each morning consistent with each bank's reserve account balances with the CBBH. These amounts had to be approved by the CBBH each day. The payment bureau could not accept any payment order that did not have sufficient cover in the payer's Giro account.

The new procedures had an important additional requirement for banks to obtain information from their customers on the amounts desired by each customer in the customer's Giro account balance with the payment bureau. Furthermore, the amounts posted to a bank's customers' accounts would be explicitly deducted from the bank's own Giro account in the morning. The sum of the bank's Giro balance and of its customers' Giro balances should match its reserve account balance with the CBBH.

I had some concern over whether banks would be able to fulfill this requirement. Their instruction each morning to the payment bureau and the CBBH would need to include the prefunded opening Giro account balance for each of their customers as well as for their own needs. The ability of the payment bureau to provide the required information on a timely basis was another concern. Those bankers who responded to my question on this point indicated that they had that information already and could comply with this requirement without difficulty. I was reassured.

Many questions were raised (and I hope clarified) at this meeting. One had to do with exchange rates. While the Central Bank Law swept away any exchange controls, the instructions to banks governing the old restrictions had not been explicitly revoked. Thus banks were not sure where things stood and wanted to know what exchange rates they could use when undertaking foreign exchange transactions with their customers. I pointed out that with the exception of exchanges between DM and KM, which were governed by the currency board rules of one for one, the exchange rate used was up to them and their customers; the market was free. Enver acknowledged that the old regulations had not been formally withdrawn, but he reassured the bankers that starting Monday they would no longer be enforced and that the CBBH would formally withdraw the earlier restrictions as soon as possible. Nonetheless, the CBBH would publish a list of reference exchange rates for accounting purposes.

The formally signed Instructions 1 through 4 and the reserve requirement regulation were passed out to the assembled bankers. In addition, copies were mailed to each bank and would later be published in the Official Gazette—a bit out of the usual order! These Instructions dealt with each of the key uses of banks' reserve account balances with the CBBH, purchases of KM with DM and of DM with KM, transfers to and from the payment bureaus, and daily settlement of net payments through the payment bureaus. The Instructions on interbank transfers were still only available as a discussion draft.

I found the meeting encouraging. I was feeling increasingly reassured that we could actually go forward with Monday's opening. There was considerable momentum. The low level of cooperation until very recently always left the impression that no one really thought it would happen. Now, within two to three days of the event, that impression was finally beginning to change.

I no longer remember exactly what occupied us the rest of the afternoon, except that for lunch we ate sandwiches from Kogos at our desks.

I had my computer on a corner of the large table at which Kim and Jean-Luc worked from opposite sides. Next to me was the PC of the interpreter/assistant. In mid-afternoon, Kim and I were walking down the stairs from our fourth floor office when we ran into Dino from Merchant Banka, one of the more articulate bankers at the morning meeting. He spoke perfect English and was clearly intelligent. We discussed the meeting and the issues. He still had questions. Was it really intended, for example, for banks to deduct the balances posted to their customers' Giro accounts from their own first thing in the morning? It was understood, of course, that any net payments by customers during the day would have to be covered from banks' own Giro accounts (and thus ultimately from the reserve accounts with the CBBH), but up front, first thing in the morning? We asked if he would be available and willing to read the as-yet-unissued Instruction 5 that would cover these issues and discuss it with us. He might help us improve the clarity of the instruction. He said he would be in his office that Friday and Saturday morning and would be happy to help. He gave us his phone numbers at work and at home.

Later that afternoon, when discussing with Alessandro our encounter with Dino, he said, "Why don't we hire him for the weekend? I have the money." We readily agreed, as did Dino the next day, and his later input proved to be extremely important.

Kim, Jean-Luc, and I spent the rest of the afternoon and evening in our fourth floor office, reviewing the things that still needed to be done, and revising the Instructions to be issued to the banks the next day. We worked through dinner and called it a day at around midnight. The clock was ticking loudly in our ears.

THE FINAL FRIDAY FOR NBBH AS A MONETARY INSTITUTION
TRANSITION TEAM REPORT

Our June mission report had recommended the creation of a transition team to study and make recommendations with regard to the transfer of monetary operations from the NBBH to the CBBH. The committee had actually been suggested by Serge as a way of sorting through the many issues involved in the transition, such as the transfer of some staff, physical premises, equipment, and supplies, not to mention the determination of the amount of monetary liabilities that would be transferred. Serge appointed Obrad Piljak, a Serb and an NBBH Vice Governor, to head the Transition Committee (he was later made the Comptroller General of the CBBH). Its members consisted of the heads of the most relevant departments of the NBBH, including Ibro. Kasim and Serge scheduled a meeting of this committee for Friday at 10:00 a.m. to discuss a progress report. Such a discussion seemed rather late in the game to me. Kasim had billed it as the time at which all would be revealed (as very little had been revealed up to that point). It would clearly reveal whether Kasim was cooperating or not. But what could we do by then if he weren't?

I was particularly worried about two points on which Kasim's thinking was not clear to us. The first had to do with the trust account arrangement (discussed more fully later). From time to time Kasim had referred to the trust account as if it were not on the books of the CBBH and as if he would continue to administer it. A separate Trust Fund, separately administered, could raise all kinds of new issues and problems, such as who owned and controlled it. The purpose for which it had been created, as we understood it, was legitimate and fully consistent with its being on the books, and under the full control, of the CBBH.

The second issue about which I worried of late was whether all of the balances banks kept with the NBBH (both required and excess reserves) would be transferred to the CBBH. We were about to find out whether I worried unnecessarily or not.

In addition to Mr. Piljak and his fellow committee members, Kasim, Serge, Jean-Luc, Alessandro, and I attended the meeting. In addition, a team from Arthur Andersen, which had flown in the day before from various countries on about a one-day notice, made a short presentation of the procedures they recommended for the transfer of financial assets and liabilities. Serge had prepared an agenda that included the draft agreement for the transfer of monetary liabilities and foreign exchange assets that were to take place over the weekend. The draft had been prepared about a month earlier by Jean-Luc and given to several senior officials of the NBBH for comment. No one had commented on it up to that point, which illustrated the degree of cooperation that we were receiving. Jean-Luc was a bit embarrassed by seeing the draft suddenly on the table without the benefit of any feedback, and indeed it became the sole topic of discussion for the rest of the meeting. The other issues of staff, building, and supplies were put off to another time.

The meeting, though a report from the Transition Committee, was really Kasim's show. What stance would he take? Would he be cooperative or find reasons to stop the process? I listened with rapt attention as he began to speak. "The Committee has done a good job ... and I would like to thank them for their work. I can generally go along with the draft agreement between the NBBH and the CBBH. . . ."

I had worried especially about whether Kasim would claim that the excess reserves of banks (their 620 account balances as they were called by the ZPP) should not be transferred to the CBBH. Banks are not required to have excess reserves with the central bank (hence the term "excess reserves"), and the ZPP itself had made a big deal out of being able to return the required reserves (account 201 at the ZPP) to the NBBH/CBBH but not the 620 balances. He did not make that point and accepted without reservation the definition of the monetary liabilities to be transferred that were stipulated in the draft agreement, with one minor exception. That exception had to do with deposits of foreign governments and international organizations. Kasim correctly argued that these could not be moved without the permission of the deposit owners, so we amended the agreement on this point to read, "[such deposits] ... shall be transferred the same way as deposits of banks, as soon as the agreement of the owners of the deposits is obtained" (we met with the USAID representatives later in the day to obtain their permission to transfer the US$200 million earmarked for aid projects in the account of the government of BiH).

The meeting to this point had been milk and honey. The final provision of the agreement dealt with the transfer of the foreign exchange equivalent to the monetary liabilities being transferred, and Serge had arranged to invest the money with the BIS until reserve management capability and internal controls were well established in the CBBH. Kasim could not accept this. His tone changed, and he launched into an attack on the BIS for not admitting Bosnia to membership and for not releasing its foreign exchange held there from the break up of Yugoslavia. His point was not well-taken, or at least not well-understood by me. The BIS had actually saved Bosnia's share of Yugoslavia's deposits at the BIS by freezing them until an agreement could be reached with the republics of the former Yugoslavia. In any event, Kasim roared to a loud conclusion that was unyielding on the point of putting money in the BIS, which he would not accept.

As Governor of the NBBH, Kasim had no real authority to say how the CBBH invested its assets; he did, however, have a more limited say as one of the CBBH's four Board members. Serge abandoned his plan to put the money in the BIS for the time being, until the CBBH Board could take it up. The meeting adjourned a great success. No roadblock had been created. The transfer was on track. Perhaps it would all happen after all.

After the Transition Committee meeting, I met with Enver to discuss a number of operational issues and to review preparations for opening the CBBH. This review included the state of preparations for transferring the foreign exchange to be received on Monday from the NBBH to new accounts abroad opened by the CBBH. It seemed that preparations were not quite complete. An account had been opened at Commerzbank in Germany, and authorized signatories to operate the account had been established; but some further checking was required before it was certain that the account was in operation. The account at Citibank was in a different situation. The account was actually in the name of the NBBH, though it had never been used; and Enver thought that the CBBH should just change the name (as an officer of the NBBH through the end of the day he was still an authorized signatory for the account). I indicated that I was not sure this was a good idea and asked him to check with Serge. In the end, the Citibank account was not used for the August 11 transfer.

FEDERATION PAYMENT BUREAU
The most challenging part of starting up the new Central Bank was to restructure the operations of the payment bureaus (initially the ZPP,

where basically all BHD payments were made) in order to settle in Convertible Marka on the books of the CBBH without the risk of the CBBH extending any credit. The number of times I have repeated this indicates how important it was and how worried we were about it. Based on the recommendations of my June mission, and of subsequent meetings with the payment bureaus by Kim and Jean-Luc, the ZPP had undertaken a number of technical and procedural changes to prepare for the opening of the CBBH. These preparations included the plans for the weekend conversion of all BHD deposits and amounts into KM (and dropping two zeros in the process).

The instruction issued by the Federation Payment Bureau (FPB), which governed both the ZPP and the ZAP, in fact dealt only with ZPP offices and banks and other depositors using those offices. It provided complete instructions for the redenomination of BHD into KM, but it only incorporated some of our earlier recommendations for dealing with the risk that a bank would need credit to settle. In particular, the instruction provided for unwinding payments by banks that otherwise would have a negative balance after the daily net clearing of payments. The unwinding option was our very last resort, and the instruction did not seem to have provided for after-hours transactions to add funds to the clearing account of a bank with a negative balance, nor for the prefunding of Giro accounts that had become our first line of defense during the June mission. I requested a meeting with the FPB to discuss these issues, and to verify when on Saturday the FPB would deliver the closing balances for Friday that would be the basis for the bank balances with the NBBH that would be transferred to the CBBH.

Our meeting was to begin at 2:00 p.m. Things were not quite as clearly organized as they might have been. Or perhaps I was still a bit jet lagged and had not caught up to where everyone was. I thought that I was supposed to meet with Enver, Ibro, Jean-Luc, and the interpreter at the front entrance to the National Bank building. Kim, who had been very active in working with the payment bureau staff, was too busy with other projects to attend. It was a very nice, warm, sunny day, but only the interpreter was there. I wasn't sure if the others had remembered the meeting and sent the interpreter to find them. As we were running a bit behind, I went ahead, arriving only a few minutes late. The Federation

Payment Bureau headquarters was just behind the National Bank building that was about to become the Central Bank building. It was more or less the backside of the (almost) same building. I was sent into the Federation Payment Bureau Chairman's meeting room where I was greeted by the Chairman, Vice Chairman, and three others from the FPB staff.

Maruf greeted me warmly. This was our first meeting during this particular visit; but conversation was difficult without the interpreter, though Maruf speaks some "social" English. The interpreter and Jean-Luc arrived ahead of Enver and Ibro, and I began a review of the issues and the need for the procedure underlying our "prefunding" of Giro accounts scheme. The others arrived after a short delay.

The FPB side of the table listened quietly; then Maruf explained the very large effort that they had underway that day and the next to collect and report the closing Friday balances as early on Saturday as possible. He asked for my clarification of the future treatment of the required reserve accounts (called the 201 accounts by the ZPP). He reported that the ZPP would be able to "return" those balances to the CBBH as requested. For some reason, however, it would be impossible to "return" the excess reserve account balances, called the 620 accounts by the ZPP, each evening to the CBBH. His words reflected the continued lack of understanding of, or dispute over, existing and future arrangements. In our view, as a "neutral," (the word the ZPP likes to use when describing itself), non-monetary institution, the payment bureaus did not hold deposits (in the sense of having deposit liabilities of its own), at least in the local currency. In the ZPP's view, they had the money, at least during the day. Maruf repeated his view that the FPB should have been the currency board rather than creating a new central bank.

The existing domestic payments law in the Federation gave no one any comfort on this issue. The law was confusing, internally inconsistent, and at variance with actual practice (which was, more or less, to require "depositors" at the payment bureau to have deposit contracts with banks). In other words, it was accepted, implicitly at least, that the deposits transferred by the payment bureaus were liabilities of banks. The draft payment law that Ben Geva had prepared during my June mission and the draft regulation on the operation of the reserve account would clarify the issue as follows: All deposits had to be with banks, even if (for a while) payments were made by going to a payment bureau that processed them. The payment bureau was a provider of payment and accounting services to banks (and their customers). They were, as we called them in our drafts, a third-party processor—an agent of the banks. Finally, they also functioned as a clearinghouse, computing a net payment to or from each bank each day.

Our general conception and plan of how payments would operate starting Monday could be summarized as follows: After sweeping all accounts at the payment bureau clean every evening, each day would begin by the CBBH setting aside an amount for daily payments on the basis of requests received each day from banks. This amount would be credited to each bank's 620 Giro account at the opening of business. In addition, on the basis of information (or instructions) from banks' customers, each bank's Giro account balance would be debited by the amounts transferred to their customers' accounts. Only banks would participate in the daily clearing, and only banks or their customers would have Giro accounts with the payment bureau. Thus all Giro accounts would be prefunded by amounts equal to or less than each bank's reserve account balance with the CBBH, making it impossible for any bank to have a negative balance after the end-of-day clearing. The new end-of-day 620 balances for each bank would again be zeroed out, i.e., transferred to the CBBH clearing account with the payment bureau, which should also then be zero again. And appropriate adjustments would be made to each bank's reserve account with the CBBH. This end-of-day posting to banks' reserve accounts would constitute final settlement for that day. The payment bureau would be processing payments on behalf of banks and their customers—not holding deposits—in such a way that ensured no end-of-day overdraft and hence no need for credit to settle the daily net payments (assuming the payment bureau would not accept and process a payment order that exceeded the customer's Giro account balance).

Maruf repeated that it would be impossible to "return" the 620 balances to the CBBH each evening. The discussion grew heated, making it impossible for the interpreter to interpret. Ibro and Enver and their counterparts in the FPB were all speaking at once. Enver pounded the table and shouted, than suddenly stood up. The interpreter said that he had just threatened to leave if they continued to waste his time with such nonsense. Enver, the war hero, could be very tough. Things calmed down; and after some considerable further discussion, Maruf offered the olive branch that they would reconsider the technical possibilities and report on them in the morning. In any event, the required reserve account 201 would be merged with the 620 and closed as requested. This would facilitate operating the reserve requirement on an average rather than a continuous basis. Another meeting was set for 8:00 a.m. the next morning.

Agreement with the ZPP: from left to right: ZPP Deputy, Maruf Burnazović (Chairman of Federation Payment Bureau and ZPP), Enver Backović (Vice Governor NBBH/CBBH), the author, and Kim Rhee (IMF).

USAID AND THE BIH DEPOSIT WITH NBBH

By the time we left the ZPP meeting, I was late for the meeting with Serge and Kasim and USAID people about transferring US$200 million in aid funds from the NBBH to the CBBH. Enver was to come with me to USAID headquarters, but needed a breather and some food (we had not had time for lunch) and bowed out. At the same time he apologized for his behavior at the meeting, saying that it was sometimes necessary to keep them serious and on the point. We laughed that we were playing good cop, bad cop.

Ivi was waiting to drive me to the USAID headquarters. It was only about ten blocks from the NBBH/ZPP and normally I would have walked. After being processed through U.S. security, I arrived late to the meeting already in progress. Craig Buck was chairing the meeting, which included Mike Sarhan and some others I had not met before and would work with again in Kosovo and Yugoslavia.

The meeting was more a formality than anything, but face-to-face meetings from time to time are essential to maintain trust and cooperation. There were some legal formalities that would need to be satisfied, but of course the U.S. was eager to cooperate in establishing and strengthening the new Central Bank. It turned out, however, that transferring the USAID deposit to the CBBH would be more symbolic that substantive because the U.S. managed the deposit off balance sheet on its own until disbursements needed to be made. Thus the deposit would not generally provide any reserves for the CBBH to manage.

I returned to the NBBH with Serge and Kasim. Kim was in the process of notifying the forty people from the NBBH who were being hired by the CBBH. Starting Saturday, two days before it's opening, the CBBH would have a real staff. Better late than never, but this was insane. What were we thinking? Transferring the payment system settlement to the new institution was not a trivial undertaking. If it failed to function, payments in the country could freeze up, or worse, violate and thus undermine the currency board arrangement. A lot was at stake. How could we possibly start under these conditions?

At this point it was around 6:00 p.m. One of our interpreters asked me if they should stay to interpret. I was so tired and jet lagged that I was unable to think. I stood there for a minute trying to find an answer to her question, and then just walked away mumbling some apology.

THE LAST WEEKEND

One of the several important events in the opening of the CBBH was the formal, legal transfer to the CBBH of the monetary liabilities of the NBBH and a comparable value of foreign currency assets. In addition, the CBBH would get the use of the building then occupied by the NBBH, the free use of its accounting software, and office supplies and furniture. Kasim's office car and driver would remain with the NBBH, and its minivan would be transferred to the CBBH. Serge was to use a new car purchased by the CBBH. We needed to establish the proper legal form for these transfers and determine definitively the monetary liabilities to be transferred. The Arthur Andersen team played an invaluable role in these areas. I had purchased a house before, but had no experience in buying a central bank.

SATURDAY'S COUNT OF MONETARY LIABILITIES OF THE NBBH

Saturday morning at 8:00 a.m., two representatives of the NBBH, two from the CBBH (one of them being Jean-Luc), and the Arthur Andersen team of five auditing and currency experts (including a counterfeit specialist) started the count of the cash in the vault in the NBBH building that contained the BHD notes, some YD coins and a few other things. Everything except the BHD notes were moved out of the vault, which was to be turned over to the CBBH as part of the transfer. I had never seen the local currency vault before, which was in the basement of the NBBH building; and I did not participate in the Saturday count.

Kasim had pointed out the day before that the BHD 2,638,343,727 (equivalent to DM 26,383,437.27) that was supposed to be in the vault was made up of over 3.1 million notes. These were checked on a sample basis for counterfeit, for the number of currency bundles, and for the correctness of the amounts in each bundle. Most of the currency notes that were not in circulation, however, were in the vaults of the ZPP and the Post Offices, which acted as agents of the NBBH in storing and providing cash. On Friday, August 8, the "unissued" notes in the vaults of the ZPP and Post Offices amounted to DM 38,276,604.43. These amounts were given to us Saturday afternoon in a special report prepared by the ZPP and could not be checked until after the transfer to take place on Monday, August 11.

FURTHER MEETINGS WITH THE FPB

We had several reasons to meet with the payment bureau that day. One was to collect the data being prepared by the ZPP on the closing balances for cash and for bank deposits with the NBBH for the day before, which would constitute important parts of the monetary liabilities to be transferred to the CBBH. Another was to continue the incomplete discussions of the day before on the arrangements that had been made to coordinate the daily settlement of payments with the CBBH under the new procedures that we had outlined in the report of our June mission.

I had asked David Whitehead of USAID (KPMG/Barents) to join us. Both sides insisted that Kim be present, as she had been present at the meetings several weeks earlier at which the now-disputed agreement on settlement procedures with the FPB had been reached (and because both sides liked and trusted her). David was waiting outside the FPB building before 8:00 a.m. when I arrived; but Kim, Enver, and Ibro were not there yet. As I was attempting to introduce David as the person with the money to finance the improvements to the FPB's infrastructure (improved telecommunications lines, and computer hardware and software) the others arrived, so I was unable to resume the introduction in the general commotion.

David was a former Fed person—the Federal Reserve Bank of Dallas. He was friendly and helped us out on many occasions, with transportation, interpreters, PCs for the CBBH, etc. However, he also had his own agenda that we were never able to fully comprehend. He had established close relationships with key officials in the Federation and RS governments. He raised issues at times that needed to be raised and resolved and at other times seemed misguided and only caused us trouble. Our primary falling out with David came over his role in the comprehensive program to reform the payment bureaus that came later, but we always enjoyed his genuinely gracious hospitality.

Maruf started the meeting by announcing "some good news and some bad news." Final figures for Friday's closing balances would be available by noon. However, the ZPP would not be able to consolidate the 201 and 620 accounts and then close the 201 account by the opening of business Monday. They would do so, however, by the close of business on Monday. In addition, he again confirmed his position of the previous day that it would not be possible to return the 620 balances to the CBBH each evening. This remained a mystery to me because in later discussions with the technical staff of the FPB (with whom things were always clearer and easier) our accounting approach (zero balances in all ZPP accounts each evening) was accepted without discussion. Given the legal ambiguity under which the system was currently operating, this probably was not a very important distinction. We would continue to view it our way and they theirs. If a bank were to fail during the day in the future, a court would have to determine whose view was supported.

Our "old friend" and gab bag Avdo (Vice Chairman of FPB) took the floor and talked on about the whole system again. We had heard this story several times before (but never fully understood his version of it), and we frankly were running out of time and patience. We attempted politely to return the conversation to its subject but without any success. After being interrupted again, Avdo stated with a pout that he was not participating in the meeting anymore. In Maruf and Avdo, the FPB had their own version of the good cop, bad cop.

Avdo's incoherent story aside, the payment bureaus knew that their time was limited, in their current form at least. They repeatedly acknowledge that banks must eventually be allowed to provide payment services, which, in fact, was already allowed by the domestic payments law of Republika Srpska. But the time was not quite yet. The payment bureau management, particularly the ZPP wing of the FPB, was quite concerned about the changes we were pushing, knowing that it would accelerate the erosion of their power.

In fact, in order to meet the deadlines for opening the Central Bank, we had postponed any attempt at serious reform of the payment bureaus. I tried to stress in my discussions with them during this and the earlier meeting that we were changing nothing about the payment bureau's operations during the day. The change was in the relationship between the bureau and the Central Bank, i.e., the opening and closing of the day with final settlement controlled by and on the books of the Central Bank. Nonetheless, the psychological impact of the very small changes that we had insisted on was tremendous—a proper foundation for future reforms was being slowly put in place, and they knew it. Over and over again, I was surprised at the importance that the banks and everyone else put on our claim that we were moving the settlement accounts to the Central Bank. As we saw it, they actually had been there all along (though more or less under the operational control of the payment bureau).

Maruf wanted to base the ZPP's new operations on the procedures it had described in the Instruction it had already issued to banks earlier in the week (the one providing for unwinding payments for banks that were overdrawn). We wanted them to operate on the basis of instructions that we had provided to them in draft weeks earlier. Neither side had carefully read the other's documents. They urged us to read theirs, and we urged them to read ours. And we adjourned. We all had a great deal to do in very little time.

In the meantime, the vault cash count was continuing in the basement; and I was trying to finish the drafting of Instruction 5, which covered the issues we had been discussing with the ZPP. I dropped by Enver's office to review these procedures and found Ibro there as well. I suggested that the afternoon conversation be based on the Instruction 5 draft. Ibro argued for something simpler and more operational, something that spelled out each step we were asking for. While I thought that that was what Instruction 5 provided, I agreed; and the three of us sat around Ibro's portable as he typed out a one-page instruction from the CBBH to the ZPP. The instruction was prepared in Bosnian from the outset, and I did not bother to have it translated into English. Ibro was being cooperative in the pinch.

The second Saturday meeting at the FPB started at 12:30 p.m. We needed to finalize the operational rules for opening and closing the Giro accounts each day (tested messages, etc.,) and to receive the data on Friday's closing balances. The one-page instruction that Ibro had typed was reviewed and quickly accepted. It provided, among other things, that the bank's Giro accounts at the ZPP would not be funded in the morning until authorized by an instruction to the ZPP from the CBBH. The content of the instruction was not specified, fortunately as it turned out.

We finished agreeing to the instruction before the data on Friday's closing balances were ready, but the data arrived after a short further delay. The clock was always ticking in my mind. When these data were combined with the vault cash data we would have the figures about which we had speculated for months (and had estimated in two of our technical assistance reports).

TRANSFER OF ASSETS AND LIABILITIES: PART 1

Late Saturday afternoon, after the BHD note count in the vault had been finished, Alfredo Bello of Arthur Andersen explained the procedures for the asset/liabilities transfer from the NBBH to the CBBH as his company saw it. He and one of his colleagues met with Serge, Enver, Ibro, and me in Serge's office at about 5:00 p.m. He presented the transfer amount, i.e., the CBBH's opening balance sheet, along with the revised text for the transfer agreement that had been prepared by Jean-Luc. Alfredo was leading the AA team that had been assembled on very short notice to assist with the transfer of NBBH assets and liabilities to the new CBBH. At the time, Alfredo was Director, Corporate Finance (Financial Sector Restructuring) at Arthur Andersen London, a very impressive position for a thirty-one-year-old. Alfredo was indeed a very impressive guy. He was a Spaniard, with a quick mind and just the right blend of high energy and calm to instill confidence immediately. He was nothing if not very professional.

Alfredo explained that the figures he was presenting, while expected to be the final ones, were only preliminary because the ZPP could not submit final Friday closing balances for the banks until later in the week (well after the legally required transfer on Monday the eleventh) and because the BHD notes held for the NBBH in the vaults of the ZPP had not been audited and verified.

Enver and Ibro seemed quite uncomfortable. Enver said that he did not think Kasim would sign his name to a document transferring provisional amounts. Serge was not sure who Enver and Ibro (especially Ibro) were really working for at this point, him or Kasim, for whom they had worked for many years until yesterday, when they officially joined the CBBH. For me, this was all a new experience. I had never opened a central bank in this way and had no idea what was acceptable and what was not. Was this the straw that would break the camel's back?

Ibro said in so many words that Kasim would not cooperate with all this unless he was a part of it. We were being told, indirectly, that we had erred in not inviting Kasim to this meeting. All of us became rather edgy, except for Alfredo, who had no experience with the ups and downs of moods, political strategies, and the cooperation we had experienced regularly in BiH. Serge asked if Kasim should be invited. "Yes" both Enver and Ibro said simultaneously. We had obviously goofed in not inviting him. It was simply an oversight in the rush.

Serge sent Lejla, who was not really needed to interpret for this English-speaking group, to see if Kasim was still in his office. She returned shortly to report that he had already left for the day (it was about 5:00 p.m., an hour after normal close of business at the NBBH). "I know," Enver said softly. It is a matter of pride among top managers in the old Soviet system, and in the former Yugoslavia as well, to always know what is going on and where key officials are at all times. Enver was chastising us. "Should we call him at home?" Serge asked. "Of course," came the reply from both of Kasim's former lieutenants.

Within half an hour Kasim was back and in the meeting. We nervously awaited indications of his intentions, of his mood, or his political instructions (it was never easy to tell the difference). Serge summarized the situation for Kasim, stressing that the Central Bank Law required us to open on Monday (or at the latest on Tuesday) but that it would be impossible to have final figures by then. "In that case," Kasim said "it is obvious that we will have to sign for the provisional numbers and indicate in the agreement that they will be adjusted later when the final one becomes available."

Alfredo confirmed for Arthur Andersen that this would be the normal procedure. Kasim was back in the circle, back in play. Once again, he mattered, even as his institution went out of existence; and thus he was prepared to forgive our stupid oversight and to cooperate. The immediate relaxation of tensions that resulted around the circular table was obvious to everyone. The transfer was actually going to occur. Kasim "would not, not cooperate" (a typical formulation of "agreement" in the region). The Central Bank would really open on Monday!

It occurred to me that there was great wisdom in the procedures that Alfredo was so skillfully leading us through, such as the transfer of the vault ritual that we were about to experience. This is especially true for formally accepting provisional numbers before having to irrevocably sign for final ones. I had earlier marveled at the genius of this psychological device in the workings of the Oslo peace agreement, and the Israeli/Palestinian Peace Process as it was rightly called (during most of 1995 and '96 when I had been responsible for providing the assistance needed to the Palestinians to create a Palestinian Monetary Authority). The Oslo agreement provided for a series of agreements—provisional if you will—on limited and increasingly difficult issues. After living with new arrangements and concessions on each side long enough to test their workability (and to adjust psychologically to the previously unthinkable), the next set of more difficult issues could then be discussed, having in the interim become at least less unthinkable. Some days or maybe weeks later when the final amounts to be transferred by the NBBH were available, it would no longer be such a traumatic step to sign them irrevocably and finally away.

Alfredo then reported on the results of the vault cash audit. His presentations throughout the day were very formal and well practiced. We were participating in an important ritual, and he knew its rules. The cash in the vault had no counterfeits, but was DM 3 million less than had been reported by the NBBH. In place of the missing 3 million, however, were two notes from the ZPP indicating that the currency had been loaned to the ZPP for the payment of their pension. This loan, which was itself a violation of the informal currency board operations of the NBBH, should have been reflected in the accounts as a reduction in cash in vaults, but at least there were the two documentations of the operation. The issue was relatively minor and explainable (in terms of accounting, though not of policy).

Alfredo pointed out that the team that had audited the cash in the vault was still waiting downstairs (it was about 6:00 p.m. by this time). The vault had been sealed shut and now needed to be turned over to its new owner. He recommended that the two governors come down to the vault and participate in a ceremony of formally passing the keys to the vault. We started downstairs. Kasim held back, prepared to sign the necessary document, but reluctant to drag things out with ceremony. I urged him to go for the sake of the symbolism. "Oh, symbolism," he said in

Passing the keys to the vault: from the left: Governor Serge Robert, NBBH vault keeper, other onlookers

Bosnian, "OK," and I understood. We all proceeded downstairs. I did not want to miss this rare event.

The actual ceremony was delayed a bit while Kasim, embarrassed by the missing 3 million, questioned and chastised the treasurer and vaultkeeper, who had, as he pointed out to Kasim, properly followed orders when presented with the signed instruction to provide the cash to the ZPP. Kasim was, however, not pleased with this minor blemish on the proceedings. And then, finally, standing in front of the vault, Alfredo recited a series of words that reminded me of the judge at a civil wedding, and Kasim handed his key to Serge (it took three keys in all to open the old vault)—the old Governor passing on his treasury to the new one. It was a poignant and touching moment. Kasim looked tired. The first tangible act in the opening of the CBBH had taken place.

THE GIRO PREFUNDING BOMB

Earlier in the day, between two of my afternoon meetings, Alessandro informed me that Dino had reviewed our instructions, especially Instruction 5, and had a number of questions that he wanted to discuss. When could I see him? Dino was the guy from Merchant Bank we had run into by chance and had hired for the weekend to ensure that we had at least some bank input into what we were doing. I was finally able to see him just before the meeting with the Arthur Andersen team described above. After I clarified some points in our instructions, what he said was very disturbing.

"In the meeting with us [all of the bankers] Thursday, you said that the new procedures represented only a modest change in the payment system at this point. Banks would have more information and control by authorizing the prefunding of their Giro accounts each morning. However, the use of these same balances to prefund our customer Giro accounts at the payment bureau is more novel. In fact, it is revolutionary and creates some problems for us."

He went on to say that, "If we must actually debit our own Giro account to credit the accounts of our customers, my bank and virtually every other bank will have a negative balance. The amounts in our customers' Giro accounts are greater than our total 620 account balances, implying that the balance for our own use is negative. We have in fact, as banks do most everywhere, used the deposits of our customers to make loans and other investments. Where will we find the money to cover that negative balance that is required by your prefunding scheme?"

I was stunned. Ibro had stated earlier that customer account balances were larger than banks' 620 account balances. His explanation was confused, in my ears at least, by the incorrect argument that the customer account balances (account 500) had

The bank deposit multiplier

The amount of money in circulation (currency plus bank deposits) is greater than the monetary liabilities of the central bank (currency issued plus bank deposits with the central bank). The reason is that when currency is deposited in banks and banks lend some of it to the public, the borrower redeposits some of the same currency in the same or another bank, which lends some of it, etc. This gives rise to what is called the deposit multiplier.

In Bosnia the deposit multiplier worked as follows: A bank customer would deposit currency in her local ZPP office. She would receive a credit to her GIRO account maintained by the ZPP for her bank, and the ZPP would credit the same amount to the GIRO account of her bank. This balance was an asset of the bank and could (and to a large extent was) loaned to the bank's customers. More or less behind the scenes, the balance added to the bank's 620 account also increased the central bank's monetary liabilities to banks while reducing its currency in circulation (thus leaving its total monetary liabilities—base money—unchanged). Some of that money loaned to the public was redeposited with a bank. If, for the sake of simplicity, we assume that the entire loan was redeposited with the same bank, that bank's deposit liabilities to the public would be increased by the amount of the loan while its own balances with the central bank (its 620 account) would remain the same (what it loaned was redeposited). Thus even after just the first round of relending, the initial deposit of currency would have increased the public's deposits by more than the bank's own 620 balances.

The prefunding schedule was an impossible nonsense because of the deposit multiplier.

to be deducted from the balance in banks' 620 accounts in order to measure base money, "because the customers' balances were already counted in the 620 balances."

This last statement, which Ibro was never able to explain to my satisfaction, was conceptually incorrect. They were included in the sense that the 620 account balance (including the required reserve part) was the sum of the customers' and banks' own Giro account balances in the ZPP. But this had nothing to do with the definition of base money (which included the Central Bank's liability to banks). What became clear was that the banks' own Giro balances were negative and thus the customers' Giro balances were larger than banks' 620 balances. I hadn't understood Ibro's message. Or hadn't I listened carefully enough? Our prefunding, if I understood the message finally, would cause a credit crunch as banks tried to cover their implicit negative balances. Every college sophomore knows that banks do not have enough reserves to cover their deposit liabilities because they lend some of those deposits (hence, the money multiplier). What should I do?

I had temporarily put these very disturbing thoughts out of my mind during the Arthur Andersen-led deposit, cash, and vault transfer rituals that followed. From the vault transfer ritual, Kim and I proceeded to David Whitehead's for dinner. David, a very congenial host, barbecued chicken while Kim prepared some sautéed vegetables. Jean-Luc had stayed in his office as usual. Kim was always amazing everyone by accomplishing more than any three other people during her long days in the office, then putting on the best dinner in Sarajevo while chatting with her guests about all sorts of things.

We had walked over to David's together after the vault transfer ceremony. It was a long walk, but we needed the exercise and a cooling down period. It was after 8:00 p.m. when we arrived. I drank a scotch, unusual for me, while Kim cooked. I began to discuss my new credit crunch fears with David. By 10:00 p.m. I was too tired and depressed to be sociable, and I walked Kim home, then on to the Hotel Bosna. By then it was clear to me that our plans would have disastrous effects and needed to be changed. I was actually near tears. I had made a serious analytical mistake, for which there was really no excuse. In retrospect it was a very stupid error.

Despite my heavy fatigue, I did not sleep well that evening. Our approach needed to be changed, but just how to go about it was not yet clear to me. My ideas began to crystallize during my fitful sleep, and around 4:00 a.m. Sunday morning I finally got up and started writing. We would scrap the prefunding, but keep all of the other elements of the procedures already agreed to. In fact, most of those procedures (CBBH authorization of opening bank Giro account balances, after hours transactions for overdrawn banks, and unwinding) had been developed before we had hit upon the "foolproof" prefunding scheme. The formal one-page agreement with the ZPP on Saturday only said that the banks' Giro accounts would be funded on the basis of the CBBH's instruction. That would remain valid. And it was not clear that any banks had really understood our proposed procedure (based on the still unissued draft of Instruction 5) to mean that the balances posted each morning to their customers' Giro accounts would at the same time (i.e., in the morning) be taken from their own funds in the 620 account balances. This one "little" feature would be removed. Our potentially catastrophic miscalculation, might be remedied without anyone really noticing. I would need to discuss this with Enver and Ibro since they had also endorsed the original plan.

It would take a few days to fully sort things out and provide the banks with clear instructions. In the interim, there was the risk that relying on bank instructions (subject to CBBH approval) for the amounts posted each morning to their Giro accounts at the ZPP could not be made operational from the first day and might result in posting inappropriate amounts. As the morning progressed, I decided that for the first week of operation the opening balances for each bank would be the closing balance of the day before (as it was currently), though it could only be posted by the ZPP after receiving the instruction from the CBBH. This would allow most of the key systems to function and be tested without much risk to the smooth function of the system. It would also allow the time for a more thorough review of Instruction 5 by the CBBH staff and by the ZPP before issuing it to the banks. Enver and Ibro embraced this proposal immediately.

Banks had been calling the CBBH with questions since the meeting with them Thursday. The CBBH owed them a clarification of what to expect on Monday. I prepared a draft letter from Enver to the banks, detailing the modified operational plan for the next week (until Instruction 5 was finalized and issued) and reminding them of the report they needed to submit on Monday for the reserve requirement calculation.

Sarajevo, 11/08/97 [August 11, 1997]

Dear Sir,

Over the weekend the National Bank of Bosnia and Herzegovina ended its monetary operations, transferring (for value today) its monetary liabilities (banks' balances in their 201 and 620 accounts with the ZPP and all BHD currency notes) and an equivalent amount of foreign currency to the Central Bank of Bosnia and Herzegovina. As of today the CBBH is in operation and the closing balances in your bank's 201 and 620 accounts with the ZPP on Friday, August 8, have been deposited in your bank's new account 38111 with the CBBH. In addition, all BHD amounts have now been converted to KM in the ZPP and the CBBH.

In order to ensure an orderly transition, your bank's opening balances with the ZPP in the 201 and 620 accounts this morning, Monday, August 11, was the same as last Friday's closing balance. At the close of business today, the balance in your 201 accounts will be transferred to your 620 account for use on August 12, and the 201 account will be closed in accordance with the CBBH regulation on required reserves: "Rules for Establishing and Complying with the Reserve Requirement of Commercial Banks in Bosnia and Herzegovina." Any net change in your 620 account during the day will be posted to your 381 account with the CBBH on the basis of the report of the ZPP, which is also provided to you.

For the purposes of determining the reserve requirement for the next ten calendar days, you must return the attached Form today and every ten days in the future. The CBBH will notify you in a few days of your bank's reserve requirement for this ten-day period (August 11 to the close of business August 20), and of the rate of interest at which the amount of required reserves above 5 percent of the deposit base will be remunerated.

This evening and in subsequent evenings, the ZPP will advise the CBBH of the net change in your 620 account for posting to your 381 account with the CBBH. The CBBH will notify you each day of your closing balance on that account as soon as possible but not later than 7:30 a.m. the next morning (though this may not be possible for technical reasons for the next few days). Again in order to ensure an orderly transition, for the rest of this week, your bank's closing balance with the CBBH each day will automatically become the opening balance in your 620 account with the ZPP the next morning.

A detailed instruction on these matters, "Instruction on Accounting for the Clearing and Settlement of Interbank Payment Orders (INST5)," is now under discussion with the ZPP and will be issued later this week for effect starting next Monday, August 18, 1997.

Sincerely yours,

Enver Backović
Vice Governor

THE FORMAL TRANSFER

Work continued throughout Sunday to finalize the CBBH's opening balance sheet (i.e., the amounts to be transferred from the NBBH to the CBBH). Separately, work continued on finalizing the CBBH's chart of accounts. The remaining details had to do with how the reserve account balances used for payments during the day were to be reflected (set aside or transferred) and exactly what the structure of the "trust account" (to be discussed below) would be and how it would be used. All of this work involved the Arthur Andersen team, Jean-Luc, and Ibro and significant input from John Dalton in Washington.

John had e-mailed us a detailed scheme for the operation of the trust account, which was accepted quickly by all involved. However, in establishing the exact details—account numbers and rules for posting entries (first to reflect the initial transfers from the NBBH, then to record any subsequent changes)—Jean-Luc, Ibro, and the Andersen team held many meetings that took many hours. Jean-Luc would report to me that they were making progress—that they were almost there—that there were just one or two points remaining, etc. On several occasions over this day and the next, I stuck my head into Ibro's office to find four or five heads bent over a low table deep in intense discussion.

An important part of this group's deliberations was over the figures for the next day's transfer of assets and liabilities from the NBBH and their presentation in the final transfer agreement. Not only was the presentation of the figures fine-tuned throughout the day (how to present the missing DM 3 million in BHD notes, for example), but also the language of the agreement was subjected to closer and closer scrutiny, resulting in minor changes here and there.

Mid-afternoon, Kim and I decided that we needed a break and walked down the stairs from our fourth floor office to the street below in order to enjoy the beautiful weather outside. We turned left outside the entrance to the Bank and walked toward Sarajevo's central market, with its lovely pedestrian area. It was a clear late summer day. The central market area was always full of walking, smiling pedestrians with an average age of about nineteen. It didn't matter whether it was summer, fall, winter, or spring, the walkways were always busy. It was one of the most enjoyable charms of Sarajevo. Young people were always walking its length. Walking was free entertainment. Only the outdoor coffee tables followed a seasonable pattern. We speculated that there was a seat at a coffee shop for every person in Sarajevo.

I will never be able to properly express on paper my admiration for Kim and the joy of working with her. On this afternoon, we said little. We were too tired, nervous, and excited. We had worked together in many places (Bulgaria, Moldova, West Bank and Gaza Strip) and, I like to think, accomplished good things. We walked almost arm in arm.

Late in the afternoon, Alfredo summoned Governors Omićević and Robert to examine the final document and to explain the procedure that would be followed in signing it. Again it reminded me of a wedding or actually more like a funeral (which I noted to Alfredo at the time as we waited in the hall for all to be ready). There was the solemn counseling from Alfredo on what this was all about and how it would proceed, followed by much waiting with little apparent action, while the wording of the agreement was carefully examined a final time in both Bosnian and English. And a few more words were adjusted. Kasim—Governor Omićević—sat quietly and patiently in his office for the final surrender of his institution's monetary functions and assets. I sat with him for a while, not knowing what to talk about. Then I paced in the hall for a while, knowing all along that I could not really afford the time but needing to be there.

Finally, Alfredo summoned us all into the boardroom for the formal signing of the agreement. The two Governors sat next to each other at the large boardroom table at which we had all met so many times over the past year. The signing began, one page after another. Kim took a picture of me standing behind and between them. Even then a few more words were being changed in the room next door, so that the signing was held up a few more minutes waiting for the last page. Glasses were lifted. Each Governor said a few words and the event was sealed with scotch (instead of the more traditional plum brandy—another sign of the changing order).

Signing the document transferring the monetary assets and liabilities of the NBBH to the CBBH on August 10, 1997. Standing: the author; sitting from left to right: Kasim Omićević (Governor of NBBH and Board member of CBBH) and Serge Robert (Governor of the CBBH).

So it was done. The amounts in the document would be transferred (in Sarajevo and abroad) for value Monday, August 11, 1997. Any adjustments to these "provisional" numbers could be settled later. The transfer on that day amounted to a mere DM 132,584,030.72. The CBBH assumed KM 31,677,144.45 in deposit liabilities and the assumed amount of BHD bank notes in circulation. On the asset side, it received DM 4,334,030.72 in German mark bank notes and coins from the vault, and the balance in deposits of German marks abroad.

All this ceremony had taken a lot of precious time. Kim, Jean-Luc, and I returned to our fourth floor office and buried our heads in our computers. Jean-Luc soon left for another meeting on the chart of accounts, in particular the precise operation of the trust account that would be established for the NBBH.

Jean-Luc returned from meeting with Ibro and reported on his very disturbing discussion of daily fluctuations in the trust account balance. Ibro had been tracking the behavior of the monetary liabilities to be transferred to the CBBH. If everything was properly accounted for, this account's balance could only fluctuate if the NBBH's foreign currency holding fluctuated accordingly (as it was also operating informally on currency board rules). However, they did fluctuate without changes in foreign currency holding of the NBBH. We were mystified and disturbed by this news.

Kim and I had a final discussion with Enver and Ibro about when staff needed to arrive in the morning to send the communication to ZPP on the first day's opening balances for each bank at the payment bureau. Following that meeting we left for dinner at her apartment, but hard working Jean-Luc never showed up. All was ready for the big day—we hoped.

MONDAY, AUGUST 11
PLANNED OPERATIONS

When the CBBH opened for business on Monday, August 11, it meant that a new system of settling KM payments commenced. All banks that had maintained Bosnia and Herzegovina dinar deposits with the NBBH (which were redenominated over that weekend to KM) had established reserve accounts with the CBBH during the preceding week. These reserve accounts were initially funded on opening day by the transfer of the deposits these banks had with the NBBH at the close of business Friday, August 8.

Considerable work at the ZPP had preceded the opening on that Monday so as to produce a Friday closing balance for the NBBH by Monday morning and to settle payments each evening, using banks' reserve accounts with the CBBH. Prior to that day, the entire operation had been conducted by the ZPP. The ZPP had not only cleared all payment orders, but had settled them as well by posting the net payments of each bank to its account with the NBBH. Despite the opposition from the ZPP to a number of issues, their ultimate cooperation and hard work helped make the opening possible. The ZPP easily could have prevented it, and there would have been nothing we could have done about it.

The procedure that was introduced on August 11 worked as follows:

- Each morning, every bank informed its payment bureau and the CBBH of the amount of its reserve account balance that it wished to set aside for settling that day's net payment bureau payments.
- The CBBH verified and recorded these amounts and confirmed them to the payment bureau as the bank's opening (Giro account) balance with the payment bureau.

- The payment bureau accepted payment orders from customers (of banks) that had sufficient balances in their Giro accounts recorded at their payment bureau office. The ZPP was not technically able to know on a real-time basis the impact of these payments on an individual bank's Giro account (and hence ultimately its reserve account) balances.
- At the end of the payment day the payment bureau netted all payment orders against the opening Giro account balance for each bank and submitted the result to the CBBH for settlement. If a bank did not have sufficient funds in its Giro account for this purpose, it was notified (by the payment bureau) and given time to borrow from another bank or to deliver cash. If all else failed, the payment bureau would withdraw (unwind) sufficient payments by the defaulting bank to permit it, and all other banks, to settle.
- Settlement was confirmed (to each bank and the payment bureau) by the CBBH when it posted the result to banks' reserve accounts.

REAL OPERATIONS

To minimize the water that seeps out of Sarajevo's ancient municipal water pipes, water was delivered through the system only from 6:30 to 9:30 a.m. and from 4:30 to 8:00 p.m. Each restroom at the National Bank/now Central Bank building had a large barrel full of water and a scoop for flushing during the day. For Kim to be in the office earlier than 7:30 a.m. (her normal time of arrival was 8:00 a.m.), meant no shower. Monday morning Kim was at the CBBH at 7:00 a.m. to help with the first instruction to the ZPP.

I slept much better Sunday night, knowing that the abbreviated procedures for the first week greatly reduced the risks to the payment system, and I did not arrive at the Bank until a little after 8:00 a.m. There was some agitation among the wonderful ladies who had been working with Kim and Jean-Luc for several weeks to prepare for their role in overseeing the daily settlement and the operation of the reserve account (including monitoring of required reserves). Their instruction to the ZPP for the opening balances in bank's Giro (620) accounts had been rejected because not all of the accompanying paperwork had been provided. "Who," the ladies asked, "should sign the instruction?" This was another of the many little, but important, details that we had not specifically addressed.

For this first day, I took one of the ladies with me to the Governor's office and asked him to sign until there was an agreement between the Vice Governor overseeing banking operations and the Vice Governor overseeing the accounting on who was authorized to sign. The information on authorized signatories for this instruction would then need to be communicated to the ZPP, which in the meantime would accept the Governor's signature. The shakeout of operational procedures and details had begun and continued through most of the week.

As time permitted, I worked on the revisions to Instruction 5 necessitated by dropping the prefunding scheme and on preparing an instruction on Interegional payments (Instruction 6) and German mark transactions against KM directly with the CBBH (Instruction 7). Both of these were adaptations of drafts that had been prepared earlier by John Dalton, the latter one only the day before via e-mail before he went on vacation.

PAYMENT BUREAU—ROUND FOUR

At the end of Saturday afternoon's meeting with the FPB, we had agreed to hold a technical level meeting on Monday at 3:00 p.m. in order to agree on all of the operational aspects of the new relationship between the CBBH and the FPB. That meeting was moved up to 2:30 p.m. so that Jean-Luc and I would not miss Serge's press conference, scheduled for 4:00 p.m.

Three of the wonderful ladies newly appointed to the CBBH staff and Jean-Luc came with me to the FPB offices. Our technical level counterparts from the FPB were knowledgeable and cooperative. We discussed communications protocols, authorized signatures, and information formats and deadlines.

Jean-Luc then requested daily data for each bank on the net cash transactions with the CBBH (purchases and sales of BHD, and eventually KM notes, against DM) that are conducted at the FPB as agent of the CBBH. We were told that it was not possible to provide these data.

Without them, important accounting items could only be inferred rather than measured directly. This was not desirable, but we never succeeded in getting the desired information from the ZPP (i.e., FPB). Without it, the CBBH continued to have some accounting issues that delayed the first publication of its balance sheet as required by the law and caused continuing questions over the impact of continuing NBBH operations on the CBBH's balance sheet.

THE PRESS CONFERENCE

Public confidence in a currency is essential to its success. When introducing a new currency, it is particularly important for the central bank to provide the public with accurate information on its operations. In a wartorn country like Bosnia and Herzegovina, where distrust remained high, good information to the public was critical. The press conference scheduled for 4:00 p.m. Monday afternoon was set later than usual to give us time to know whether things had gone well or not. This meeting with the press was very important for these reasons and because the struggle among the political leaders of the three regions over some aspects of the Central Bank and currency note design had resulted in some misunderstanding in the press and among the public. Serge's press conference was an important opportunity to help launch the new Central Bank properly.

To help the Governor prepare for the questions that were expected to be raised, Alessandro had prepared a briefing paper—a traditional Q & A brief. In addition, the new American Deputy to the High Representative (then Mr. Westendorp), Jacques Paul Klein, joined Serge and Kasim at the front of the room facing the TV cameras and international and local print media reporters. The Governor concluded his comments by saying:

> *The start up of the CBBH represents an institutional change that will not disrupt in any way the activities of business and the everyday lives of ordinary people. At the same time, however, it is of great importance in two aspects; first, it represents the fulfillment of a condition needed to mobilize further external support from the international community, and second, it lays the groundwork for a sound financial system throughout Bosnia and Herzegovina. On both accounts the CBBH will contribute significantly to strengthening the prospects for sustainable economic growth in all parts of the country.*

Serge's remarks were followed by a statement from General Klein commending the establishment of one of the common institutions called for in Dayton and putting the event in its broader context. Ambassador Klein urged the three nations of Bosnia and Herzegovina to get on with the task of designing new notes and as an amateur numismatic, he volunteered to settle the note design problem himself.

Kasim made a few remarks about the importance of the event for the unity of the country. I didn't think his remarks would give offense to anyone, but one must always listen carefully.

A question-and-answer session followed. The initial questions were tough—with no agreement on note design, no restoration of proper telecommunications links throughout the country, how serious could everyone be about the new Central Bank? etc.

I was called out of the press meeting for a while to confirm with Enver and Ibro the modifications to the payment scheme that I had introduced over the weekend. They liked the changes but wanted to be sure that they had properly understood them, as indeed they had.

The press conference was followed by a reception, and I took the occasion—a moment of considerable pride in what we had accomplished so far—to grab a scotch and carry it into Enver's office to join the small gathering of new CBBH staff. His office, which later became Kim's office, was next to the boardroom in which the press conference had just been held, at the end opposite to Kasim's office. Now Serge would have to ask Kasim to relinquish the office to the new Governor, setting off a whole set of related and unwanted issues to resolve (where to put Kasim and the other Board members during their periodic visits).

Kim soon joined us in Enver's office with a drink already in hand and a broad, very well-earned smile on her lips. Around 6:00 p.m. she and I succeeded in dragging Jean-Luc off to dinner at Kibe, a restaurant on the hill at the north end of town with a beautiful view of the now peaceful hills of the Republika Srpska. Kibe specialized in lamb roasted over an open fire.

The executive summary of my back-to-office report a week later summarized the accomplishment of this day as follows:

The Central Bank successfully started operations as required by the new law on August 11. The National Bank of Bosnia and Herzegovina transferred to the CBBH about DM 133 million in monetary liabilities and an equivalent amount of foreign currency assets. All account Bosnia and Herzegovina Dinar (BHD) were converted to Convertible Marka (KM), and net KM payments through the payment bureaus are now settled everyday on the books of the CBBH.

TUESDAY, AUGUST 12

The procedures between the CBBH and the ZPP for opening banks' Giro accounts at the ZPP in the morning and closing them at night continued to encounter minor problems that required some attention. But on the second day—which was really the first with the fully consolidated reserve accounts—they were more quickly resolved than they had been the day before. Everything was being tested out under operation—on the fly. This was NOT a proper way to introduce such important new systems, but our only alternative would have been to delay the opening.

THE TRUST ACCOUNT

The trust account mechanism was one of several things added to the Central Bank Law in the spring when I was away from Sarajevo. It was a provision in Article 72.2 covering the transition to the new Central Bank, where it was stated that:

> a. The monetary liabilities of the National Bank of Bosnia and Herzegovina will be transferred to a trust account at the Central Bank together with, and only to the extent of, the available, liquid, convertible foreign exchange assets held by the National Bank of Bosnia and Herzegovina. The liabilities so transferred will include, and may be limited to, the outstanding bank notes in Bosnia and Herzegovina dinars and the required reserve deposits of commercial banks. The foreign exchange assets so acquired shall be transferred to the ordinary accounts of the Central Bank whenever the Central Bank carries out a conversion of the corresponding liabilities into Convertible Marka, up to the amount of the liabilities so converted, within the rules and regulations set by the Governing Board of the Central Bank for these purposes. Any net assets remaining in the trust account following the conversion of all such liabilities will be used in the liquidation of other liabilities of the National Bank of Bosnia and Herzegovina.

The trust account's purpose was to protect the NBBH from transferring more foreign exchange to the CBBH than was really justified by the BHD notes actually in circulation. Kasim thought that the accounting records of currency in circulation, which would be the basis of recording the amount of that particular monetary liability transferred to the CBBH, overstated what was really in circulation because he thought that some notes had been lost, some had been carried out of the country as souvenirs, and some had been worn out without being replaced. As a result, when KM notes were issued and the BHD notes were redeemed, Kasim quite reasonably thought that the amount redeemed would be less than the amount initially recorded as in circulation. The trust account provided a mechanism for making a final adjustment in the amount. If a smaller amount was actually redeemed than the amount in circulation on the basis of accounting records, the CBBH would return the excess foreign exchange it had received to the NBBH (or its successor and creditors).

At my suggestion, in June the transfer agreement between the NBBH and the CBBH also provided that if the amount redeemed for some reason was greater than the recorded amount (e.g., if undetected counterfeit notes had been redeemed) the NBBH would have to transfer additional amounts to the CBBH.

Thus the trust account would be used in the first instance to record the monetary liabilities and foreign exchange assets transferred to the CBBH and all but the amount representing cash in circulation would be immediately converted into KM (reserve and BiH government deposits with the CBBH) and moved permanently out of the trust account. Aside from a possible correction to the amounts a few days later after Arthur Andersen's audit of the final numbers was complete, no other change in the trust account would be made until the redemption of BHD notes, expected to be near the end of the year. Thus Ibro's insistence that the trust account balances could go up and down every day and would require periodic adjustments in foreign exchange holdings (by further transfers between the CBBH and the NBBH) was disturbing and objectionable. Had he misunderstood the proper working of the trust account? Or had we misunderstood something?

THE NBBH PROBLEM

Two events in the first two days of the CBBH's operations rang alarms that something was seriously wrong. Sometime during the day (the second day of the CBBH's operation) someone (probably a government agency in the Federation, but I had no information on that at the time) sent a message to the CBBH requesting KM currency (interpreted as meaning BHD notes, since KM notes didn't exist yet). The cash was needed to pay upcoming payrolls, and the party wanted to know how to get the cash now that the CBBH was responsible for providing it. This set in motion discussions that eventually revealed a serious problem and clarified Ibro's persistent trust account statements.

This cash request "issue" was handled by Enver, and to this day I do not know whether the problem was one of the distribution of notes around the country—not enough in the region from which the request came—and the need to arrange a transfer from one region to another (which would be completely routine), or, as I now suspect, the problem was that the party had its deposits with the NBBH and the question was how it could pay the CBBH for cash out of deposits with the NBBH. Whichever it was, it forced our attention on the consequences of the NBBH continuing to hold deposits (other than banks' deposits, which it had transferred to the CBBH).

The other event was the discovery that within a few days after the CBBH's opening, its monetary liabilities had increased without an increase in its foreign exchange assets, thus violating the currency board rules (and the Central Bank Law). This is exactly what Ibro had said would happen, but I still did not understand how or why it was happening. However, it clearly had to do with the fact that the NBBH was continuing to operate even though all of its "monetary liabilities" had been shifted to the CBBH.

We had expected Entity government deposits at the NBBH to be transferred to the CBBH, and the NBBH to be liquidated. Because of last minute changes to the draft of the Central Bank Law, the CBBH was not allowed to accept Entity government deposits unless both Entities agreed, which they did not. My June mission report had warned of the need for Federation government ministries and agencies to find a depository when the NBBH ended its monetary operations.

In fact, no such provision was made and these deposits remained with the NBBH (along with a small amount of other enterprise deposits). Naturally, they were still being actively used for the needs of government, as if the NBBH were a solvent bank. It was also another instance of the RS acting more quickly and cleverly than the Federation by creating a State bank to which it had transferred the government's deposits nine months earlier.

My analysis of the requirements for starting up the CBBH had assumed that government and enterprise deposits would be moved to other (i.e., commercial) banks and that the NBBH would stop functioning altogether. Thus I had not given much thought to the implications of its continued operation. From the very first days of the operation of the CBBH, its assets and liabilities became unmatched and mysteriously fluctuated from day to day. We suspected that this strange phenomenon was related to the continued operations of the NBBH. However, I did not clearly understand the nature of this link for several days.

Jean-Luc and I met again at 7:00 p.m. with the Arthur Andersen representatives and Ibro to discuss the continuing problems with the operation of the trust account. In retrospect, the problems resulted from Ibro's conception of the trust account as being the place to reflect the daily fluctuations in the CBBH's monetary liabilities that seemed to result somehow from the continuing operations of the NBBH. He had to account for and reconcile what was happening somehow in his accounting system. A few days later I came up with a simpler and more appropriate approach to this problem, but on Tuesday my understanding of the problem wasn't there yet.

WEDNESDAY, AUGUST 13
BOARD MEETING

As noted above, the Governor had taken many actions without the explicit approval of the Board in order to allow the CBBH to open on time. In fact, all of the Instructions and Regulations issued by the CBBH had been submitted to the Board earlier, but the Board had not formally approved them. The operations of the Board up to this point had been such that it was sometimes unclear whether the Board had actually approved something or not, since Serge had been reluctant to take formal votes, preferring to arrive at decisions by consensus.

Board meetings in the past had been very unpredictable events. The Board meeting that started at 10:00 a.m. August 13 fell more or less in the middle of the spectrum. Representatives of Arthur Andersen and I had been invited to attend. The agenda and supporting documents had been sent to Board members the day before. As a practical matter this meant that Board members had not seen the material before the meeting began.

After the Governor opened the meeting, the first thing that Manojlo Ćorić noticed was Enver's signature on all of the four Instructions that had been issued to the banks in the area of the Sarajevo Branch. He was angry. While he often started meetings by delivering a cold shower to everyone else, these opening blasts seemed more often the result of a political obligation, about which he often seemed genuinely embarrassed. On this occasion, I think that his anger was quite genuine and was indeed justified up to a point.

The pace of events (resulting from the lack of earlier cooperation and the deadlines in the law) had been brutal and had not allowed the Governor time to properly inform the Board of every decision. No other central bank board would have tolerated the approach that our circumstances forced on us in this case. I would have been angry too if I had been Manojlo.

Manojlo accused the Governor of taking actions contrary to the Board's wishes. In particular, he charged that the agreed-upon decentralization of the Branches—that was required by the law and that had been approved by the Board—had not been observed in the opening actions. He seemed angered that the Central Bank had opened at all. Following this initial blast, the Arthur Andersen representatives, who were in attendance for the initial part of the meeting, presented the results of their work in supervising and monitoring the transfer from the NBBH to the CBBH.

At the end of their presentation, Manojlo continued his venting. He politely and carefully explained to the Andersen representatives that he was not questioning or doubting their professional competence, but he did not understand how the liquidity of an economy the size of Bosnia's could be supported by the DM 133 million that had been transferred from the NBBH to the CBBH. Could they explain that? I didn't really understood Manojlo's question, and the Andersen representatives clearly did not understand it either, or were diplomatically evading it. They answered by repeating the process they had followed and its appropriateness.

It is often difficult to pin down what lies behind a particular comment or question in these circumstances. I assumed that Manojlo was expressing his general distrust of Kasim and Kasim's Bank. Had the NBBH really transferred all of the monetary liabilities required by the law?

One major part of the NBBH's deposit liabilities that had not been transferred (which was almost equal in value to what was transferred) were the deposits of the Federation and municipal governments. In fact, the transfer of these balances was not possible under the law (one of those last minute changes to the draft negotiated with the assistance of the U.S. Treasury) unless both Entities agreed to it; and the RS was not about to agree. I responded to Manojlo's question by pointing out that because of the public's lack of trust of the banking system most of the liquidity in the economy was in cash (DM, YUD, BHD, and Kuna bank notes). In addition, BHD, Kuna, and especially YUD bank notes were not that trusted either. Thus it was not that surprising that the amount of BHD deposit and currency liabilities transferred to the CBBH were relatively small.

Manojlo's comment about Enver signing the Instructions was more important. We had in fact been somewhat careless on this point. I must stress in our defense that as our recommendations for the start-up were put into practice, hundreds of detailed issues not considered before arose and needed to be resolved. One was who issued which communications and who signed them. The Branches (Main Units) of the CBBH, other than the almost notional Sarajevo Branch, had not yet been established, except on paper. In drafting the Instructions for opening reserve accounts and settling payments, we thought we were preparing Instructions for all of BiH, but in fact only banks with BHD deposits (i.e., those in the Sarajevo Branch area) were affected in the first instance. Enver was the Vice Governor responsible for the Sarajevo Branch AND for the Banking Services Department responsible for the payment activities involved in these instructions. Thus, in fact, we had not been terribly clear even in our own minds whether the Instructions were addressed to the Sarajevo Branch banks or to all banks.

Prior to this meeting I had pointed out to Kim that the reserve account monitoring and payment settlement activity being done by the wonderful ladies, was properly a Branch activity and requested that she show them as staff of the Sarajevo Branch rather than the Head Office. The working relationship between these ladies (i.e. the Sarajevo Branch) and the Banking Services Department and the Accounting Unit of the Administration Department would also define the working relationship and procedures for the other two Branches as well, once they opened. This whole subject had been so sensitive and had gone through so many revisions that at Kim's request, I had repeated this point to Serge to be sure that he agreed, which he did.

Thus as I listened to Manojlo's attack, I was well prepared with a response. Mr. Backović had signed the Instructions because they were meant only for banks in the Sarajevo Branch area. The same instructions were being adapted for the circumstances (differences in the ways the payment bureaus in each area worked) of the banks in the areas served by the other two Branches and would be signed by their Vice Governors. We had not acted contrary to the decentralization principle but entirely in keeping with it. In fact, Serge decided later that he would cosign all of these and other important documents issued by the CBBH to help ensure that the Branches did not act too independently. We were also hoping to preempt trouble over Branch stationery and other potential symbols of nationalism by preparing standards for all such things for the HQ and Branches. Before this plan was implemented in the weeks ahead, we decided that it would be more appropriate for the Governor alone to sign CBBH Instructions and other official statements, and all Instructions were reissued over Serge's signature.

Following these initial exchanges, the meeting began to settle down into something more normal and constructive, a pattern I had seen at a number of earlier meetings of this Board. I excused myself to pursue other priorities.

MANAGEMENT BOARD AND OTHER MEETINGS

My time left to consult with counterparts was running out. Midday I met with the Management Board of the CBBH, chaired by Serge. The operational opening of the Bank seemed to be proceeding well, but the development of the organization itself was only beginning. After all, beside Kim and Jean-Luc, Serge had only had a staff for the past few days. By-laws and procedures were discussed as were stationery, authorized signatories, personnel policies, and ethnic mix of the staff, to name but a few of the pressing issues. None of my previous training or experience had prepared me for the level and number of details we were forced to resolve under great pressure in a very short period of time.

At 2:30 p.m. I met with the Vice Governors and discussed issues relating to the distinction between the Main Units and the Headquarters of the CBBH and the administrative relationship between them and the Vice Governors.

As mentioned earlier, we had changed the reserve requirement by consolidating banks' previously frozen required reserve account balances with their settlement accounts into one account at the CBBH and by allowing them to use the full balance at any time as long as the daily average was maintained over each ten-day maintenance period. In addition, the CBBH had the responsibility to monitor the banks' compliance with this new requirement. To help staff with this new activity, I had hired a programmer from our computer support department at the IMF to prepare software for making the appropriate calculations and to produce the needed reports.

Our timetable was so rushed that I had not had time to check the software in Washington myself, but the programmer assured me that she had—and that it had—met all of my specifications. I brought it with me and gave it to Nasef, the newly appointed head of the CBBH Information Technology Unit. For the past several days I had been promising to stop by his office to answer some questions about the program. I finally found the time to do so after my meeting with the Vice Governors.

The program was not working. The CBBH IT unit was missing a necessary file, which the programmer had overlooked. After several hours of telephone calls to Washington with the programmer, and after installing the missing 32bit ODBC file, the program was so poorly designed that we decide to trash it and ask the local programming staff to build their own. I was furious with the sloppy work that had been done in Washington and frustrated with the self-imposed pace with which we were forced to bring up these new operations. This experience was sadly typical of far too much software design in the IMF. Programmers worked far too independently of users and were thus not sufficiently responsive to user requirements, and users were too busy to spend the time with programmers to change the process.

I continued to brood about the NBBH problem.

THURSDAY, AUGUST 14

By morning I was almost clear on what was going on with the NBBH and what to do about it. Part of my thinking went on as I slept and part while staring at the dark ceiling from my bed. What was happening was that deposits with the NBBH were being debited for cash (which now belonged to the CBBH) and to make net payments to other banks. At the end of the day the CBBH posted the increase in reserve account balances of the other banks but not the reduction in balances in the reserve account with the CBBH that the NBBH did not have. As a result the CBBH's net monetary liabilities increased without any change in its foreign currency assets.

The accounting system of the ZPP had been designed around the treatment of the NBBH as the central bank—a function that had been transferred to the CBBH. Because not all of the NBBH's deposits had been transferred to the CBBH (or to other banks), this left the NBBH's treatment by the ZPP in an awkward limbo. The ZPP was not sure how to handle a payment order from a depositor with the NBBH. Without discussing the problem with us, the ZPP decided to accept payment orders drawn on accounts with the NBBH and process them like any other. The net end of day increases or decreases in the NBBH's Giro account balance with the ZPP resulting from these payments were necessarily at the expense of—or in favor of—all other banks. However, the NBBH did not have a reserve account at the CBBH so that an increase in reserve account balances of these banks at the end of the day that resulted from a decline in the NBBH's Giro account balance did not produce an offsetting decline in the NBBH's reserve account (because it didn't have one).

The fact that the ZPP was processing payment orders drawn on deposits with the NBBH and the additional fact that the NBBH did not have a reserve account with the CBBH also resulted in a gap in the operating procedures previously described (*Monday, August 11, Planned Operations*). Under these procedures the Giro balances of all banks with the ZPP were funded each morning on the basis of instructions from the CBBH. These instructions reflected the wishes of each bank subject to the limit imposed by its balance in its reserve account with the CBBH).

Because the NBBH did not have a reserve account with the CBBH for settling payments between itself and other banks, there were two circuits of payments, and payment orders could transfer funds between the two creating a hole (i.e., a gap between monetary liabilities and foreign exchange backing) in the circle operated by the CBBH. Every time the deposits held with the NBBH dropped, the CBBH's monetary liabilities increased because it reflected the increase in currency in circulation or reserve deposits of other banks without reflecting the decrease for the NBBH. The NBBH was outside the loop. Thus its net payments or receipts were leakages from or injections into the CBBH that were not in accord with the rules of a currency board. Here was a serious problem, only partially and imperfectly foreseen, about which urgent action was needed.

I planned to discuss these understandings with Enver who was coming with me and Kim to Mostar that day.

I met Enver and Kim in front of the CBBH building at 7:00 a.m. for the drive to Mostar. The Mostar Main Unit had not opened yet, and there was grumbling that they were actively resisting the embrace of the KM and the CBBH. Thus we would meet with ZAP staff and bankers to promote the CBBH and to discuss remaining issues before opening the Mostar Main Unit of CBBH and introducing KM payments to the Croat ethnic majority area.

As we left the Sarajevo area and started into the mountains that separated Sarajevo and Mostar, I relayed my understanding to Enver of what became known as "the NBBH problem," though the expression took on added meaning as time went on. The solution, I suggested, was to treat the NBBH like any other bank and give it a reserve account at the CBBH that would have to have sufficient funds for the settlement of each day's net payments through the system. We discussed how the NBBH might be made a bank for this purpose. I suggested that it be given a special license by the Federation Banking Agency. Enver seemed to understand my explanation and accept my solution. The mystery had been resolved and like most mysteries, once it had been explained, we wondered why it had taken us so long to understand what was happening.

The Mostar meeting again started with complaints of inadequate preparation. They again had not had sufficient time to review the documents we intended to discuss. And once again the lost shipment of BHD bank notes from a few years earlier was raised. I concluded that their complaints indicated a hole in the "balance sheet" of the Mostar ZAP that the Bosnian Croats wanted to explain in advance. As any central bank functions of the ZAP were unwound in connection with shifting settlements to the new CBBH, any balance sheet problems would have to come to light. However, this traditional initial venting was milder than before and we got down to business fairly quickly. To save time, sandwiches were served for lunch, after which the group was divided into working groups on different issues that needed to be addressed in connection with finalizing Instruction 5 (interbank settlements).

I slept in the car most of the way back to Sarajevo. When we arrived, Kim and I returned to the CBBH where Jean-Luc was working away as usual. I worked until almost midnight on the inter-regional clearing and settlement sections of Instruction 5.

FRIDAY, MY LAST DAY

Over the preceding two years, many days before this one had been spent working on the monetary system of Bosnia and Herzegovina, and many more would be spent in the same way following; but my last day in

Sarajevo of this visit captures well the nature of the work. The first twenty minutes of the day (midnight to 12:20 a.m.) consisted of my waiting with increasing anger for the guard of the Central Bank to return to his post and let me out of the building so I could sleep. At 11:50 p.m., after working through the evening without dinner, I had finished (or at least tired of) work on the remaining draft Instructions (Instructions 6 and 7 to banks) and a final memo to the Governor summarizing priority actions that still needed to be addressed. However, when I tried to leave, the guard was nowhere to be found; and I was forced to wait. I even shouted "HELLO" loudly several times (quite unlike me), each time louder. Eventually he appeared, full of apologies in his limited English vocabulary, and unlocked the door. I walked the one block to the Hotel.

By 8:00 a.m. I had dressed and breakfasted and begun to pack my bags for the "2:30" flight to Zurich. I was back in the office by 9:00 a.m. and finished up the work of the previous evening. I needed to go to a bank to change some traveler's checks into cash in order to have enough to pay my interpreter. But first I met with Alessandro and reviewed my current thinking about the NBBH problem.

THE NBBH PROBLEM SOLVED

A meeting was called for noon with Kasim, Serge, Enver, Ibro, and me to explore solutions to the NBBH problem. I had to leave by 1:30 p.m. at the latest to catch my flight, and the Governor had arranged for his car and driver to pick me up in front of the Bank at 1:30 p.m. (my bags were packed and hotel bill had been paid). I barely had time to run to the bank to cash traveler's checks and pay my interpreter. The very slow pace of service at the bank seemed even slower than it probably was. While waiting, the manager, having been informed of my presence, came down and invited me to his office for a discussion. I explained the reasons for my great haste, so he proceeded to question me in the lobby of the bank; but at least I was able to escape the minute my cash was ready.

The noon meeting began by my reviewing the implications of payments being made by depositors at the NBBH. There was a big hole in the operation of the currency board. The points were readily understood by everyone there and had been understood by Ibro for some time. His solution was to transfer foreign exchange between the NBBH and the CBBH every day (or periodically) through the trust account in order to close the resulting mismatches. The proper way to do so in my view was for the NBBH to open a reserve account at the CBBH and to be treated like any other bank.

In my discussion of this approach the day before with Enver, I had assumed that the NBBH would need to obtain a special license from the Federation Banking Agency, and I had proposed a temporary special (very limited purpose) license until a more permanent solution could be found. It seemed to me that Ibro's approach might be more complicated to operate because there were other factors that might cause changes between monetary liabilities and foreign exchange assets of the CBBH that should not be removed by foreign exchange transfers with the NBBH. Furthermore, it granted the NBBH special treatment in managing its reserves. It could transfer any foreign exchange needed to settle net payments after the fact rather than in advance, as was required for other banks. In addition, the ex post transfer implied credit from the CBBH to the NBBH, however short-term, which was not permitted by the law.

Kasim accepted quickly that I had a point and that he could accept my proposal in principle. After a moment's reflection, he added that he did not want to have to satisfy a reserve requirement on the NBBH's deposits. I pointed out, to everyone's relief, that the requirement did not apply to government deposits, which were the bulk of the NBBH's deposits. Thus the reserve requirement would apply only to the other non-government deposits, which were large in number but small in amount. I said that there was no excuse for these non-government deposits to be held by the NBBH anyway and that these depositors should be required to move their deposits to banks after a short warning. Kasim agreed to this point immediately, saying that he had no problem with such a withdrawal. On the issue of a banking license, he argued that none was needed since the NBBH was already chartered as a bank under the special law that created it—a point I accepted immediately, wishing a lawyer were present.

There followed a discussion of what should determine the amount that the NBBH transferred to the CBBH and maintained there. The NBBH had never had to be concerned with the issue of liquidity management before, and Kasim and the other former NBBH employees in the room (Enver and Ibro) did not readily conceive of what was involved or required.

"The question of the amount of reserves on deposit with the CBBH [established by transferring an amount of foreign exchange] is completely up to the NBBH to determine," I pointed out, "on the basis of its estimates of the net settlement needs each evening. If it fails to have enough, the system's payments for the day (for every bank) cannot be settled until it comes up with enough."

Kasim, always alert, then added that he didn't see why he should forego the interest on the foreign exchange he would give up when making deposits with the CBBH. He wanted to earn a market interest rate on them. I am a strong supporter of market interest rates on required reserves deposited with central banks, but the law (against my advice) had restricted the payment of interest (though at a market rate) to the required amount above 5 percent of covered deposits. Furthermore, I had to point out that the NBBH would (after getting rid of the non-government deposits) have no required reserves and was not entitled to remuneration of excess reserves (at least not if it was to be treated like any other bank). An argument ensued on this point and in the end Serge agreed to the compromise that the CBBH would pay a market rate on any NBBH deposits with it.

I reviewed the points that we had discussed and the approach that I thought we had agreed to, and I looked around the table. Kasim asked his former advisors, Enver and Ibro, what they thought. Enver paused and said—through Lejla (Serge's interpreter)—that he did not disagree with my approach, and Ibro nodded his agreement as well. Lejla looked at me and said, "that means that they accept your proposal."

Until the NBBH Giro at the ZPP and Reserve Account at the CBBH were in full, proper operation, currency board rules could be (and probably already were being) violated as a result of the NBBH's Giro balance rising or falling in the daily settlements between August 11 and 15. I recommended that the Chief Accountant prepare an accounting of this one-time further adjustment needed in the transfer of assets and monetary liabilities between the NBBH and the CBBH, and that it be reviewed by the MAE accounting expert (Jean-Luc) and by Arthur

Andersen and included in the final figures for these transfers through the trust account created for this purpose.

I left this meeting at 1:30 p.m. sharp to Serge's waiting car for the drive to the airport. I was filled with a great sense of accomplishment. An important problem, potentially disastrous to the currency board, had been discovered, analyzed, and solved. The key parties had agreed to implement the solution. I was running on adrenaline, with no lunch, and felt exhilarated. When I arrived at the airport, I discovered that the plane was leaving at 3:30 p.m. not 2:30 p.m. as I had thought and that it had always been scheduled to leave at 3:30 p.m. Run and wait. So I took advantage of a new feature at the airport—a snack bar—to eat a sandwich.

I boarded the "Cross air" flight to Zurich "on time" and taxied to the end of the runway. The engines were revved (a smallish turbo prop plane) full throttle and we charged down the runway only to abort the take-off half-way. A cargo door had not been shut properly. We taxied back, sat in the plane for fifteen minutes while it was checked out and finally were on our way. In Zurich, I met my friend Einar, who managed to be there at the same time, and we drank and talked into the wee hours.

8 THE MORE COMPLETE "OPENING"

IMMEDIATE ISSUES

The opening of the CBBH was, of course, more the beginning than the end of the story, but it certainly concluded an important chapter. The CBBH was open and operating, but only in the Muslim region (the area served by the ZPP) and without its currency. MUCH was left to do. Several days after leaving Sarajevo, I sent Serge the following memo:

> To: Serge Robert   August 17, 1997
> From: Warren Coats
> Subject: **High Priority Actions for Monday, August 18**
>
> I have safely returned to Washington and after sleeping through most of "The Marriage of Figaro" I am now wide awake at 5:00 a.m. full of thoughts about the CBBH. I herewith am sharing those thoughts:
>
> 1. The issue of the CBBH's preparedness to both buy and sell DM for KM (raised by Alessandro) has presumably been resolved. No bank or other person must think for one minute that they cannot buy DM from the CBBH without delay. I sent a draft instruction on that subject (along with other draft Instructions) to Mr. Backović on Friday. These transactions are done directly between banks and the CBBH, not through the payment bureau.
> 2. Instruction 5 should have been issued on Friday, as banks will not know how to open for business on Monday without it. I provided the draft to Mr. Back-

ović on Tuesday (late) with the request that his staff review it, and send it to and thoroughly discuss it with the ZPP BEFORE it was issued. I have some doubts that this happened (because of all the other things going on and taking up Mr. Backović's time). The Instruction contains two after hours transactions that can be used to remove negative clearing balances of banks (selling DM cash in ZPP vaults—[i.e., a bank's DM Giro balances] to the CBBH, and borrowing from another bank). Both of these are done via the payment bureau, but at this point the ZPP has no procedure for processing these after hours (though they indicated strong willingness to do so). As part of the general discussion of Instruction 5 with the ZPP, IT IS CRITICAL THAT THE NEED FOR THE ZPP (and a bit later the ZAP and SPP) TO PREPARE SUCH FACILITIES BE DISCUSSED WITH THEM and prepared by them. In fact (and this may not be fully explicit in the instructions issued so far), the CBBH must reject the settlement of a payment bureau if it would include a bank with a negative 620 (or equivalent Giro accounts in the SPP or ZAP) Giro account balance. Thus the instructions should provide that the payment bureau would not submit an end of day clearing statement to the CBBH unless it had all positive (or zero) balances and that the payment bureaus would be responsible to notify any negative banks and to help them (via the above after hours facilities) to remove the negative balance. Failing that, the PB would unwind payments by that bank in accordance with its procedures (as already issued by ZPP last week).

3. We arrived at a good solution for payments by depositors with the NBBH, but there are several important follow-up actions that must be dealt with quickly:

   a) The ZPP must be involved in the discussion of clearing NBBH customer payment orders. This might be in the context of discussion with them (and the ZAP and SPP later) of the VERY IMPORTANT regulation (not yet issued) for operating the Reserve Account. This regulation (an earlier draft of which was Appendix VI of Vol. II of our last report) is very relevant to this issue as it provides that only licensed banks participate in the clearing and settlement (on behalf of the customers and themselves). Section 2(c) of this Draft Regulation may need to be amended to include the NBBH as a bank authorized by a special law (rather than a license). I suggest that all of this also be discussed with the Federation Banking Agency urgently. This same section needs some modest adjusting to reflect the fact that bank reserve accounts in the Sarajevo Main Unit area all have their reserve accounts already. I have also asked Ben Geva to suggest other changes that might be appropriate in light of differences between the SPP and the ZPP— in particular the fact that banks may offer payment services directly in RS. This regulation should be issued soon (especially as the payment law is not yet adopted), but the ZPP must fully understand and provide for the way we have agreed to bring the NBBH into the system.

b) Until the NBBH Giro at the ZPP and Reserve Account at the CBBH are in full, proper operation, currency board rules could be (and probably already have been) violated as a result of the NBBH Giro balance rising or falling in the daily settlement between August 11 and now. Any change in the NBBH Giro balance this past week (on behalf of its customers) has as its counterpart the opposite change in the collective Giro balances of all other banks in the clearing. However, and this is the problem, it does not produce a fully comparable shift of reserve account balances at the CBBH because the NBBH does not yet have one. Thus any net change in the NBBH's Giro balance during this period will have caused a change in banks' reserve account balances with the CBBH for which there was no comparable change in the FX backing of those balances. I recommend that Ibrahim prepare an accounting of this one-time further adjustment needed in the transfer of assets and monetary liabilities from the NBBH and the CBBH, and that it be reviewed by Jean-Luc and Arthur Andersen and included in the final figures for these transfers.

4. When I left Friday, the Agency Agreement between the CBBH and the Federation Payment Bureau for BHD (and later KM) cash purchases and sales on behalf of the CBBH had not been signed. Based on the letter from Maruf of Aug. 14 there seems to be some confusion over the use of CBBH cash deposited with the ZPP as agent and cash deposited in Giro accounts by others. Mr. Backović correctly (as far as I can tell not having been directly involved) has been insisting on a correct statement of the Agency arrangement. Jean-Luc had also complained that the ZPP was seemingly not able to provide daily data on such cash transactions (those involving CBBH cash). The two issues seem related and need a quick resolution. I suggest that the Legal Section of the CBBH become involved in assisting Mr. Backović in finalizing the agreement (and in reviewing other Instructions and Regulations issued by the CBBH).

All the best,
Warren

Two weeks later, I sent Serge another memo:

To: Mr. Robert
From: Warren Coats
Subject: **Priority Items**

August 30, 1997

Please forgive me if I worry from the great distance of Washington about things that may well have already been done. But as I have no confirmation that they have been done I will bring them to your attention in the following checklist (which makes no effort to be comprehensive) just in case:

1. Opening the reserve account of the NBBH, requiring all net payments by the NBBH and its depositors each day to be settled via the balances in that account (meaning the understanding of and cooperation of the ZPP with regard to this point), and the adjustment in the FX backing—i.e., a transfer between the NBBH and the CBBH—of any net increase or decrease in monetary liabilities as a result of net settlements by the NBBH and its depositors between Aug. 11 and whenever the above steps have been completed. NOTE: One implication of the Federation's deposits being in a bank (NBBH or some other bank) rather than at the CBBH is that they need not be fully backed by DM (as they would if they were at the CBBH). Is this a part of Pelivan's problem?

2. Issuing the CBBH regulation on operation of the reserve accounts (Interbank payments), which establishes the requirement for the ZPP to cooperate with the above. This draft must be carefully discussed with all three payment bureaus before it is issued and can be the vehicle for clarifying a number of payment system issues.

3. Issuing Instruction 7 on DM/KM transactions directly between banks and the CBBH.

4. Opening the account of BiH. This includes the transferred USAID funds at B of A. I would like to see the entries in the books for this balance to ensure that there is no violation of the tight limit on holding non-DM foreign exchange.

5. Issuing Instruction 6 on inter-regional payments. This MUST be carefully discussed with the Main Units and the three payment bureaus before it can be finalized and issued. But every effort should be made to have it in place by the time the branches open in Mostar and Pale and their banks open reserve accounts with the CBBH.

6. Adopt FX reserve investment guidelines and move the FX to the BIS or diversify investments out of Commerzbank.

cc: Mr. Zanello
Mrs. Rhee
Mr. Couetoux

Between these two notes to Serge, he sent the following letter to my boss, which I am more than happy to share with you:

Mr. Manuel Guitian   August 22, 1997
Director
Monetary and Exchange Affairs Department
International Monetary Fund
Washington DC

Dear Manuel:

Today marks the two weeks existence of the Central Bank of Bosnia and Herzegovina. I would like to take this opportunity to thank you for providing technical assistance to the Central Bank. Mr. Warren Coats came to Sarajevo during the week of opening of the Central Bank, and he worked long hours. He brought good analytical understanding of a very complex situation to the resolution of problems with the payment bureau and the commercial banks. He provided excellent leadership to the MAE experts who have been working with the staff of the Central Bank and gave directions and guidance on introducing the new procedures to the banking community of Bosnia and Herzegovina.

As you may be aware, all 37 commercial banks working in Bosnian Dinar have opened the reserve accounts with the Central Bank on August 8, the last working day before the starting of the Central Bank. We now communicate twice daily with all the banks on the status of their reserve requirements. Arrangements were made with both the commercial banks and the payment bureau so that the final settlement takes place on the books of the Central Bank each evening and the closing balances of the day for each bank are transmitted to them.

I have appointed, with the approval of the Governing Board, the key management position: three Vice Governors, the Comptroller General, three Deputy Comptrollers, and the Secretary General. With these appointments, we are implementing the infrastructure of the organization and beginning to elaborate the operations of each unit. In addition, we plan to open the Pale Main Unit and the Mostar Main Unit on September 15.

At this point of the Central Bank operations, I wanted to express my personal gratitude for the outstanding technical assistance your office has provided to the new institution.

Serge [Robert]

In addition to the issues I worried about, Serge had dozens and dozens more in bringing the CBBH into full operation. One of the first was to ask Kasim to turn over the Governor's office to Serge and to decide what alternative space to provide him and the other two members of the Board. Another problem concerned the distribution of new CBBH staff (many former NBBH staff) and remaining NBBH staff throughout the building. Eventually, the NBBH staff, most of whom had nothing whatsoever to do, were moved into the large banking hall on the first floor, where they could be seen chatting and playing cards for many more months.

In addition to the establishment of the CBBH, other important and difficult issues included adoption of a new flag and a new system of license plates that would not identify the residence of the car. After the new flag was adopted, I remember well the day Serge replaced the old Bosnia flag with the new flag for Bosnia and Herzegovina in the boardroom. We held our breaths as Kasim walked into the room for the first time with the new flag. He said nothing and another step in nation-building was taken quietly.

I didn't return to Sarajevo for six months. During that period I led technical assistance missions to Croatia, Bulgaria, and Andorra. I kept in constant touch with Serge and Kim by phone and email. Much of the intervening story until February 1998 can be told through the letters and memos that were exchanged. Five main issues dominated the period: protecting the currency board rules from the impact of the continued operation of the NBBH; the liquidation of the NBBH; agreeing on and publishing the balance sheet of the CBBH; and the opening of the Main Units in Mostar and in the RS; the design and issue of KM bank notes. The first two of these seemed to be major factors in the controversy that swirled around the start-up of the CBBH; most of them were related to "the NBBH Problem." The delay in publishing the CBBH balance sheet had the same source.

Most of these issues were running in parallel. Understanding them, however, is easier if I take up and complete each topic one at a time.

CROAT COMPLAINTS

One day after my August 15, 1997, departure from Sarajevo, Jure Pelivan, the Croat member of the CBBH Board, and Dragan Kovačević, the Croat Vice Governor, sent a three-page letter to Serge, bitterly complaining about some aspects of the operations to date. I reproduce the first page (and first of three points) so that you can see how difficult it was to understand what they were really complaining about. All of the points raised are restated in a somewhat clearer later letter from even higher Croat officials, which I reproduce in full in a few pages.

The letter from Jure and Dragan began:

Sarajevo, August 16, 1997

Dear Mr. Robert,

We—signed officials in the Central Bank of Bosnia and Herzegovina, representing Croatian people—are stating our concern in regard to the way that the first two important steps in the implementation of the Law on the Central Bank have been made.

1. First of all, the issue concerns denomination and conversion of the money deposits that were in BH dinars into konvertibilna Marka (KM) which were at the accounts at ZPP and other banks, as well as the part of liabilities at the National Bank of Bosnia and Herzegovina accounts on the day of 08.08.1997. You gave the instructions to denominate all of the deposits that were in BH dinars into KM, along with that only a part of the NBBH liabilities has been taken over by the CBBH with the simultaneous transfer of the foreign exchange security account in the CBBH in a freely convertible foreign currency for the part of liabilities that has been taken over.

   This way, the situation has been created, on one hand, that one part of the NBBH liabilities (so called, central deposits and some others) has automatically been converted to KM and in the same time the currency security transfer to the account of the CBBH has not been executed. On the other hand, all of the deposits of the legal persons which are kept at the ZPP accounts in BH dinars have been converted to KM by automation although only a part of those deposits of the foreign exchange currency is covered through banks' Giro accounts whose status is registered on the accounts at the NBBH and that part has been transferred on the CBBH account with the simultaneous foreign currency security.

   By this method, on the day of August 1l, 1997, actually on the first day of operation of CBBH, big part of the KM deposits have been left uncovered. The consequence of that can be increased demand (in the short run) of the account owners in KM, by the banks, the increased DM withdrawal from the CBBH and the weakening of it's foreign exchange reserves. Created excess of deposits comes from the issue (primary through the NBBH or secondary by the banks credit multiplication).

We were persistent in informing at the meeting of the Governing board that such problem could be created but our view has not been considered . . .

The primary complaint in these paragraphs seems to be that the fractional reserve banking system used everywhere in the world (in which only a fraction of the public's deposits at banks are actually kept at the central bank as liquid assets) was also in use in BiH. As a result, all depositors would not be able to withdraw all of their deposits at once. This is true of all banking systems whether their deposits are in dollars, German marks, or some "weaker" currency. The banking system in Bosnia was made no more or less solvent by converting BHD to KM than it was before. The currency board rules governing the CBBH—the requirement that all of its monetary liabilities be fully backed by liquid DM assets—ensured the integrity of the unit of account (KM) defined by those monetary liabilities. It did not extend further to ensure that others (e.g., banks) extending KM liabilities could always satisfy them. Firms in the U.S. with dollar liabilities, including banks, can and do go broke.

Limits of currency board arrangements

Currency boards ensure the discipline of "monetary policy." The stock of money will be what the public demands with the inflation rate of the anchor currency, and the central bank will always have sufficient foreign exchange backing to defend the fixed exchange rate to the anchor currency.

Currency boards do not ensure the financial soundness or solvency of other entities in the economy. Commercial banks can fail under a currency board regime as easily as under any other monetary policy regime, though the currency board will spare them the monetary shocks sometimes imposed by regular central banks. Argentina's currency board could not protect or prevent the Argentine government from overspending and defaulting on its debt. The government's default was delayed temporarily by abandoning the currency board rules and raiding the assets of the central bank and commercial banks.

The Argentine government, with (in effect) dollar liabilities, can (and did) default on its debt.

Beyond the difficulty in understanding the English translation of their letter (I have only corrected obvious typos), we were very disappointed to see Dragan's name on it. Dragan was a very likable academic, who, we thought, believed in the central bank project. At this early stage—he had only been on the job a few weeks—we still didn't know how far to trust him, or anyone else for that matter. Were the Croats simply trying to prevent the effective operation of the CBBH, with its single currency for the country and loss of power for the Mostar ZAP, or did they have genuine concerns over problems that might harm the CBBH? And while I became good friends with Dragan over time, he didn't really know how far to trust us either. A great deal was at stake here. Suspicions ran high all around.

Only history could decide whether our decision to go ahead with the CBBH opening on August 11 was wise or not. Preparations were far from satisfactory, and misunderstandings were bound to arise when the pace was driven by such a tight timetable. My assessment of what was behind the first complaint in the letter is that the Croats were unhappy that the Kuna was being treated differently than the Bosnia Dinar and that they were also mixing up the problems of bank insol-

The author and Dragan Kovačević (Bosnian Croat Vice Governor of CBBH) in Mostar—February 1998

vency (especially the insolvency of the NBBH) with the conversion of BHD into KM and the choice of the conversion rate. They had diffi-culty accepting the fairness of converting BHD assets and liabilities into KM and not Kuna (or Yugoslav dinar).

The Croats were right that the NBBH problem was serious and could undermine the CBBH. However, redenominating its (and other banks') assets and liabilities into a new unit, such as KM, neither improved nor worsened its financial condition. If its liabilities were greater than its assets before the conversion (whatever the rate) they would continue to be afterward.

What was "real" about the conversion rate was that it established a value of BHD and subsequently for KM in terms of German marks that the CBBH was legally committed to honor for anyone wishing to con-vert BHD or KM bank notes (or KM deposits with the CBBH) into German marks. Kuna could be converted into German marks as well but at exchange rates that might (and did modestly) vary in the mar-ket. Two important points need to be noted. (1) The BHD were liabil-ities of a domestic monetary institution (the Kuna and YUD were liabilities of foreign central banks), which needed to be honored as they were liquidated; (2) the CBBH was getting from the NBBH the German marks needed to fully cover the BHD liabilities it was assuming.

The "tone" of the time is well represented by the following letter to the Managing Director of the IMF from the Croat member of the Joint Presidency of BiH, the Vice-President of the Council of Ministers of the BiH, and Jure Pelivan, the Croat member of the Board of the CBBH who had cosigned the above letter to Serge:

Dear Mr. Camdessus,

Due to the extraordinary efforts of the international community, especially the personnel of the International Monetary Fund, Parliament Assembly of Bosnia and Herzegovina has adopted the Law for Central Bank of Bosnia and Herzegovina.

Central Bank, like all other common institutions in Bosnia and Herzegovina should be a source and expression of trust of all parties in Bosnia and Herzegovina in a new Bosnia and Herzegovina. Trust in mutual relations and common future. Therefore the opening of the Central Bank of BiH, despite all the difficulties, was expected with great anticipation. With hope that reconciliation process will gain a strong momentum with the establishment of the Central Bank and that impartial, strict as well as lawful common monetary institution will be one of the bearers of integration process in BiH.

Unfortunately, two months after adopting the Law for the Central Bank, action that has been taken until now in regard to methods of work are not the guarantee that the Central Bank will achieve the role given to it by Peace Agreement. On the contrary, it can become an initiator of new misunderstandings, and enhancing of mistrust and conflict between the sides in BiH.

In fact, Central Bank has started with its work as a central monetary institution without establishing basic preconditions and is not in accordance with adopted Law:

- Central Bank of BiH does not have an official premises (it operates in the National Bank premises without any defined rules);
- Central Bank has started its work without initial capital, which is not in accordance with the Article 25 of the Law;
- Central Bank is operating without resolved issue of inner structure of organization and systematization of personnel, which is not in accordance with the Article 7. f), g), and i) of the Law, where in fact the Managing Board should have made the decision on this issue;
- Central Bank, that is the Governor, gives guidelines, instructions and other

regulation, without acceptance of the Managing Board, which is not in accordance with the Article 7 b) of the Law;

- Central Bank is not publishing guidelines and instructions in public media (all official papers), which is not in accordance with the Article 70 of the Law.

Despite all mentioned negligence and omissions in its work, Central Bank is entering on 11th of August 1997, into the most delicate operation of establishing the new monetary system in Bosnia and Herzegovina, that is conversion of Bosnian-Herzegovinian Dinar (BHD) to Convertible Mark (KM).

General instruction of application of the Article 7. of the Law (conversion of BHD to KM), without the decision of the Managing Board, which is bound by the Article 7.b and Article 72 of the Law, is given by the Governor, along with surprising co-signature of the Governor of National Bank of BiH, even though the instruction is carrying the symbols of the Central Bank of BiH. Based on that instruction, without the complete report of the Payment System Bureau of the Federation of BiH, and without any decision taken by Managing Board, plus without it being announced in public media, instruction was conducted and all accounts and records were transferred to Convertible Marks. The result is that in the very beginning of work of the Central Bank of BiH the basic principle of full coverage of the Convertible Mark by foreign currency was undermined, because in the accounts of the payment system bureau there exists the Convertible Marks for over 70 mil. DM more than the foreign currency coverage that exists on the accounts of the Central Bank. The explanations offered are only there so that National Bank can keep on operating, where in fact it should have ceased its operation 45 days after the Law on the Central Bank of BiH was adopted, in accordance with the Article 72. of the Law dated 11th of August 1997.

The "urgency" in which these activities were carried through without an insight to the particularize by the Serb or Croat side with all the data necessary for carrying out the conversion, are an obvious attempt for this activity to happen in high secrecy in order to cover up the discrepancy between the actual value of BHD in regard to official exchange rate of the National Bank of BiH.

Activities regarding the sudden employment of 45 persons, during the weekend without previously making a decision on the structure of the organization at the Managing Council meeting, without the knowledge of Serb and Croat representative in the Managing Council, personnel being employed from the ranks of the National Bank of BiH personnel, which has as a result an unbalanced nationality structure, only confirms the above mentioned scheme. Out of the 45 employed, 37 are Bosniac, 5 are Serbs and 3 Croats. With that, in accounting and computer operating departments, all the positions were given to the Bosniacs. It is important to underline that through these departments a complete insight into the Central Bank's transactions is gained.

All above mentioned facts indicate that the Governor accepted the opinion of the Bosniac side as well as the co-operation with them exclusively, and that under the cloak of respecting the given due dates, beginning of the Central Bank's work is occurring outside the Law, and under the influence and to the benefit of only one side in Bosnia and Herzegovina, with the intention that Central Bank becomes a bare follow up of the National Bank of BiH (this bank is not even that according to the Law). This is the way in which all of the eventual short-comings in the business transactions of the national Bank of BiH are restored, about which the Serb nor the Croat side or the media-public have no accurate information. The Governor of the Central Bank of BiH, along with the "Governor" of the National Bank of BiH, who is by the way at the same time the Bosniac member of the Managing Council of the Central Bank of BiH, is attempting to "change," take-over and interfere with the Managing Council of the Central Bank of BiH.

Meanwhile, the Croat side has on many occasions pointed out and warned the Governor as well as the Mission of the International Monetary Fund in Bosnia and Herzegovina about that. However, in the media this was presented as an obstruction by the Croat side, which was most certainly the opposite to what the Croat side in the managing Council was attempting to do.

The Serb side in the beginning assumed that the question of the conversion of BHD is exclusively the matter of Federation side in BiH, so they did not wish to discuss it, but after the above mentioned activities and confrontations with the consequences as well as the method of work, they refused to accept what has been done.

This is why we are writing to you with the hope that you will use authority to prevent this negative approach in establishing the Central Bank and the work of introducing the new currency in Bosnia and Herzegovina. We are hoping that you will give a new initiative to the attempts of the international community in implementation of Peace Accords in BiH and the necessary process of strengthening the trust between all sides in BiH. We hope that you will help with the application of "balanced accounts" as an only possible principle in the process of building Bosnia and Herzegovina in accordance with Dayton Agreement.

We hope that you will accept this letter to be of the most sincere intentions.

Sincerely Yours,

Mr. Krešimir Zubak, Member of the Presidency of BiH;
Mr. Jure Pelivan, Croat member of the Managing Board of the Central Bank of BiH;
Mr. Neven Tomić, Vice-president of the Ministry Council of BiH.

Sarajevo, 4th of September 1997

The letter was copied to the Ambassadors to BiH of the U.S., U.K., Germany, France, Italy, and Russia and to the European Commission and the Office of the High Representative. It was a serious matter and quite devastating for us. It was also an example of Pelivan rhetoric at its clearest (yes, clearest). It reflected the deep distrust that existed, but also Jure's particular view of the world. He was boiling with anger over the continued operation of the NBBH and the "hole in its balance sheet," about which we would learn much more later. He had been the governor of the NBBH at an earlier time and knew its operations very well. We also assumed that he simply didn't understand the workings of the "money multiplier" under fractional reserve banking, which exists everywhere in the world. The "hole" in the NBBH's balance sheet refers to the fact, not fully appreciated by us at the time, that the NBBH did not have sufficient foreign assets to cover all of its deposit liabilities (the difference being the BHD claims it had on the Bosniac government). Jure knew the reason for that "hole," and it was a serious sore point with the Croats. We were yet to learn about it.

We took all arguments and criticisms very seriously, but we were not really able to be sure when there was a legitimate problem deserving our attention or when our counterparts from one region or another were just stalling for political reasons. I had to remind myself that our counterparts no doubt had a similar problem: knowing how far to trust our good intentions and our judgment. Fortunately, this was to change over time as we all got to know and respect each other better.

Serge promptly sent the following letter to Mr. Camdessus:

September 6, 1997

Dear Mr. Camdessus,

First of all, I would like to thank you very much for your letter of August 26. I hope that I will have soon the opportunity to express more directly my gratitude for your extremely kind words.

Starting up the Central Bank—within the tight time frame of the law and the work plan suggested by the IMF staff—has not been easy. In addition to the intrinsic difficulties of the task, the complex internal and external dynamics of local politics have added to the challenge. As late as a few days before the start-up of the CBBH, the Croat member of my Board was urging that the operation be postponed indefinitely, although he sent a congratulatory message the day of the opening.

Political interference has never abated, as evidenced, for instance, by the recent letter to you from senior officials of the Croat community in Bosnia and Herzegovina stating their misgivings about the way the new Central Bank of Bosnia and Herzegovina (CBBH) has been established.

These criticisms are not new. I have repeatedly tried to address them and elicit the full cooperation of their expounders. However, it appears that these efforts have not succeeded and I feel it is my duty to correct the record—most importantly, to safeguard the credibility of this important new institution. To this end, the attached note addresses in some detail the points mentioned in the letter to you.

At a personal level, it is important to me that you be convinced that my actions have been transparent, impartial, and correct. I share with you your pride in the fact that the new Central Bank has been established, despite severe obstacles. The future of this institution holds a promise of peace.

Sincerely,

Serge J. Robert
Governor

Attachment

The purpose of this note is to offer a rebuttal to the criticisms expressed by Messrs. Zubak, Tomic, and Pelivan to Mr. Camdessus, Managing Director of the IMF, in a letter dated September 4, 1997.[1]

I. I will first respond in some detail to five specific points mentioned in that letter. I will then address two more general criticisms.

1. Contrary to what is claimed, the CBBH does have "official" premises: as was agreed explicitly by the Governing Board (including Mr. Pelivan) and later by the Presidency of Bosnia and Herzegovina (including Mr. Zubak), the CBBH has begun its operations in a building formerly occupied exclusively by the National Bank of Bosnia and Herzegovina (NBBH), and where—incidentally—USAID and the IMF Resident Representative also maintain offices. Perhaps, the official's uneasiness refers to the still unresolved ownership status of those premises. They should know, however, that this is a complicated legal issue at the core of the relationship between State and Entities, and that concerns all other public buildings in the country. Its resolution is not in the domain of the Governing Board of the CBBH. I am pressing for it to be addressed by the competent State and Entity authorities, and by a Liquidation Commission in charge of the divestment of the NBBH. Also contrary to what the letter says, there are "rules" to share occupancy costs between the CBBH and the NBBH (they are shared in proportion to the area occupied by the two institutions.)

2. It is well known that the CBBH still does not have a capital base, as mandated by the Law. This reflects a failure of the central government to provide the needed resources, and it has been expected that part of the first purchase under a stand-by arrangement with the IMF will be used for that purpose. However, operationally the lack of capital is of no consequence for the immediate future, since the CBBH can finance its operations from interest income earned on its foreign exchange deposits. Moreover, under the Law the CBBH cannot extend credit to anyone and therefore cannot treat its capital as "free reserves" earmarked to support bank liquidity, if need be.

3. The Governing Board of the CBBH approved its organizational structure and its 1997 budget on August 1, 1997, with the Croat representative voting in favor of the tabled proposals (CBBH Decisions 97–2 and 97–3). This is exactly what the referenced Article 7, items (g) and (j) of the CBBH Law stipulates, contrary to the claim that it has been violated. It is true that the by-laws of the CBBH—which contain provisions about the hiring policy of the institution—have not yet been approved by the Board as required by Article 7, item (f), despite the fact that I have asked for such approval since mid-July. (The by-laws, drafted by an IMF monetary expert and the Resident representative, were first circulated to the Board on July 3, 1997.) The delay has arisen because of the unwillingness of some Board members to discuss the proposal on the grounds that items of higher priority had to be discussed first. This viewpoint has been endorsed by the Croat representative at the last Board meeting on August 20, when he asked that the discussion of the by-laws—which I had again scheduled for that occasion—be postponed to the next Board meeting on September 8.

4. No guideline, instruction or regulation has been issued by me without prior notification to the Board. A package of instructions, drafted by an IMF team in collaboration with Sarajevo banks and the Sarajevo payment bureau and concerning exclusively Bosnian dinar transactions, was circulated to the Board on July 2, 1997. Despite my request to voice promptly any concern on the substance of the instructions, some Board members—including the Croat representative—preferred to postpone their formal discussion and approval. Two of such instructions were issued on July 7 and August 7, in order to proceed with the establishment of the CBBH. Not doing so would have implied a violation of the deadline to start CBBH operations on August 11, as decided by the Parliament of Bosnia and Herzegovina with unanimous approval of all voting members. To date, no member of Governing Board has expressed substantive reservations to the proposed instructions. The letter to the Managing Director mentions explicitly the first instruction issued. This concerned the conversion of Bosnian dinar deposits prior to their redenomination in the new currency. Because this instruction included provisions that spanned two

monetary regimes, it was appropriate, in my view, that it be issued by both myself, as the Governor of the CBBH, and the Governor of the NBBH, then functioning as a central bank with jurisdiction over Bosnia dinar regulations.

5. The letter to the Managing Director mentions that these instructions have not been published in the relevant Official Gazette. This is absolutely right, for the simple reason that no such Official Gazette exists for Bosnia and Herzegovina, pending a decision by the Council of Ministers. The absence of an Official Gazette is, incidentally, also a major impediment to the work of the Parliament and Council of Ministers of Bosnia and Herzegovina. The instructions have, nevertheless, been widely circulating among the intended recipients, both in draft form and in final prior to their being issued. They are also scheduled for imminent publication in the Official Gazette of the Federation, although this is not the proper legal venue for the diffusion of State-level directives.

II. Besides these specific points, the letter to the Managing Director raises two broad and troublesome criticisms: that the transfer of assets and liabilities from the NBBH to the CBBH failed to meet the legal requirement of full, foreign exchange backing of Convertible Marka liabilities; and that the hiring policy of the CBBH has been biased against personnel with a Croat ethnic background.

1. As for the first topic, on August 11 the CBBH took over all monetary liabilities of the NBBH that the law allowed it to assume on its books—namely currency in circulation and commercial banks' reserve deposits at the NBBH—with the corresponding counter value in liquid Deutsche mark assets. Thus, contrary to the claim in the letter to the Managing Director, all liabilities of the CBBH are fully backed as the law requires. The opening balance sheet of the CBBH is being certified by an external auditing firm, Arthur Andersen, which has supervised the financial aspects of starting up the CBBH. Other liabilities left with the NBBH may fall short of its liquid foreign exchange assets, which would be one more reason for not taking these items on the balance sheet of the CBBH, should this be possible. This is not of direct concern for the CBBH and it is consistent with the NBBH continuing non-monetary operations for its depositors, pending its liquidation.

As for the alleged lack of full Deutsche mark coverage of all deposits at commercial banks, it should be well known that commercial banks worldwide have liabilities greater than their immediately available "good funds" since they operate in a fractional reserve system. Perhaps, the intricacies of the local payment system tend to obscure this obvious point.

The letter refers also to the continuing operations of the NBBH, which are interpreted as a violation of the Law. In fact Article 72 of that law simply calls for the NBBH to cease its central bank operation—something that happened—and does not prejudge its ongoing role in other activities. However, these will soon be clarified within the framework of an ongoing audit of the NBBH prior to its liquidation.

2. As for the hiring policies, I have long cherished the idea that the CBBH will reflect the multi-ethnic character of Bosnia and Herzegovina. There is no initiative underway to undermine that ideal. Of the envisaged 100 employees of the CBBH about 60 have been hired. Necessity has required that the pool of the NBBH personnel be taped first, because only there one could find the expertise and familiarity with the Bosnian dinar financial system needed to start the new central bank under a tight time constraint. Even within that constraint, preferential treatment has been granted to non-Bosniac staff of the NBBH: 10 Bosnian Croats—and not 3 as claimed in the letter—are currently employed by the CBBH.

    The complaint about ethnic bias in hiring would be more credible if the officials had offered a list of qualified applicants who had been rejected. In fact, the only nomination made by the Croat member of the Board has been for one of three positions of Vice Governor, and this came through as a firm proposal only on August 20, although that nomination had been solicited by me since early July. Incidentally, this Vice Governor is in charge of the Administration and Financial Services department of the CBBH[2]—a department that the signatories of the letter single out as of key strategic importance to gain "complete insight into the transactions of the Central Bank."

3. Finally, the letter makes the unsubstantiated claims, for instance that the media have portrayed the Croats as intentionally delaying the establishment of the CBBH. It also imputes to the member of the Board from the Republika Srpska an attitude vastly at odds with his—publicly and privately—expressed opinions. For lack of evidence, both claims should not be taken seriously.

The IMF's Managing Director (MD) replied to the Croat President on September 11:

September 11, 1997

Mr. Krešimir Zubak
Member of the Presidency
Bosnia and Herzegovina

Dear Sir:

I have received your letter of September 4, 1997, conveying your concerns about the way in which the Central Bank of Bosnia and Herzegovina was established. I would like to thank you for your courtesy in bringing these matters so promptly to my attention.

Let me assure you that the Fund and Governor Robert have sought to be impartial and even-handed in all matters concerning Bosnia and Herzegovina. I am convinced that Governor Robert not only complied with the relevant legal provisions but also, given the practical circumstances, met that standard of fairness. More generally, Governor Robert has kept me informed of the difficulties he has faced in trying to open the new Central Bank in a timely manner despite the complex political dynamic in Bosnia and Herzegovina, and I can assure you that he has operated at all times with my complete confidence and backing. To have opened the Central Bank at all under these circumstances is a noteworthy accomplishment.

Against this background, I very much hope that we can count on your whole-hearted support to the effort to make this crucial institution fully operational throughout the country. In this way you will be making a major contribution to economic reintegration and a better future for all people of Bosnia and Herzegovina.

Sincerely yours,

Michel Camdessus

Jure had raised most or all of the points expressed in the letter to the MD many times over the preceding months. Jure's arguments were so difficult to understand that few bothered. His continued insistence that the CBBH was not meeting its currency board obligation to fully cover its liabilities with foreign exchange confused us because, of course, its monetary liabilities were fully covered. The deposit liabilities of the NBBH were not fully covered with foreign assets, however. But they were not required to be. The prevailing view on our side was that he didn't understand the nature of banking, by which a large part of a bank's deposits are lent or invested and thus not immediately available if all depositors tried to withdraw their money at once. I took the time, however, on several occasions to meet with Jure and to try to get to the bottom of his concerns. I became convinced that his concerns were genuine, if misstated and very poorly explained, and deserved serious attention. He appreciated these efforts and our mutual respect grew.

We would learn later that the NBBH had made a loan to the Bosnian government during the war to support its war effort against the Croats and Serbs and that it might be difficult for the government to pay it back. The loan was now the liability of the Federation

Government to the NBBH and there was no way the Croats were going to help pay off a loan taken to finance the fight against them. Thus the real problem for the NBBH was that it would have difficulty paying off all its depositors if they withdrew their deposits and transferred them to other banks. In short, the NBBH was probably insolvent. Its insolvency, however, also depended on whether it owned the building now being used by the CBBH and what the value of that asset was. I became convinced through my discussions with Jure that he understood the situation correctly and that he was concerned, as was I, that the financial condition of the NBBH posed risks to the CBBH if satisfactory arrangements where not made. He seemed to accept that what I had proposed (opening a reserve account for the NBBH, etc.,) would be satisfactory. However, he could not be fully satisfied until the NBBH stopped all operations and was liquidated. And who could disagree with that?

As with other problems of understanding, such as with the ZPP over their cash operations for the CBBH, you might wonder why we just didn't take the time to get to the bottom of the issue. The simple answer is that time was limited, and we had other priorities. No one seemed to be operating from the same inner understanding of how these things worked. Thus communication was difficult, even when in the same language, as between, say, Enver and Maruf. I would invest just enough time to an issue to think that I understood the arguments on both sides and then pass on the rest of the work to Enver or some other local. Giving more time to really get to the bottom of something meant not having the time for many other pressing tasks. The concerns of Jure haunted us for a long time and in retrospect taking more time in the beginning would have been wiser.

At the time the MD was responding to the letter from Jure and his Croat colleagues, I was in Croatia with a team providing technical assistance to the Croatian National Bank (as the National Bank of Croatia was now named). At my suggestion, Kim and Dragan Kovačević, the Croat Vice Governor of the CBBH, came to Zagreb (where his family had lived since the war) so that I could introduce him to Governor Marko Škreb and others at the CNB. Dragan was a very likeable and gentle man and like all of us he adored and respected Kim. We saw an ally in Dragan. If I couldn't understand the Croat objections to the

CBBH through Dragan, there was something wrong with me. We had extensive discussions of Jure's problems during evening dinners with Dragan, his wife, and son. Dragan was born near Tuzla in Bosnia, where he and his family had lived until the war. Not only had the Croat Vice Governor been born in Bosnia, his graduate studies in Economics had been in Belgrade. The Serb Vice Governor had been born in Sarajevo. This war had been insane, and had done enormous damage to a fascinating society.

Jure's problems had translated into passive Croat resistance to opening the Mostar branch of the CBBH, scheduled for September 15, and thus to full cooperation with Dayton's monetary plans for Bosnia and Herzegovina. He stated that my solution to the NBBH problem had not been implemented. I was furious. I sent Serge the following memo (following the rule of not letting anger show in writing):

To: Mr. Serge Robert   September 13, 1997
From: Warren Coats
Subject: CBBH Branch in Mostar

As you know Dragan Kovačević (CBBH Vice Governor for Administration and Financial Services) is here in Zagreb with Kim to meet with the Governor and selected staff of the National Bank of Croatia and the Croatian payment bureau (ZAP). He has indicated that these meetings and contacts have been very helpful.

His visit here has given me an opportunity to discuss with him the opening of the Mostar Branch of the CBBH, which he will also oversee. It goes without saying that if the CBBH does not have the full participation of the Mostar Branch (Croat Majority) area, we will have failed in our efforts to fulfill the Dayton mandate for a statewide central bank. While cooperation and participation of the Croats is a decision only they can take, we must, of course, continue to make every effort to address their concerns. With this in mind, I am sharing my thoughts with you on the three points that Mr. Kovačević says need to be addressed before the Mostar office can be opened. By the way, he assumes that they could be satisfactorily addressed and the office opened within one to two weeks from now.

1. The area served by the Mostar Branch must be defined. This is obviously necessary, but need not, I think, wait for or be tied to the broader political issue of the Cantonal organization. Along with temporary, transitional, currency note designs (coupons, etc.), the CBBH might adopt temporary boundaries of operation for each of its three Branch operations. The functional purpose

of each branch is to service the reserve accounts of banks in its area. These are tied to the settlement of net payments each day in the clearinghouse (payment bureau) operating in its region. Thus it should not be too difficult to agree on a temporary definition of the region such that it includes all banks that submit their payment orders to and maintain their domestic payment Giro accounts with the ZAP headquartered in Mostar.

2. The conversion of BHD accounts to KM. The resolution of this issue requires more background information than I have, but we will naturally wish to preserve the principle of fairness. My guess is that conversion is not the issue, but rather the collectibility of the underlying claim whether it is denominated in BHD or in KM. Thus, while more facts are needed, we should seek agreement that the resolution of any existing claim now denominated in BHD, will need to proceed through normal legal (and maybe political) channels and that the validity of these claims and their collectibility are not likely to be affected by whether they have been redenominated in KM or not.

3. Backing of NBBH deposits. As noted in my back to office report following the opening of the CBBH last month and in a subsequent memo to you of August 30, 1997, the currency board rules are potentially being violated each day by the settlement of payments to and from deposits maintained with the NBBH, until it opens a reserve account with the CBBH for such purpose. You will recall that on my last day in Sarajevo August 15, you, Governor Omićević, Mr. Backović, Mr. Smajlagic, and I met to discuss this problem and agreed on a solution. The solution was that the NBBH would open a reserve account with the CBBH immediately (as a bank already established under a special law), all non-government depositors at the NBBH would be given a short period (several weeks) to withdraw their deposits and find other banks, and the payments of the remaining governmental depositors would be processed by the ZPP and settled like all other payments by banks and their customers on the books of the CBBH. We further noted that as the reserve requirement did not apply to government deposits, the NBBH would not have a reserve requirement. The only special treatment of the NBBH would be (in a compromise agreed to by you) the payment of interest on the NBBH's deposits with the CBBH. Mr. Kovačević assures me that the agreement just summarized above completely addresses the Croat concern about currency board rule violations. The problem is that it has apparently not been implemented. As I urged in my memo of August 30, the agreement should be implemented with great urgency and any under or over coverage of foreign exchange that may have resulted during the intervening period should be removed by an additional one-time transfer between the NBBH and the CBBH.

I hope that these suggestions are helpful, and wish you the very best.

cc: Mr. Guitián
     Mr. Ryan
     Mr. S. Brown
     Mr. Zanello
     Mrs. Rhee

THE NBBH PROBLEM SOLVED AGAIN

This being the Balkans—an expression we always used when things went inexplicably wrong—the solution to the NBBH problem that everyone had agreed to on my last day in Sarajevo the week of the CBBH's opening was aborted. The ZPP was not prepared to accept the instructions that they treat the NBBH like any other bank (in part, I assume, because it would have made explicit the need to block payment orders that would overdraw the NBBH reserve account). Instead, the NBBH transferred an additional DM 10 million to a special deposit with the CBBH (a "guaranteed deposit account") to cover the potential net use of its deposit liabilities on the assumption that, as the government maintained a balanced budget, over time inflows would match outflows.

I always thought, but cannot prove, that the failure to implement the agreement I had worked out for a reserve account was the result of the persistence of Ibro in using the trust account in the way he had always had in mind. But the ZPP may have played a role in this as well since it struggled to preserve as much as possible its place at the center of the monetary universe. I must say, however, that as difficult as the FPB/ZPP was to deal with, I believed throughout (and believe even more now) that they fought fairly. I think that they were honest with us and in fact delivered more of the changes we wanted than we should probably have expected.

When I saw what was being proposed to deal with the NBBH problem instead of what we had agreed on, I was beside myself. After receiving a draft of the Instruction that would implement it, I sent the following memo to Alessandro:

To: Mr. Zanello   September 19, 1997
From: Warren Coats
Subject: NBBH in the payment system

Thank you for the opportunity to comment on the draft Instruction on the NBBH's deposits with the CBBH. I can appreciate what it attempts to do, but I have strong objections to the approach it takes. While I fought for some modest flexibility in the Central Bank Law, that position was not accepted and I cannot support creating it outside the limits of the law.

Our agreement with Mr. Omićević, repeated in my memo to Mr. Robert earlier this week, was that the NBBH would be treated like every other bank. Thus it would not have a special "guaranteed deposit account," which I don't think the law permits anyway, but only the reserve account that every other bank would have. While it would be possible to structure an arrangement whereby the guaranteed deposit account could be automatically drawn on to cover a clearing shortfall in the NBBH's reserve account, it definitely would violate the law to permit a daily settlement for the system in which the sum of the NBBH's reserve and guaranteed deposit accounts were negative. Article 4 explicitly provides for such a possibility.

The Instructions governing all banks should apply equally to the NBBH, as long as it has deposits from clients that participate in the payment system. No special agreement is needed for that purpose. What is needed, as I have stressed before, is an arrangement in place for any bank (not just the NBBH) to adjust its reserve account balance (by an interbank transfer or sale of DM to the CBBH) after the daily netting has been computed and communicated by ZPP.

The draft Instruction that you sent to me for comment, in my opinion, would be very inappropriate and illegal. The one special concession agreed to by Mr. Robert was that interest would be paid on the NBBH's deposits. An Instruction would be needed for that.

cc: Mr. S. Brown
     Mr. C. Ryan
     Mrs. K. Rhee

A NEW GOVERNOR

The resolution of the NBBH problem was slowed by Serge's resignation in October. The previous spring, Serge had shocked me with the revelation that his agreement with the IMF's Managing Director to accept the governorship of the CBBH extended only through May 1997. My department and I had been completely unaware of that understanding. It had not been easy to find a sufficiently senior central banker, with appropriate credentials and reputation, who was willing to move to Sarajevo for six years (or even, it seems, for one year). Serge's revelation meant that we needed to undertake the search again. However, after some prodding, he agreed to extend his stay until the new Central Bank was established. He remained in Sarajevo until October 3.

September 28, 1997

Mr. Serge Robert
Governor
Central Bank of Bosnia and Herzegovina
Sarajevo

Dear Serge:

I wish that I could be with you today to convey these greetings more personally, but I am certainly there in spirit. It has been most enjoyable working with you this past year. Your job has been a very difficult one, and your hard work and winning manner are documented by the existence of the now functioning CBBH. The IMF and Bosnia and Herzegovina are fortunate to have had your services for this past year, I only wish it had been longer. It has been a privilege for me to have helped you. I wish you the very best in your next challenge, and hope that we will remain friends.

Very truly yours,

Warren Coats

Serge's careful non-confrontational style had resulted in slow, sometimes very slow, progress. However, it was probably just what was needed at the time, when distrust was very high and building confidence seemed the most important contributor to long-run progress and success. Serge was always a gentleman and gained respect and eventually trust from his counterparts as he patiently prodded them on. When it became essential to take bold decisions to open the new Central Bank—when the Board was dragging its feet and not taking needed decisions—Serge rose to the occasion. By October 1997, however, the time had come for a more aggressive governor.

Fortunately our search over the summer had found one. Peter Nicholl—then an Executive Director at the World Bank, representing

New Zealand, Australia, Korea, Cambodia, Mongolia, and seven Pacific Island countries—had been Deputy Governor of the Reserve Bank of New Zealand from 1990 to 1995. He had agreed to accept the post in Sarajevo starting the last week of November. Peter had overseen the RBNZ's internal reforms and had thus worked through the fundamental questions of the purposes of a central bank (mission statement) and the appropriate means for achieving them, with the detail that characterized New Zealand's structural reforms of the late 1980s and early '90s. Following his two years at the World Bank, Peter might have expected to be tapped to become the new governor of the RBNZ, but he was not. No doubt this helped him say yes to our offer.

Recruiting a new governor had taken up valuable time. Finalizing Peter's contract took even more. He was a tough negotiator. He wished to bring with him his partner of some years. This would be normal in a "normal" country, but the security situation made Bosnia a non-spouses duty station. The best we could do was to pay for her to live in Rome or some other nearby city outside of Bosnia. In the midst of these discussions, it came to light (though Peter had not hidden the fact) that Peter and Glynyss were not married. Thus our human resources department stated that he was not entitled to the Fund's spouse benefits.

Further discussion brought into consideration (as Peter and our Legal department exchanged views on the situation) that by the laws of New Zealand, he and Glynyss were common-law spouses and the Fund would hardly want to discriminate against the laws of one of its member countries. In any event, they wanted to live together in Sarajevo (and in fact, Glynyss had been an economist at the RBNZ and would be a valued resource for Peter), which they could always do at their own expense. But Peter argued for medical coverage and made special arrangements with the American Embassy for Glynyss's evacuation in the event of a medical or security emergency.

About the time these issues seemed on their way to resolution, we became aware that Peter was still married to his first wife (again, the fault for the oversight had been ours; Peter had never hidden the fact). Even in New Zealand you can't be married to two people at once (the IMF had resolved the polygamy issue long ago by paying benefits for only one wife), however many you might legally have in your own

Central Bank autonomy and accountability

In the decade leading up to the establishment of the European Central Bank, central bank independence became generally accepted best practice. In the U.K., for example, the Chancellor of the Exchequer dramatically relinquished control over interest rate policy to the Bank of England in May 1997. Throughout Europe and much of the rest of the world central bank laws were adopted or amended to protect central banks from political interference with the implementation of monetary policy. Independence came with the need for greater accountability as well.

The objective of monetary policy remains the responsibility of the government and is most often expressed through the mandate given to the central bank in the central bank law, generally to maintain price stability. However, the central bank is responsible for determining how best to achieve its policy mandate. The most common provisions in the law to protect the central bank's operational autonomy are:

a. fit and proper board and governor appointed for relatively long (and staggered), fixed terms and unremovable except for very good cause specified in the law;
b. limited or no lending to government;
c. restriction against government direction;
d. establishment and control of its own budget;
e. obligation of government to cover negative net worth.

To protect the public from misuse of its autonomy, central banks must also be accountable for their performance. The most common provisions in the law of accountability are:

a. publish annual report that assesses performance against objectives;
b. publish financial statements periodically;
c. external audits of financial statements;
d. excess profits remitted to government.

country. The formality of divorce was already underway, however; and the divorce was completed in time for a happy conclusion of all these discussions. I had not met Peter in person yet and was not at all sure what I would think of him when I did.

Peter's personality was the opposite of Serge's. He was very animated and gregarious. He was impatient with failure and not shy or slow to express his views or anger. However, everyone in Bosnia quickly saw that he was driven by his perceptions of what was right and fair. Thus no one could think him partisan (Bosniac, Croat, or Serb) for very long. After a short learning period, Peter began to "kick butt" and the pace of the CBBH's development quickened.

Serge's early October departure and Peter's late November arrival left an unfortunate gap in leadership during a critical period. More than anything, progress during this period was maintained by the efforts of Kim Rhee, the real power behind the throne anyway. I have also said little of the very important contributions of USAID and EU PHARE in providing training, equipment, and organizational and procedural assistance. These programs, as well as our own technical assistance from Kim and Jean-Luc, kept things generally moving in the right direction. But there were many serious problems still to overcome, and the NBBH problem was one of the biggest of them.

PUBLISHING THE BALANCE SHEET

The NBBH problem made its liquidation difficult, held up the opening of the Mostar Main

The Board of the CBBH in 1998: standing: Peter Nicholl (Governor); seated from left to right: Kasim Omićević, Manojlo Ćorić, and Jure Pelivan

Unit of the CBBH, and threatened to undermine the currency board arrangement. In addition, it contributed for a while to the CBBH's failure to publish financial data required by the law.

The Central Bank Law required the CBBH to publish monthly a statement of its monetary assets and liabilities in order to provide evidence to the public that it was complying with currency board rules. It did not do so for many months. The failure to publish the required balance sheet was not simply an oversight. It was held up because of the failure to get agreement on its format, and because it would have revealed currency board violations. Neither is an acceptable excuse, of course.

We had adopted the "plunge ahead and clean up and polish later as you go" strategy. Most of the detailed procedures were developed through experience and as needed—as illustrated in the following letter from Jean-Luc in mid-October 1997. My reply to him took the form of inserted comments in brackets and in bold.

From: Jean-Luc Couetoux
To: Warren Coats
cc: Alessandro

Dear Warren,

Alessandro gave me your comments on my draft monthly report discussed with him. Please find enclosed a draft letter to the Official Gazette and a new version of the report (the English at least must be corrected) and answers to the three points you mentioned.

The article 35 of the Law on the CBBH provides that "every month the Central Bank shall publish monthly information concerning <u>the total amount of Convertible Marka in circulation</u> and the official foreign exchange reserves of the Central Bank, with a breakdown of the holdings of Deutsche Marks and other currencies." That is the reason why I chose this title for the report. Nevertheless, this is still a draft and the template of the report is likely to be revised in the near future to include other items if needed. I do agree, as we suggested, that we should add capital and reserves and BiH deposits other than USAID. The point is to decide if we include these items from now on or only when there is an amount for each of it. I thought that from a psychological point of view, it was maybe better not to mention zero capital or reserves.

[WC: **The purpose of Article 35 was to reassure the public that the rules of the currency board have been followed. Some last minute changes in the law were unfortunately not reflected throughout and this is one of those places. We can repair some of that damage by sticking with the spirit of the law rather than its exact wording. In other words the relevant concepts here are Monetary Liabilities and Net Foreign Assets. If we introduce these more relevant concepts here they will last forever and correct the oversight in drafting the law. I agree with you that capital and reserves present a problem at the moment as they are very small—assuming there has been some net profit by now. It might easily be added later or called surplus at this point to reflect the difference between assets and liabilities.**]

I included in the report your suggestion on FX reserves. The only point concerns the deposit of the NBBH with the CBBH. In my mind, this deposit should be denominated in KM to be merged with the amount due to or by the NBBH (I obtained the abbreviation "KM" [in addition to DEM] to be included in the agreement signed between the NBBH and the CBBH; thus the agreement gives the choice for the deposit between the two currencies). Nevertheless Ibrahim thought that this deposit should be in DEM and is recorded as such in the bookkeeping. Therefore, in the present situation, the FX liabilities are DEM 10 million, instead of zero, which should be the case. [WC: **As I wrote earlier, I agree with you that the NBBH deposits should be in KM. As we did not foresee liabilities to residents in anything but KM, the definition of Monetary Liabilities—after the last minutes changes—did not need to be explicit about the fact that they are all liabilities to residents. Thus all liabilities to NBBH must be shown and the counterpart FX must be included in the total NFA.**]

Regarding the note on currency in circulation, I added in the comment that the ZPP and the Post Office were acting as agents of the CBBH. As for the second point of your section 3, I was told by Market Banka and the ZPP that no cash was kept by the ZPP on behalf of banks. [WC: **I have my doubts, but it is not a big deal.**]

Please find some other comments on the report.

For USAID funds, I included the relevant data in a separate table called "Third Party Money" in a previous version. Alessandro thought we should not publish them. Mr. Robert, who I called yesterday, agreed, because in his mind the liability and the corresponding assets can be considered as those of a customer for which we must not give any information. I also discussed this point with John, who considers that we can offset liabilities and assets, which gives a zero balance. Therefore I deleted this additional table and added some comments in the explanatory notes.

For the way of publishing the information, Mr. Robert finds Alessandro's idea to publish it in the Official Gazette very good, as far as we are sure it is now the Gazette for the whole country.

Another point I discussed with Alessandro was the relevance to publish data at the end of August. We agreed not to publish them because it was part of a month. The point on which we should now agree is if from next October we refer for each month to the previous month's data.

I called John yesterday and sent him this morning the last version of the draft report. I took already his comments into consideration but he will probably have other remarks after receiving the document.

On the issue of the settlement CBBH/NBBH, I met Mr. Backović and Ibrahim on Monday. Mr. Backović agreed on the necessity to document the amount due to or by the NBBH. He told me that he would organize a meeting with the payment bureau on Thursday (that is tomorrow). He will attend this meeting with Ibrahim, Alessandro (if he is available) and myself. [WC: **Good, keep it up until they have it right.**]

I hope you received the note on required reserves [WC: **No, though it may have come after I left.**] and you had the information you needed. I finished the one on USAID funds. Would you want me to send it to you or to John? [WC: **Both.**]

Thank you for your comments on the report.

I hope you are fine and you have an interesting mission in Andorra.

Yours sincerely,
Jean-Luc

In addition to the need to iron out the accounting and presentational issues, no one was eager to publish the fact of the currency board violations. In practice, the alternative scheme, using the "guaranteed deposit account," was not properly monitored in accordance with the procedures we had put in place more generally. The above shortcomings in the procedures for settling payments involving deposits with the NBBH resulted in the end-December 1997 monetary liabilities of the

CBBH exceeding its monetary assets by KM 16.6 million. An additional DM 10 million was transferred from the NBBH to the CBBH in March 1998, but it proved to be inadequate to cover the net outflow of deposits from the NBBH. The situation was beginning to create a public scandal that was undermining confidence in the new Central Bank. Prior to the end of the year, banks in RS and Mostar areas had not been asked (by the regional political authorities) to open reserve accounts. Thus the Mostar and Pale main branches had not opened on September 15 as planned, in part because the authorities in those areas were concerned about the integrity of the currency board operation as a result of payments by depositors in the NBBH. The main branch in Pale opened in a formal sense September 22, but was not functioning operationally.

Proper implementation and use of the NBBH's reserve account required the cooperation of the ZPP and the NBBH. The ZPP had to provide daily information on the NBBH's Giro account balance in the same way it did for other banks and had to provide the CBBH with daily information on changes in its holdings of KM (BHD) bank notes (held as agent of the CBBH) that resulted from deposits and withdrawals of cash from the CBBH (i.e., from the payment bureaus as agent of the CBBH). When I returned to Sarajevo in February 1998, I obtained a new agreement to implement the original proposal while waiting for the liquidation of the NBBH to begin. The NBBH opened a reserve account with the CBBH on March 20, 1998; but the related settlement procedure was suspended several days later when the CBBH's accounts suggested that the NBBH was overdrawn, while those of the NBBH showed a positive balance. A new problem had come to light.

As a result of these delays, the monthly balance sheets of the CBBH continued to show currency board violations in February and March. The local press was becoming more loudly critical. We were all getting quite concerned. On Sunday morning, April 12, Peter called me at home from Sarajevo, pleading with me to send John Dalton back to help them get to the bottom of this never-ending problem. That option was totally impossible. John had returned to Washington the week before from several unexpected weeks in Indonesia and had five days to catch up on his preparations for an accounting workshop he was delivering in Vienna that started Monday, April 13. At this point he was in Vienna, with good phone contact with Sarajevo.

At the end of the previous week Scott Brown had concluded his long-sought agreement with the authorities in BiH for a standby arrangement with the IMF. It had as prior actions the full operation of the CBBH (the opening of all reserve accounts throughout the country) and the resolution of the NBBH/CBBH problem that had been hounding me since the CBBH was opened in August. The morning of April 15 I was on the phone first thing with Kim Rhee, who had just returned to Washington from Sarajevo over the weekend, to continue discussing our latest refinements to some of the Instructions to banks and payment bureaus. New instructions were needed covering interpayment bureau payments and end-of-day settlement of payments when more than one Branch of the CBBH was in operation. Kim had also taken over the efforts to resolve the NBBH/CBBH problem in Sarajevo after John Dalton and I had left in March, and until she had left for Washington a week earlier.

While talking with her (and just before I was to call Peter Nicholl in Sarajevo for an update on progress), Hasseneli Mehran called to tell me that the European I department director (Scott Brown's boss) had contacted him a second time for help in resolving the never ending NBBH/CBBH problem. Hasseneli had led the very first MAE mission to Bosnia, in December 1995 (arriving three days after the signing of the Dayton agreement in Paris on December 14). Hasseneli, himself a former Governor of the Central Bank of Iran during the Shaw's rein, asked what we should do about it. We had already determined that if John couldn't go, the second best would be to get help from the Arthur Anderson team that had returned to Sarajevo to audit the CBBH's year-end balance sheet the week before (just as we were determining that it really was impossible to send John) and to finalize the liquidation balance sheet for the NBBH.

When I called Peter, it was clear that with all of the other things on his plate, particularly the preparations for issuing the new bank notes that would be delivered at the end of May, he was having trouble nailing down the resolution to the NBBH/CBBH problem. My mind slowly and painfully began to review my plans for the next few days as I began to consider going myself.

I was already planning to leave for Bulgaria the following Monday evening in order to arrive there Tuesday and start work on Wednesday, April 22. I was under great pressure to finish the preparations for that mission and other duties in the office. I had a haircut scheduled for 6:30 p.m. and was trying to figure out when to find the time to see my doctor about the reoccurrence of an allergy-based skin rash that was getting rather serious again. I had dinner plans for that evening with a Russian friend. Minutes before I had made plans with Juan Herrera for dinner Thursday evening. Another friend, Laurent Cartayrade and I had just gotten theater tickets for the Source Theatre for Friday evening. And Saturday I was expecting to take Tu Tran, a young member from the Minister of Finance of Vietnam I had met a few weeks earlier at an APEC meeting in Vancouver BC, to dinner. We had established e-mail contact after Vancouver, and he was coming to Washington for the APEC Deputy Minister's meeting that coincided with the IMF's Interim Committee meetings that took place every spring. Sunday evening was a concert at the Kennedy Center—the reason why I wasn't leaving for Sofia earlier (I could have spent the weekend in Europe). In short, I had a full schedule.

I reluctantly suggested to Peter, that if he felt it was really needed I could come for a couple of days right away. He accepted the offer immediately, as I knew he would. It was 10:15 a.m. at this point and I had a 10:30 a.m. meeting with Marko Škreb, the governor of the Croatian National Bank, who was in town because of the Interim Committee meetings. As I left for that meeting, I informed my staff assistant of the need to start preparations for my departure for Sarajevo—UN security clearance to visit Bosnia was still required and usually took several days—and to find out from our travel office how quickly I could be there.

When I returned from the meeting with Marko at about 1:00 p.m., Rose had flight reservations for 6:10 p.m. that would have me in Sarajevo at 2:30 p.m. the next afternoon (8:30 a.m. Washington time), with just one stop for five hours in Zurich. The efforts to obtain the security clearance, without which my tickets could not be issued, were underway, but were made more difficult because the UN office in Sarajevo had already closed for the day. By the time I had gathered up what I had hoped were the needed documents (for Bosnia and Bulgaria), canceled various things (including my haircut), picked up my ticket and travel money and arrived home to pack, it was 4:00 p.m. At 4:30 p.m. I was out the door to the waiting cab for the forty-minute drive to Dulles Airport, without, I later discovered, my skin rash medication, or casual pants.

I had just enough time at the airport for a last call to Rose with a few more instructions (I miss Rose, who had to leave the IMF because of a stupid rule regarding a typing test). The plane, Swiss Air to Zurich, left on time. Unlike the Lufthansa flight I had been scheduled to take to Frankfurt Monday evening, Swiss Air's flight had no first class, and business class seats are more difficult to sleep in. I arrived blurry-eyed in Sarajevo, in the rain again, a bit over fourteen hours later and was met by Peter's wife, Glynyss, and driver. She informed me that my first meeting with Peter, Enver, the manager of the Sarajevo Branch, and the new Chief accountant was at 3:30 p.m. They dropped me off at the Hotel Bosna at 3:10 p.m., which gave me just enough time to check in, brush my teeth and get to Peter's office by 3:30 p.m.

Formal liquidation of the NBBH had been launched on April 7, 1998. An experienced American liquidator, William Duddly, had been recruited by KPMG consulting—then called Barents, and now called BearingPoint—and appointed liquidator by the Bosnian court. He had many challenges in this former Yugoslav republic, which, as part of Yugoslavia, had developed some unusual forms of public, private, and social ownership of property. I have discussed at length by now the various steps we were trying to take to keep the NBBH's insolvency (or at least illiquidity) from creating a violation of the CBBH's currency board rules. Mr. Duddly's appointment added a new interim tool, since he was able to freeze any deposit withdrawals that could not be covered by the NBBH's deposits with the CBBH.

Duddly arrived in Sarajevo on a plane from Vienna at the same time I did from Zurich, though I hadn't realized it at the time. He joined the 3:30 p.m. meeting, a bit late. The meeting lasted until 8:00 p.m. As if I could really handle anything more, Alessandro stopped in during the meeting with the message to call Bob Feldman in Washington about a meeting with Marko and Stan Fischer, the IMF's First Deputy Managing Director. When I returned to my hotel room, Tony Lybek called from Zagreb about a payments seminar and asked me to speak with his payment expert from N.Y. sometime the next day.

Exhausted, I fell asleep without dinner and managed to sleep, quite well in fact, until 4:30 a.m. Knowing that it would be futile to try to sleep again, I got up and wrote the diary notes you have just read above. It was a great pity I didn't record the details of my activities more often. After breakfast at the Hotel Bosna, I walked the block to the Central Bank at about 7:30 a.m., checked my e-mail, and sent a few messages. The rain of the day before had stopped, but it was still overcast and cool.

The Central Bank was quiet at that hour, and the guard at the door gave me the key to the IMF office door. Though I am sure he recognized me, I was concerned about the state of security at the Bank. Considerable work in the past two months had gone into improving Bank security. Not only did its old vaults in the basement contain over KM 22 million in BHD bank notes (equivalent to the same amount of DM) and DM 5.6 million in DM bank notes, but they would soon hold a large amount of the new KM bank notes that were to be delivered near the end of May. Considerable additional work had yet to be completed.

At what I thought was 9:00 a.m., but turned out to be 8:00 a.m., I walked into the Governor's office to discover that he wasn't there yet. I stayed to enjoy another cup of coffee. When he arrived, we met with Mr. Duddly and discussed his side of the NBBH/CBBH problem.

During breakfast it had occurred to me that if the NBBH liquidator froze all balances at the ZPP and instructed the ZPP to open new accounts for these depositors into which limited amounts (as authorized by the liquidator) would be transferred for the free use of the depositors, the whole operation would be cleaner. These amounts would have to be limited to something less than the NBBH's reserve account balance, which by that time reflected almost all of the remaining foreign exchange that had belonged to the NBBH. The establishment of new accounts and the freezing of the old would add a very comforting additional layer of protection for the CBBH.

The ZPP's first duty was to verify and ensure that any payment order it accepted was fully covered by the balances of the payer. If the sum of all deposits with the NBBH was less than the NBBH's reserve account balance with the CBBH, the day's net payments from these deposits could not exceed and thus overdraw the reserve account. So even if the ZPP failed to make the second check—the check at the end of the day of the sum of net payment from the accounts of depositors with the NBBH—the CBBH could be confident that the NBBH's reserve account would not be overdrawn. Mr. Duddly, who in his second day in Sarajevo was still gathering information and formulating his plans, agreed in principle with this approach.

He also agreed that this first step should be taken within a few days. Even if the ZPP did not cooperate with the CBBH in enforcing the procedures of Instruction 5, the liquidator's actions could prevent any effort of depositors to transfer out of the NBBH more than the NBBH could cover with foreign exchange.

I left Peter and Mr. Duddly at 10:00 a.m. for the meeting with the ZPP management that Enver had arranged.

Peter had asked Anka Musa to drive over from Mostar to meet with me. Later in the morning, I also had separate meetings with Nino and Sadik. I discussed their concerns about which number to use for NBBH reserve account, theirs or ZPP's. I was finally overcome with hunger and broke for lunch at 2:30 p.m. To my disappointment, after I returned from lunch Anka was gone, driving back to Mostar.

However, the separate technical meeting between Nino, Sadik, and ZPP produced good results. Contrary to their earlier statements to us, it turned out that the ZPP was not able to process some payment orders completely within the same day, giving rise to payment-system float (some debits were made to the Giro accounts of paying banks one or two days before the credits were made to the receiving banks). Thus, the category of "items in transit" was added to the CBBH's accounts to reconcile the difference in the CBBH's and the ZPP's versions of bank reserve account balances; and the ZPP agreed to treat the NBBH like any other bank.

The next day, I summarized the problems and their prospective solutions in a memo to Peter:

Office Memorandum

To: Governor Nicholl   April 18, 1998

From: Warren Coats

Subject: **Prior Actions for IMF purchase**

Three prior actions are required before Bosnia can purchase foreign exchange from the IMF. Two of them pertain to the Central Bank: a) the credits that were implicitly extended by the CBBH to cover payments by depositors with the NBBH must be repaid and procedures must be in place to ensure that they are not repeated, and b) all banks in BiH must have usable reserve accounts with their Branches of the CBBH. During my visit to Sarajevo from April 16 to 20, I addressed primarily the first of these.

As you know, the NBBH has now transferred virtually all of its foreign exchange assets (an additional DM 40 million after the initial opening of the CBBH on August 11, 1997) to the CBBH. These additional transfers more than cover the additional monetary liabilities of the NBBH transferred to the CBBH since August 11, 1997 (which as of Thursday, April 16 amounted to KM 22 million). The difference is the current reserve account balance of the NBBH. The CBBH acquired additional monetary liabilities from the NBBH as the result of purchases of BHD bank notes and payments to other banks by the NBBH and its depositors. Thus the (overdraft) credits that the CBBH had extended to the NBBH have now been repaid.

Furthermore, as of Tuesday, April 21, 1998 the CBBH will have opened the reserve account of the NBBH agreed to by you and Mr. Omićević in early March and Mr. Burnazović, Chairman of the Federation Payment Bureau (ZPP), has agreed to adhere to the requirements of CBBH Instruction 5 and to apply those instructions to the NBBH, thus treating the NBBH like any other bank (since August 11, 1997, the only functions of the NBBH have been those of a bank). When combined with the control over daily settlements held by the CBBH, these procedures should make it impossible for the CBBH to permit new overdraft credit to the NBBH.

I would like to note, however, that the full success of the above procedures requires faithful daily adherence by the CBBH to clearly established internal rules for the daily settlements of payments cleared through the payment bureau. Within the CBBH, the authority to settle these daily payments falls under Vice Governor Backović's Banking Operations Department. You might wish to ask the Comptroller General, Mr. Piljak, to review the procedures for daily settlements (which presumably include the requirement that Mr. Backović or his officially authorized alternate sign the authorization for the daily settlements) and report on his findings to you. If all banks participating in the payment bureau clearing do not have zero or positive clearing balances (taking into account the reserve account amounts set aside for that purpose), it is essential that the CBBH refuse to settle that day's payments for all of those banks.

The procedures for daily settlement are about to get more complicated with the addition of settlements in two other clearinghouses (the payment bureaus in Mostar and RS) involving reserve accounts in three CBBH Main Units rather than just one. These new procedures are discussed in MAE's April 1998 technical assistance report and in the drafts of Regulation 2 and Instructions 5 (amended) and 9 contained in that report (final version). This regulation and these Instructions need to progress through the review process and be adopted by the CBBH Board with some urgency. In fact, they are required for the operation of reserve accounts on a countrywide basis and are thus part of the fulfillment of the prior actions for the purchase from the Fund (which will provide the resources for the CBBH's capital).

In addition to the above safeguards, the NBBH is now officially in liquidation and the actions expected imminently by the liquidator, Mr. Duddly, to limit the use of deposits with the NBBH to something less than the NBBH's reserve account balance, provides a second guarantee that the CBBH will not extend new credit to the NBBH. With the implementation of the above, I am fully satisfied that this condition for the program with the Fund has been fulfilled. You may wish to more formally establish Mr. Burnazović's agreement to the procedures. One possibility is for you, in the company of Messrs Burnazović, Omićević, and Duddly, to report to the Federation Prime Minister and Finance Minister on the new agreement and arrangements. To assist you with the important public relations aspect of correcting the many misunderstandings reported in the press, I have prepared a draft press release for your use (attached).

As an aside, I understand from Mr. Backović that he issued an instruction to the ZPP with regard to the treatment of the NBBH, which he numbered Instruction 8. This document was apparently (I have not seen it) based on what was meant to be a guidance note to the ZPP prepared by my mission last month (no new instruction is required because the actions required of the ZPP are fully covered by Instruction 5). I may not have the facts correct on these points, but as Instructions must be approved by the CBBH Board and signed by the Governor and must be numbered in accordance with an established procedure, it appears that there is a lack of understanding of these procedures on Mr. Backović's part.

On this visit I have not addressed the second prior action—opening and operating reserve accounts for all banks. As in the past, delays in opening reserve accounts may be related, in part, to the NBBH overdrafts discussed above so that the success in resolving that problem, once fully communicated to the officials

and the public, should remove that source of delay. I understand that the opening of reserve accounts and the training of staff in their operations is progressing
satisfactorily. Arrangements for opening accounts in Banja Luka and Pale and their
operation (in Pale?) need to be moved along quickly (starting with the reissuance
of the instruction to banks to open their accounts). As noted above, once reviewed
by the banks and cleared by the managers of the CBBH Main Units, Regulation
2 and the amended Instruction 5 and the new Instruction 9 must be approved by
the Board before countrywide settlements can be undertaken. The new accounts
and internal procedures for national settlement at the Head Office of the CBBH
must be quickly developed. I assume that Mrs. Musa, working with Mr. Backović
and Mr. Gregović, the acting chief accountant, is overseeing this process.

Exciting progress is being made at the CBBH and I look forward to seeing
the new KM bank notes in circulation when I return in July. Thank you for your
kind hospitality during my stay.

Attachment

cc: Mr. Guitián
      Mr. Blejer
      Mr. Mehran
      Mr. Scott Brown

I left for Bulgaria April 20, four days after I had arrived.

The NBBH's reserve account was finally put into full operation on
April 21, 1998; and the NBBH issued instructions to transfer an additional DM 20 million to its new reserve account with the CBBH. Aside
from the fact that most of the additional foreign exchange did not arrive
at the CBBH, the new arrangement worked properly; and the funds in
the NBBH's reserve account at the CBBH proved sufficient to settle all
net payments by its depositors until May 5, when another modest overdraft occurred. On that occasion, both the ZPP failed to adhere to the
settlement instructions requiring it to unwind the excess payments; and
the CBBH failed to hold up the settlement of payments for the day. On
the following day the overdraft was reversed on its own. As a result of
these combined failures, which again caused the currency board rules
to be violated, the IMF postponed the meeting of its Executive Board
to consider approval of the financial package that had been negotiated
with the authorities by the IMF staff.

The summary page of the draft press release that I had attached to
my memo to Peter follows:

Recent Currency Board Violations
Summary

The year-end financial statement of the Central Bank of Bosnia and Herzegovina (CBBH) shows its monetary liabilities in excess of its foreign exchange assets by about KM 16 million. Its end January, February, and March balance sheets also show that it failed to fully cover its monetary liabilities with foreign exchange assets as required by the Central Bank Law. This development is the result of credit inadvertently extended by the CBBH to cover payments made by depositors at the National Bank of Bosnia and Herzegovina (NBBH). These credits were the indirect result of technical problems between the NBBH, the ZPP, and the CBBH in the daily settlement of payment orders processed by the ZPP. The problems have now been resolved and these credits have been repaid. The procedures now in place will prevent the reoccurrence of such settlement credits.

In addition, as was announced earlier, the NBBH is now under liquidation, which will completely eliminate the initial circumstances (payments from deposits with the NBBH) that were the root source of these difficulties in the first place. While it is likely that the NBBH has sufficient assets to honor all of its financial obligations, it does not currently have sufficient foreign exchange assets to permit the withdrawal of all of the deposits made with it. As a result, some limitations have been placed on the uses of these deposits. The details of these restrictions are now being discussed with the authorities by Mr. Duddly, who has been appointed to liquidate the NBBH. These shortfalls of foreign exchange at the NBBH will not be transferred to the CBBH, which will no longer permit payments to be made from deposits with the NBBH for which the NBBH has not deposited sufficient foreign exchange with the CBBH. Thus the shortfall in foreign exchange backing of deposits with the NBBH will not affect the full foreign exchange backing of deposits with the CBBH (and currency in circulation).

Now that the NBBH is under liquidation, virtually all of its remaining foreign exchange assets have been deposited with the CBBH. Since the initial transfer of monetary liabilities and an equivalent value of foreign exchange assets from the NBBH to the CBBH on August 11, 1997, the NBBH has now transferred an additional KM 40 million in foreign exchange to the CBBH. These additional transfers more than cover the additional monetary liabilities of the NBBH transferred to the CBBH since August 11, 1997. The difference in the amounts of these subsequent transfers of assets and liabilities is the current reserve account balance of the NBBH with the CBBH. The CBBH acquired additional monetary liabilities to the NBBH as the result of purchases of BHD bank notes and payments to other banks by the NBBH and its depositors. Thus the (overdraft) credits that the CBBH had extended to the NBBH have now been repaid and the NBBH has a positive balance in its reserve account with the CBBH with

Net settlement payment systems again

The NBBH problem resulted from the ZPP (and CBBH) implicitly extending overdraft credit to the NBBH in order to allow net payments to the other banks to be settled. This becomes explicit if the NBBH is part of the closed circuit of banks whose net payments among themselves are being settled on a periodic net basis. In this case the NBBH would have a settlement account with the CBBH (as it eventually did). When more payments are made from accounts with the NBBH than are received, the balance of the NBBH's settlement account is reduced. If the net outflow is more than the NBBH has in its settlement account, net settlement cannot take place unless the NBBH account is overdrawn (i.e., unless the CBBH extends credit to the NBBH).

When the NBBH problem was first encountered, the NBBH did not have a settlement account with the CBBH. It was in effect outside the system. However, payments from its depositors were being credited to the settlement accounts of banks within the system. In principle, net amounts should only be credited to the system (i.e., to settlement accounts) by deposits of KM currency, which replaces one monetary liability of the CBBH with another (cash for deposits), or by deposit of DM (either cash or deposit balances abroad), which increases the monetary liabilities and foreign currency assets of the CBBH by the same amount. In the case of net payments from NBBH depositors to depositors with banks within the system, settlement account balances were increased without any increase in the foreign exchange backing required by the law. This was possible because the CBBH was implicitly extending overdraft credit to the NBBH.

which its depositors can continue making net payments, subject to the rules adopted by the liquidator of the NBBH for the pay out of deposits.

NBBH LIQUIDATION

The failure of the CBBH accountants to fully reconcile their deposit data with those of the ZPP because of float was a nuisance. The real issue, however, was the potential for depositors at the NBBH to withdraw their funds or to transfer them to other banks in amounts greater than the foreign exchange the NBBH had (or had with the CBBH). Our procedural safeguards, while important, were like a bandage on a festering wound. The only fully secure solution to that problem was to liquidate the NBBH.

During my visits in 1998, we worked closely with Duddly to find workable solutions to these problems. The NBBH had about 19,800 non-government accounts of small depositors (shops and other small businesses) who collectively had only modest amounts deposited, and a much smaller number of accounts (about 9,000) of municipalities and other government entities, who had collectively rather large deposits. The NBBH had sufficient resources (German marks) to cover the complete withdrawals of the non-government deposits. These depositors were given a deadline for transferring their deposits to commercial banks. The more important government deposits could operate without difficulty if government payments were limited to its receipts (i.e., if it had a balanced budget and if its receipt preceded its payments). In these ways the NBBH shrank and continued in limited operation without further violation of the CBBH's currency board rule while the liquidation process got under way.

The key political resolution of the problem, which centered on the inability of the government to repay its wartime loans from the NBBH, came when the predominantly Bosnian municipalities (Cantons) agreed to an arrangement whereby over the period of several years they provided the funds to pay off the loan. This had been a very difficult and contentious issue. It had taken some time and debate to resolve. It was clear to everyone from the outset that the Croats could not be asked, much less forced, to finance the repayment of a loan that helped underwrite the soldiers they had fought. Any repayment directly by the Federation, the successor government to the loan, would be using funds partially provided by Croats. Thus a way had been found for Bosnians to repay what Bosnians had borrowed so that the full liquidation of the NBBH and the payout and closing of all of its depositors could proceed. The above solution was only possible because the local authorities actually wished to resolve the problem. It satisfied the need for the government to continue operating within the limits of its ongoing revenues without dipping into its previously existing deposits (which had no foreign exchange backing).

Following the acceptance of a liquidation plan, which included the principles for loss sharing by creditors, and the freezing of all deposits with the NBBH for which there was not sufficient foreign exchange backing, the IMF approved its financing package with Bosnia on May 29, 1998. However, well-laid plans had been thwarted so many times before that none of us would be comfortable until the loans were paid off, all deposits at the NBBH paid out or transferred to other banks, and the NBBH fully liquidated. We remained concerned about the risks throughout the year, and we sought firmer arrangements to ensure that no uncovered deposits would be withdrawn until funds were available to cover them. After all small non-government deposits had been withdrawn, we proposed that new government deposits be opened at commercial banks for the ongoing activities of government and that their remaining uncovered deposits with the NBBH be frozen.

This discussion went on over the entire year. The deposit freeze promised by Bill Duddly was delayed pending a decision from the OHR on Duddly's list of priorities of claims. When he and the CBBH finally announced the freeze as of July 16 and called a press conference for 3:00 p.m. on July 17, the freeze was rejected and ignored by the ZPP, which had operational control over the accounts. Subsequently, the Federation Prime Minister, Edhem Bicakcic, publicly complained about the freeze, claiming that "freezing the government's deposits would affect the budgets of seven cantons and the Federation, preventing the Federation government from performing even a minimum of its functions." This outburst precipitated a press release from the CBBH on October 13, 1998, in which Governor Nicholl countered, in part, that "This is a major exaggeration. The 'freeze' would affect only that part of the NBBH's deposits that are not covered with assets. . . . The cantons and Federation entities would open bank accounts in another bank and all of their future revenues flows would go into them. The 'freeze' should therefore have little impact on Federation government functions and services." I felt a bit like a foot soldier who digs a fox hole in order to secure hard fought ground, and who then fights forward a few more meters and digs another fox hole.

During the year, Scott Brown, who had brought Bosnia to its first Standby Arrangement with the IMF (our traditional and standard lending program), was replaced as mission chief from our European I department by Juan José Fernandez Ansola. Juan José had risen through the ranks of the IMF, and this was his first assignment as a mission chief. He was a citizen of Spain but spoke English flawlessly and with a bit of an aristocratic enunciation. He was tall and almost always had an optimistic smile. Above all, and at all times, he was polite—a gentleman.

Like all IMF mission chiefs, he was determined to do his job well. He was nervous, but at the same time confident that he would master the complexities of Bosnia. At the time he took over, he was beginning to see just how complicated Bosnia was, politically, institutionally, and economically.

At the conclusion of the first quarterly review of Bosnia's compliance with its Standby Agreement with the IMF, Juan José set out in his concluding note on December 12, 1998, our requirements to secure the NBBH's continued limited operations without forcing the CBBH to violate its currency board rules:

Closure of the National Bank of Bosnia and Herzegovina (NBBH)

5. Substantial progress has been made on the closure of the NBBH, which continues to be a key issue for completion of the first review under the stand-by arrangement. The mission has been informed about a plan prepared by the Federation government, in consultation with the ZPP and the CBBH, whereby the covered government deposits at the NBBH will be moved to commercial banks. As part of the plan, the uncovered deposits at the NBBH will be frozen in an NBBH account. In addition, the plan contemplates that selected Cantons and public institutions, and the Federation Government will make weekly payments over a period to be determined to the NBBH account at the CBBH to provide cover for the full amount of the uncovered deposits. As these payments are made, the corresponding amounts will be credited to the respective accounts at commercial banks. The mission is encouraged by the proposed approach to closure of the NBBH and would like to stress that the following principles must be applied: (1) all financial operations on accounts with the NBBH must end immediately following the transfer of **covered** government deposits at the NBBH to commercial banks and (2) **illiquid (uncovered)** deposit balances must be frozen **within** the NBBH-in-liquidation.

6. Specifically, the mission considers that it is essential that: (1) The uncovered deposits be frozen at NBBH, and all financial operations on those uncovered accounts by the ZPP end immediately. (After discussions with ZPP officials it seems that this recommendation is technically feasible: a new account will be opened by the ZPP at the NBBH, to which all uncovered amounts will be transferred; and this account will then be frozen.) (2) Government depositors that currently have accounts at the NBBH would open new bank accounts at a bank of their choice. The total amount now available to be credited to these accounts would be equal to the sum of the "free" funds in the NBBH account at the Central Bank of Bosnia and Herzegovina (CBBH), a residual payment of about KM 0.5 million from CBBH on account of seigniorage obligations, plus payments made under the agreement between Cantons and selected public institutions, and the Federation government. To minimize the risks to government account holders, it is critical that commercial banks maintain the counterpart of government deposits as deposits in their reserve accounts at the CBBH at all times. (3) In this process, banks should not be allowed to

extend credit to Cantons or to accept the uncovered deposits held at NBBH. There are at least four reasons for this: (a) the insolvency that is now contained within the NBBH, and might be resolved, could contaminate more widely the banking system, which is already suffering from illiquidity and undercapitalization; (b) overly close relationships between banks and the Federation government raise important governance issues, which have been highly detrimental to the financial system in other countries; (c) the blocking of deposits at commercial banks conflicts with the strict implementation of prudential requirements by the Federation Banking Agency as well as with the strengthening of the banking system; and (d) the extension of credit by banks to the Cantons violates the undertakings under the IMF program. (4) Any funds recovered by the NBBH liquidator under the agreement with Cantons, selected institutions, and the Federation government, would be used to pay off government depositors as these funds become available. The mission welcomes the Federation authorities' efforts to find resources to compensate for lost financial assets of the NBBH. Ultimately, however, to the extent that the total amount of funds from all sources falls short of the full amount of liabilities, the uncovered part of deposits at NBBH must be written-off, as would be the case in any normal bankruptcy procedure.

7. In sum, we would support an approach to the NBBH liquidation along the above principles, which should enhance the credibility of the currency board and the KM, without further weakening commercial banks. Moreover, we would not be able to propose the completion of the review under the stand-by arrangement if the approach adopted was found to be inconsistent with these principles. Accordingly, the mission urges the Federation authorities to take rapid and concerted action to solve this issue, as it is essential to close the NBBH. Until a solution is reached, we would suggest that Cantons continue to make payments to NBBH according to plans. Regarding the management of the liquidation itself, we understand that the previously appointed liquidator will not be available to complete the process. There is an urgent need to appoint a new liquidator to facilitate a prompt, orderly liquidation of the NBBH.

The Federation government agreed with the IMF, and in December 1998 the freeze was finally implemented. The new arrangements avoided any further overdrafts of the NBBH's reserve account with the CBBH. Following the redemption of the old BH dinars for the new KM bank notes (discussed below) in 1998, the provisional transfer of monetary liabilities and matching assets from the NBBH to the CBBH—made on August 11, 1997, followed by the several additional transfers of DM in 1998—was finalized on August 9, 1999, with a return of DM 4,569,903 to the NBBH. This figure represented the amount of BH dinars that had been issued (and covered with DM) but were never redeemed. With this liability thus canceled, the extra backing was returned to the NBBH as had been foreseen when the trust account arrangement was set up. It was used toward satisfying the NBBH's remaining liabilities as part of its liquidation.

PROMDI BANK FOOTNOTE

As mentioned above, the instructions issued by the NBBH in April to transfer an additional DM 20 million to its reserve account at the CBBH was never fully executed. Only a few million were actually received by the CBBH. This episode is a long story by itself. It resulted in the firing of Mr. Fetahovich, head of the Foreign Exchange Department of the CBBH (and previously of the NBBH), the forced resignation of Enver, and a criminal case against both of them and against Kasim, which is ongoing at the time of this writing.

The full and correct statement of facts is now the job of the court in Sarajevo, but in general terms the NBBH invested part of its foreign exchange reserves in Promdi Banka, a Croatian bank with offices in Sarajevo. When NBBH issued the instruction for Promdi Bank to transfer its DM 20 million deposit there to CBBH, the funds were not delivered. When the bank was contacted, it indicated that it was having some difficulty (or misunderstanding) with the German bank in which it had invested the money. When contacted, the German bank said the money was no longer there. Promdi Bank then said that it was waiting for a payment in DM and to please be patient, etc.

This went around in circles a few times. A partial payment of a few million DM was received by CBBH. The rest never came. Eventually Promdi was put into liquidation by the Croatian National Bank and no further funds were recovered by NBBH/CBBH.

Promdi Bank's President, Ibrahim Dedić, claimed that he was the first person to open a privately owned bank in the former Yugoslavia in the late 1980s. He was a controversial businessman. I remember walking by Promdi's main office in Zagrab on several occasions after these problems surfaced and noticing several spiffy BMWs parked in front. The office was more or less between the Sheraton where I always stayed and the Croatian National Bank to which I was usually walking. The bank president had gained some attention by claiming that he was the target of an assassination attempt. He once stood outside the Croatian National Bank shouting for entry and protection from the assassins. Several years later, he was in fact shot to death in his home by unknown assailants.

OPENING THE MAIN UNITS

As I indicated earlier, the Serb and Croat Main Units of the CBBH— I have finally given in to that strange terminology—did not open as scheduled. The mere opening of offices and hiring of staff were not very important beyond the politics of it. What mattered was building an integrated, homogeneous monetary and banking system. This was an essential part of the foundation for an efficient and integrated economy. We strongly believed that a healthy and prosperous economy would contribute to the peaceful reuniting of the country. National healing would, we hoped, be promoted by the self-interest of people in improving their material standards of living. An open and integrated economy should promote both the standard of living and the desire, or at least willingness, to once again live harmoniously together.

Thus our goal was to promote and accelerate the spread of the use of KM and the displacement of the Croatian kuna and Yugoslav dinar within Bosnia. In addition to building up the branches of the CBBH, this goal also required dismantling its predecessors, the NBBH in Bosnia, the National Bank of the Republika Srpska (NBRS) in the RS, and the ZAP in Croat majority areas of the Federation.

In early 1998 there were still no KM bank notes, and non-cash KM payments were only being made in the Bosniac region formerly serviced by the NBBH. The technical arrangements and instructions for interregional clearing and settlement of non-cash KM payments had been prepared. To implement them, the Main Units in Mostar and the RS needed to be operational. Their actual operation in settling KM payments depended on the banks in their areas opening KM reserve accounts with them and the public opening and using KM accounts with these banks. We knew that it would take time for KM to take hold in these areas, which still used the currencies of the countries they each identified with politically. However, there would be no political nod to move forward in these areas until the NBBH problem was resolved. Thus its pending liquidation opened the door for the next step in the rollout of the new nationwide Central Bank.

PALE

The Serbian government always managed to be better prepared and to move more quickly in preserving its interests. RS Main Unit in Pale was formally opened September 15, 1997, almost on time. But as no Serbian banks had KM deposits, no KM payments were settled through this branch for some time. More importantly, in some respects, the NBRS went out of existence as of January 1, 1998, something that took the NBBH over a year to achieve. The National Bank of Republika Srpska was the existing central bank of the RS that was being replaced by the Main Unit of the CBBH. The Serbs accomplished this feat by turning its version of the payment bureau, the SPP, into a state bank (the Serb State Bank) and transferring the assets and liabilities of the NBRS to the reconstituted payment bureau. The problem of the NBRS's insolvency, which was so problematic for the NBBH in the Federation, was absorbed by the new SSB and postponed to a later day.

The Serbs had planned and executed this clever maneuver without consultation with us or anyone else that we were aware of. Down the line, RS banks began to complain bitterly about unfair competition from the SSB. All depositors with any bank had to maintain a Giro account with the SSB for the purpose of making payments (this is how the payment bureau system worked), and the separation of the new state bank from the RS payment bureau became a policy goal of the international community.

The RS Main Unit of the CBBH was established in Pale, the quiet ski village only a twenty-minute drive from downtown Sarajevo, because the hardliners who dominated Serbian government at that time had moved the RS capital from Banja Luka in a purely political power play. The Research and Statistics Department of the CBBH was set up there under the Serbian Vice Governor, Ljubiša Vladušić.

Ljubiša had been born and raised in Sarajevo, and lived there until he was driven away by the war. Like the Serbian member of the Governing Board, Manojlo Ćorić, he had graduated from the Faculty of Economics in Sarajevo. Though he was a cousin of Momčilo Krajišnic, the Serb President of the Joint Presidency of Bosnia and Herzegovina, now an accused war criminal (I guess Tobias Asser was right in wanting to arrest him while we were preparing the central bank law in Pale in December 1996), he had been one of Sarajevo's young liberal leaders and a strong supporter of its intellectual tradition and diversity. After being driven out of Sarajevo by the war, he had been Minister for Refugees in the Government of Republika Srpska from 1995-97, before his appointment as Vice Governor.

Ljubiša was handsome, immensely likable, and impressively well organized and competent. He was the person in the CBBH that Kim and I thought most likely to grow into the governorship when the time was ripe. During my first visit to the newly opened Main Unit offices in Pale, Ljubiša proudly pointed to the sign over the door. It read (in Serbian Cyrillic) Central Bank of Bosnia and Herzegovina. The Central Bank Law (much against our wishes) stated explicitly that the Serbian Main Unit would be called:

Main Bank of the Republika Srpska
Of the Central Bank of BiH

All letters in this name will be of the same size font;

The translator's note in my copy of the law stated that: "in local language, this name is: Glavna Bank Republike Srpske Centralne Banke BiH." As stated earlier, apparently the translator also had trouble believing what was written there.

"No one even remembered the stupid language in the law that you had fought over two years ago. When I put up this sign, no one said a word," Ljubiša said with a smile. Here was someone who could help rebuild this shattered country.

During these years we had many dinners as Ljubiša's guests in Pale. He had an interesting way of seeming to transcend emotionalism yet

revealing deep emo-
tions almost at the
same time. At one din-
ner in late 1999, fol-
lowing a particularly
nice example of Ser-
bian cuisine in a guest-
house outside of Pale,
he literally brought us
to tears with his stories
of earlier life in Sara-
jevo and the tragedy of
its loss. I had a wonder-

Dinner in Pale with Ljubiša: from left to right: Ljubiša Vladušić, Kim Rhee, John Dalton, Dragan Kovačević, Simon Kappelhof (De Nederlandsche Bank), Peter Nicholl, and the author—October 1998

ful reunion dinner with him and his family at a floating restaurant on
one of the two rivers in Belgrade after I had started working on the
rebuilding of Yugoslavia's monetary and banking system in early 2001.

MOSTAR

The Croatian part of the Federation had never had its own central bank.
When the war broke out, the NBBH—which had been the whole country's central bank—became, in effect, the central bank of the Bosniac
part. The RS already had a branch of the National Bank of Yugoslavia
in Banja Luka, the NBRS, which took on the role of the central bank
for the RS. Thus the Mostar Main Unit had no direct counterpart to
replace. Instead, it replaced the quasi-central bank functions that were
being performed by the regional payment bureau, the Mostar ZAP. These
are discussed in more detail later in this chapter in the section on pro-
moting the KM.

Once the general features of the resolution of the NBBH problem were
understood and agreed, preparations for the opening of the Mostar Main
Unit progressed more rapidly. The Mostar branch was officially opened on
April 6, 1998, one day before the formal start of the NBBH's liquidation.

BANJA LUKA

The first of my four visits to Bosnia in 1998 started on February 18. During that visit, we drove once again from Sarajevo to Banja Luka. With each trip more and more of the temporary army bridges were replaced with new permanent ones, and by this trip the border between the Federation and the RS had all but vanished. More and more of the bullet-riddled homes along the way were being repaired and lived in again. Winter travel on these roads was always a bit worrying. However, we arrived in Banja Luka with no difficulties.

Our primary goals were to establish the CBBH office and to make progress toward broader use of KM. While there, we met again with the chairman and management of Agroprom Banka. The questions they raised told us a lot about what the public understood (or didn't understand) about what we were doing. For example, what would be the preconditions for their bank to accept deposits of KM? How could KM be obtained? Could YUD deposits with the Serb State Bank (as the payment bureau in the RS was by then called) be converted into KM? Would their bank's balance sheet be converted to KM and at what exchange rate for the YUD? And on what date? Will enterprises be required to convert their accounts and financial statements? etc. Will the bank's KM reserve account be with the CBBH or the SSB (old thinking dies hard)? Will all KM payments be made through the SSB? We were surprised and disappointed at how little they knew about what we were doing.

With the CBBH now launched in the Federation, we were trying to give more attention to the RS. Until the CBBH branch was established there, our usual counterparts had been the management and staff of the payment bureau (SPP) and of the NBRS, until these merged, in effect, into the SSB. We also increasingly met with the Finance Minister, Mr. Nevan Kondić, and his staff. The NBRS no longer functioned as a monetary authority, but its research and statistics department had been the source of IMF data on the financial sector. Much of its staff was slated to move to the new CBBH branch office. Kim worked with Petra Marković, the deputy governor of the NBRS, in preparing for the opening of the CBBH branch. While the RS Main Unit was already well established in Pale, most of the banking activity in the RS would actually be centered in Banja Luka, the traditional capital.

With the full resolution of the NBBH problem more or less in hand, and the opening of the CBBH's Main Unit in Mostar, all banks had opened their reserve accounts with the CBBH by May 20, 1998; and nationwide payments in non-cash KM became possible. The Banja Luka branch of the CBBH was formally opened June 16, 1998, which further prepared the system for real countrywide payments.

Len and Kim had worked for some time with the three payment bureau staffs to prepare the rules and procedures by which interregional payments would be cleared and settled. Ensuring that a failure to settle in one regional clearinghouse (payment bureau) did not spill over to the whole system added another layer of complexity to the procedures. In June 1998, the ZPP, ZAP, and SSB signed the Protocol Agreement and the Implementation Agreement between the payment bureaus of Mostar, Banja Luka, and Sarajevo for settlement of payments across regional boundaries. The first inter-Entity transaction under this new system took place on September 22 using fax messages. An electronic file transfer message system for inter-payment bureau payments was implemented February 1, 1999. These inter-branch payments were settled the same day as part of the evening settlement of intra-branch payment orders.

When money was moving on net from one bank and region to another, the paying bank's reserve account would be debited and the receiving bank's reserve account would be credited. If the bank losing money didn't have enough in its reserve account at the CBBH to cover the outflow, it would buy additional balances for its CBBH reserve account by selling DM assets abroad to the CBBH. This finally replaced the interregional settlements by physically transporting DM bank notes between payment bureaus several times a week. What we called the "bank notes in the truck of the Mercedes" settlement system, which had been in operation since 1996, was history. A very important milestone had been reached.

The final element for the full operation of the CBBH—which was proceeding in parallel with the opening of the Main Units of the CBBH—was the introduction of KM bank notes.

NEW BANK NOTES
BANK NOTE DESIGN

Naming the currency proved an easy task compared to agreeing on the actual note designs so that they could be printed and issued. Without bank notes the CBBH was half a central bank at best. The notes would be the most tangible and visible symbol of the integrated country. Thus the three ethnic groups dragged out the process. Work on note design had preceded the opening of the CBBH and continued in parallel with the other activities already discussed.

The Central Bank Law had some very unusual and specific provisions governing the new bank notes:

Article 42. Currency features and interim notes (Coupons)

1. The Governing Board of the Central Bank shall determine the face value and size of bank notes and coins in accordance with Article 7, paragraph e, of this Law. The design of the bank notes and coins shall be decided by the Governing Board with the approval of the Presidency of Bosnia and Herzegovina.

2. As an interim measure until a permanent solution for the design of the notes has been agreed upon, and as legal tender for cash payments, the Central Bank will put in circulation "Coupons." The Central Bank shall not issue coins as long as the Coupons are in circulation.

3. The Coupons will have common design elements as well as distinct design elements for the Federation of Bosnia and Herzegovina and the Republika Srpska. The two versions of the Coupons will be of the same size for a given denomination, and will have also the following common elements:

   a. the word "Coupon" will be on the note; and

   b. the sentence: "To the bearer of this Coupon, the Central Bank of Bosnia and Herzegovina will pay upon demand [__] Convertible Marka" will be on the note in readable terms;

   c. the denomination of the Coupon will appear in highly identifiable numbers on both sides of the note;

   d. as a technical security feature, the Coupon will bear serial numbers. Both versions of the Coupon will have equal status as legal tender throughout the territory of Bosnia and Herzegovina.

4. The Federation of Bosnia and Herzegovina and the Republika Srpska will each have its own design features on the Coupons. The design of the notes shall be fully consistent with the Dayton Treaty and will not include elements offensive to the other Entity. The text on the Coupon may be written in different alphabets at the choice of the Entities, one being in the Cyrillic alpha-

bet and the other in the Latin alphabet. The names of the Federation of Bosnia
and Herzegovina and the Republika Srpska will not appear on the Coupons.

5. The Governing Board of the Central Bank will undertake all the necessary
   endeavors to ensure that the Coupons will be available for circulation in both
   the Federation of Bosnia and Herzegovina and the Republika Srpska within
   three months from the adoption of this Law.

The provision for Coupons was not in the draft we had originally proposed. It was one of those last minute additions in the final round of discussions with the U.S. Treasury that I was not part of. Its purpose, I assume,
was to make it easier for the three groups to agree on a design, knowing
that it could be replaced down the line. In short, it was a potentially useful psychological tool, like the interim agreement on the assets and liabilities to be transferred from the NBBH to the CBBH that was accepted in
August 1997. After agreeing to an interim design, it would be easier later
to agree on a permanent design (there is no such thing anyway)—perhaps
by simply agreeing that the interim design could be made permanent.

The work to agree on a design had been started many months earlier by Serge Robert and was then taken up by Peter Nicholl. Serge had
arranged for Banque de France to print the notes at no cost. As required
by the law, there were to be two sets of notes—two versions of each note.
However, the two versions were designed to look like the same currency
with only modest variations.

Each Entity submitted designs for one, five, ten, twenty, fifty, and
one hundred KM notes. The first designs submitted by the Federation
were unobjectionable (except, of course, to the RS), while the designs
submitted by the RS were more provocative, with two faces of Serb
heroes. One of its notes depicted the Serb retreat from Kosovo, which
is not even in Bosnia and Herzegovina. This was the event that was precipitated by the defeat of the Serbs by the Ottomans in the battle of
Kosovo Polje on June 28, 1389. Six hundred years later to the day, on
June 28, 1989, Slobodan Milosević addressed half a million Serbs on
the site of the defeat just outside Prestina in a speech that deeply fright-
ened non-Serb citizens of Yugoslavia. It is often referred to as the event
that eventually led to the collapse of Yugoslavia and its attendant wars.

The selection of note designs was not progressing very fast. The
international community's patience was wearing out. On November 18,

1997, Robert S. Gelbard, then U.S. Envoy to BiH, sent the following letter to Bosniac President Izetbegović, who at that moment was the obstructionist of the day:

Dear President Izetbegović:

In recent days, President Krajianik conveyed to your office a revised set of designs for the Republika Srpska (RS) version of the temporary currency Coupon. In his written proposal, he also accepted in full the Croat version of the Federation Designs.

We believe that the new proposal is reasonable and fully consistent with the Central Bank Law and the Dayton Agreement. The valid objections of your side have been taken into account, leading to removal of six personal images and the shield with the "4 S'S" from the previous RS designs. The RS flag and Coat of Arms remain. Unlike the shield, these are official RS insignia, which we find to be beyond reasonable objection. The Central Bank Law contemplated distinctive features on the respective sets of designs. Names of the entities were prohibited, but official insignia were not. The required common elements, including the promissory sentence of the Central Bank of Bosnia and Herzegovina, were clearly stipulated and the current RS Designs adequately reflect them.

I understand that President Zubak has informally accepted the new proposal, and I would urge you to do the same. As you know, agreement on a temporary currency is one of the necessary preconditions for an IMF program for Bosnia and Herzegovina. The temporary currency design has already consumed too much time and energy on all sides. It is imperative that we resolve this matter promptly. I would strongly urge you to undertake to resolve this issue with your co-Presidents before the December 3 Peace Implementation Council Steering Board meeting in Paris so that it does not become an issue at the Bonn Ministerial.

Let me underscore that we are talking here about temporary coupons. Permanent currency will follow in due course, but it is not practicable now.

If these negotiations fail—and the responsibility now lies with you—the international community may decide to impose temporary currency designs. If that happens, I will ensure that any imposed designs are consistent with the Central Bank Law and based on the reasonable proposals already on the table, including the latest submissions from the RS. It is only fair that no party will be rewarded for obstructing the negotiation process.

I look forward to seeing you soon in Sarajevo.

Sincerely,

Robert S. Gelbard

The pressure to settle on a design and get on with it was mounting. In the next round, the Serbs submitted designs with the faces of writers on one side and art objects on the other. The Federation liked the idea of writers and submitted their own list of writers to Peter Nicholl, by then in place as the Governor. Two of the Federation writers, Meša Selimović and Ivo Andrić, were also among the Serb choices. When the RS authorities heard that the Federation notes would also have writers, they indicated that they would replace the writers on their notes with something else. Gelbard's December 3 deadline was not met.

At this point, mid-December, Peter went to Jacques Klein, the deputy High Representative, and asked whether the OHR would support and impose his own design if the local authorities were not willing or able to comply. Klein agreed. Peter then obtained pictures of the writers on each list (by this time one of the two writers on both lists had disappeared from the Federation list) and flew with his wife, Glynyss, to France after Christmas and just before New Years. They stayed in Rhone with an executive of the French printer. Peter had instructed the note designers in France to prepare good quality designs that would look a bit like a German mark and to leave blanks for faces and objects on each side. Both versions of each denomination were to be identical except for the difference in the face and the object and the fact that the name of the Central Bank in Latin letters would be placed on top in the Federation version and the Cyrillic version would be on top in the RS version. The idea was that you would need to look carefully to see that there was any difference.

During the first several days of 1998, Peter sat at the computer terminal with the note designers in France to refine the designs. The writers and objects supplied by the Federation and the RS were inserted into their respective versions. The five KM note used the same writer, Meša Selimović, and object for both versions. Thus the Federation and RS versions of the five KM note differed only in placing the Cyrillic spelling of "Central Bank of Bosnia and Herzegovia" above the Latin version on the RS notes. Faces were rotated electronically so that all faced the same direction. Other elements were also refined until Peter was satisfied. One set was printed, and he flew back to Sarajevo to present it to his Board. Glynyss waited a day in order to bring two more sets so that each of the

Presidents of the Joint Presidency would have one. Due to fog in Sarajevo, her plane landed in Split in Croatia in the middle of the night, where she was met by a CBBH car and driven to Sarajevo (about a four-hour drive).

The new designs were generally acceptable to all sides, but the Serb President wanted the Serb coat of arms on the RS version. The Bosnian and Croat Presidents replied that they would then want their coats of arms on the Federation version. There was also an issue over signatures on the notes, traditionally in most countries that of the governor. Peter refused to add coats of arms and submitted the resulting designs to the High Representative who on January 18, 1998, approved them and imposed them on the Joint Presidency.

In a very clever move, as long as the choice was being forced by the international community anyway, the note designs were approved as the new currency rather than as interim coupons. The word "Coupon" did not appear on the notes, and it meant that coins could be issued whenever they could be readied.

This proved to be a very well timed intervention. No one really objected. We knew very well that it would be impossible to force any of our counterparts to take actions or participate in actions they strongly opposed. Consider how long it had taken to open the Mostar Main Unit. NATO strikes were no longer on the table (we occasionally joked in desperate moments that if all else failed we would threaten a NATO air attack). But there were times when it was difficult for the three groups to explicitly agree to something for political reasons when they otherwise really didn't mind. At these times, an externally imposed decision might be acceptable (and probably welcomed). This was one of those times. (For more information on the KM Bank Notes, see Appendix III.)

The delay in introducing bank notes was potentially dangerous. Until the currency notes were introduced, the balance sheet of the CBBH barely changed. In fact, if you excluded the capital that the BiH government paid into the CBBH from the proceeds of its first loan from the IMF, the foreign assets of the Central Bank (and its monetary liabilities) where a bit lower in June 1998 than when it opened ten months earlier. This was a source of considerable nervousness within the CBBH. Tensions between the regions, even within the CBBH, remained high.

The Comptroller General of the CBBH and others in senior management were increasingly expressing concern about some banks that were consistent net buyers of DM from the Central Bank. The Comptroller General seemed to be hinting that restrictions should be placed on such withdrawals, which gave me considerable concern.

During a short visit in June 1998 for the launch of the new bank notes, Governor Nicholl asked me to discuss their concerns with this senior management group. I pointed out that while some banks were always withdrawing (buying) DM, other banks were doing the reverse (i.e., they were net sellers of DM to the CBBH) so that net purchases and sales of DM were more or less balanced. There was no reason for an individual bank to have a balance of purchases and sales with the Central Bank. Importers in Mostar tended to receive KM payments from Sarajevo banks for import from Croatia and further abroad that had to be paid for with DM. These importers deposited the KM in their Mostar banks and bought DM. As long as others were receiving DM from exports or aid there would be no problem.

As we discussed the issue, I was relieved to conclude that the group's real concern was whether the Central Bank would survive and succeed in establishing the KM. I agreed with the group's suggestion that the CBBH should actively encourage the international community and the Entity governments of Bosnia and Herzegovina to use KM. However, I urged delay in terminating the foreign currency deposits with the payment bureaus until banks were stronger. I took this position reluctantly, because termination of the foreign currency deposits with the payment bureaus would surely increase the use of KM to some extent and thus increase the CBBH's balance sheet. However, I felt strongly that the public's savings should not be put unduly at risk and that the KM's success would be better served by allowing the public's confidence in the new KM to be established voluntarily. Under no circumstances should the CBBH fail to honor its legal obligation to sell DM for KM to anyone, including a bank that was a persistent net buyer of DM.

These concerns were about to vanish with the introduction of the new bank notes. However, nothing comes easily in Bosnia. Printing bank notes takes time. As there was great urgency to replace the very tattered Bosnian Dinar and introduce KM bank notes, Peter decided to print the three, low denomination notes first and to undertake the redemption of Bosnia dinars for these notes. These were the denominations most relevant for day-to-day transactions. Larger amounts that people might save as cash were generally kept in German marks anyway.

One, five, and ten KM notes were printed in two versions each and delivered to Sarajevo. A small delay set the start of the exchange back one week to June 22, 1998. Shortly before that date, CBBH staff found three errors in the notes. Unfortunately they were all on the Serb version.

The most serious error was that the name of the Serb writer on the 1 KM note, Ivo Andrić, was misspelled. The Cyrillic spelling of his last name ended in the Cyrillic of g rather than c, which in Cyrillic it resembles.

The errors on the 5 and 10 KM notes were less serious. On the 5 KM note the word "five" was printed four times. Three of them were in Latin letters and one of them in Cyrillic rather than two and two.

These errors were an enormous embarrassment, and it was particularly unfortunate that all of the errors were on RS versions. Peter apologized humbly to the Joint Presidents and promised to replace the defective 1 KM notes. He refused to replace the defective 5 and 10 KM notes since the errors were so minor. In fact, while the defective 1 KMs were never issued, replacement versions were never printed either. Strangely, a few of the RS 1 KMs were found here and there as collectors' items, but never in significant quantities. By the end of the year, coins (including a 1 KM coin) were available, making the issue of the 1 KM note moot.

BANK NOTE EXCHANGE

Once the designs were chosen, the CBBH went into high gear with its preparations for the exchange of the old BH dinar for the new notes. The team I brought to Bosnia from February 18 to March 4, 1998, devoted a significant amount of its time to helping the CBBH prepare for the introduction of the new currency. While it took the European Union almost four years to prepare for the introduction of the euro bank notes and their exchange for existing national currencies, it took us about four months.

For the exchange itself, decisions were needed with regard to the length of the exchange period, exchange rules, exchange points, financing of the operation, handling of possible counterfeits, public information about the new currency, and the exchange arrangements (to name a few). In addition, arrangements needed to be finalized for the ongoing exchange of KM for DM after the official redemption period had ended. This was the core of the currency board arrangement. Making the arrangement operational entailed its own set of issues. What role would the payment bureaus and banks play as agents of the CBBH? What commissions or spreads should be charged?

We also provided advice on strengthening the security and cash handling procedures in the CBBH's values and the transportation of currency to banks and other distribution points. I had gone through this process several times before, in Kazakhstan, Kyrgyzstan, and Moldova and was well aware of what was involved.

One issue we had not previously considered was how to manage the stocks of the two versions of the currency over time. Should they be mixed from the beginning and both versions issued in all regions, or should they be kept separate in the beginning and over time? It was obvious that the Serbs (especially) wanted to keep the two versions as separate as possible.

Anka Musa, the Croat head of the Mostar payment bureau (ZAP), provided the wisdom that guided Peter on this question. She told us that it would be very important to the acceptance of the new notes that each group saw its own version initially. She suggested that after a few days of close scrutiny no one would pay much attention after that. Thus only the Federation version was used in the exchange (which only took place in the Federation as no one held BH dinars in the RS) and only the RS version was provided in the RS. However, after the notes were issued, no attempt was made to keep the two versions separate. Over time they were mixed in the market and I never heard the subject discussed again.

Low denomination KM bank notes were introduced in Bosnia and Herzegovina starting June 22, 1998, and BH dinars ceased to be legal tender July 7, 1998. Because of a delay in transporting the notes to Bosnia by the French printer, this was one week later than the June 15 date announced in May. During the exchange period, small denomination

KM bank notes (1, 5, and 10 KM notes plus a 50 Feninga note worth one-half KM) could be acquired from the CBBH in exchange for BiH dinar bank notes at the rate of 100 dinar per KM. After July 7 BiH dinars were demonetized and no longer redeemable, though a somewhat longer redemption period was allowed with good cause.

After June 22, KM could be acquired at any time for German marks at the rate of one for one. Needless to say, they could be returned to the CBBH at any time for German marks at the same rate. These exchanges were actually made through banks and payment bureaus as agents of the CBBH. As with KM deposits, the new notes could trade freely in the market for any currency at market rates.

The redemption of old Bosnian dinars had a few rough spots—generally long lines at exchange points—but by and large went well.

After the first two weeks, no notes had been issued in the RS; and Peter asked the Director of his RS Main Unit in Pale what was going on. The Director, Marko Radović, told him that because of the errors in the RS versions of the notes, the RS Parliament had ruled that they could not be issued. I had met Marko on my very first, disappointing trip to Sarajevo in June 1996, when he showed up at our first meeting to represent the Serbs. We had expected someone more senior. Marko was very likable and competent. He knew the monetary system of Yugoslavia inside and out. His ready smile was disarming. He was a survivor through good times and bad. Peter asked Marko whether he wished to work for the RS government or the CBBH, saying that the choice was his. But if he wanted to continue in his post with the CBBH, the notes should be issued immediately. And they were.

Following the official exchange period, modest problems began to arise with the normal currency board activity of exchanging DM for KM and vice versa. The problem arose because the law—in another of its little peculiarities introduced behind my back—forbade banks to charge a commission or spread for its service of making the exchange.

We had debated this issue extensively when the law was drafted. A one-to-one exchange with no spreads was simpler for the public to understand, and it potentially contributed to the credibility of the currency board arrangement. However, it also tended to undercut market development of the foreign exchange market.

We had proposed originally that the CBBH deal only (or mainly) with banks in buying and selling KM for DM, using a very small spread to leave some room to encourage banks to deal with each other. Banks in turn (and initially the payment bureaus) would deal with the public in these transactions and could charge a spread or commission sufficient to remunerate the activity. The restrictions in the law on commissions and spreads (see the earlier discussion in Chapter 4) caused banks to complain that they were being forced to provide a costly service for free. Some banks refused to provide the service at all. There was some public grumbling.

Peter held several meeting with the banks to seek a solution and on July 6 announced that the CBBH would pay a commission "to commercial banks from its resources until such time as a longer-term solution is agreed."

Obviously, I had never liked this change in the law, and I knew it would cause problems. Stretching the law to its limits, I suggested that the transactions covered by the law be interpreted as standard foreign exchange spot exchanges. Foreign exchange markets settled a spot exchange with two-day value (two business days later). But it was also possible to transact for foreign exchange with one-day value or even same-day value at a higher cost. I exploited this distinction and suggested that the law could plausibly be interpreted to refer only to standard spot exchanges. Thus immediate exchanges were free to take place with a commission. The CBBH debated this idea for awhile and accepted it.

On July 16, 1998, the CBBH issued the following statement:

> The Central Bank of Bosnia and Herzegovina has clarified for commercial banks in Bosnia and Herzegovina, the meaning of the CBBH Law article 33 paragraph 2, in order to resolve a dispute over the charging of commissions for the exchange of KM into DM and DM into KM. This dispute has led some banks to decline to provide these services, which has consequently led to considerable inconvenience for people.
>
> The language of the CBBH law specifically refers to "ON DEMAND" exchanges. "ON DEMAND" transactions between a domestic and foreign currency typically require a waiting period of 48 hours. For these exchanges, the CBBH stands firmly behind the Law's prohibition of charging taxes, commissions and other charges, so that will be at 1 for 1.
>
> However, it has been decided for "over the Counter" transactions, or imme-

diate exchanges, the banks will be allowed to charge up to a maximum of 1 per-cent handling charge or commission. This is consistent with the CBBH law.

The CBBH understands that banks in Bosnia and Herzegovina do incur costs in carrying out these transactions. Allowances should be made to compensate them for these costs, if we want banks to provide this service to the public.

On the other hand, consideration for the CBBH law and for those citizens wishing to make a one to one exchange between DM and KM has been preserved by prohibiting any fees for the "ON DEMAND" transaction. The CBBH real-izes that this may be inconvenient for some citizens, and will require them to allow more time and planning before exchanging their Konvertable Marks into Deutsche Marks or vice versa.

These minor problems passed quickly. On July 27, 1998, the CBBH released the high denomination bank notes (20 KM, 50 KM, and 100 KM) that had not been available for the BH dinar redemption. Coins were introduced in December of the same year. In the initial months we monitored the movement of currency between regions closely. There was some initial concern as to whether the RS and Mostar regions would really embrace the KM.

PROMOTING THE KM

Opening the Main Units of the CBBH constituted important and nec-essary steps, but they would be ultimately empty if there were no KM payments being made beyond the Bosniac region. Public acceptance of a new currency is naturally a gradual process. Trust is earned over time as the currency fulfills its promises (stability of its value). However, conven-ience plays a very important role as well. We argued that the artificial sup-port given to foreign currencies by the payment bureaus should be phased out (while preserving the freedom for all persons to hold and use what-ever currencies they wanted by mutual agreement) and that the use of KM should be encouraged by its rapid adoption by all levels of govern-ment in all of their financial dealings (taxes, fees, wages, pensions, etc.).

We initially emphasized the need for the payment bureaus to end their foreign currency activities. Their acceptance of DM bank notes for safekeeping and facilitating their use in domestic payments was strictly an emergency wartime measure. We argued that the practice should be ended. A politically (and perhaps economically) more diffi-cult step would be to end similar practices with regard to the other "for-eign" currencies in general use (kuna and Yugoslav dinar) because of their psychological/political significance.

MOSTAR REGION

Unlike the SPP in the RS (or the ZPP in Sarajevo), the Mostar ZAP had no relationship with any central bank and thus had no claims on any cen-tral bank.[3] As a result, the balances in the Giro accounts it maintained rep-resented actual deposits and hence liabilities of the ZAP itself. In short, the ZAP was a quasi-central bank. The ZAP had DM deposit liabilities to banks and the public (Giro account balances) and an equivalent amount of DM bank notes. It also had Croatian kuna deposit liabilities to banks and the public and an equivalent amount of kuna bank notes. In the case of the kuna deposits, however, the balances with the ZAP represented only about 45 percent of the kuna deposits of the public with banks. Thus the public's deposits with the ZAP (excluding the negative balances of banks on their own account, which represented kuna loans extended by banks) were more than twice the amount of the kuna bank notes held by the ZAP.

Stated differently, the Croat-majority area banks had a 100 percent "reserve requirement" against DM deposits, and a 45 percent "reserve requirement" against kuna deposits, both of which were held with the ZAP in cash. Hence, Croat banks had a very large share of their deposits held in non-interest earning cash and stood to improve earnings signifi-cantly by a switch in customer deposits to KM, which only had a 10 percent reserve requirement (half of which was remunerated by the CBBH). I stressed these points whenever I met with banks in the Mostar area. Furthermore, although the kuna had been a highly stable currency over that period, it depreciated almost 7 percent against the DM in 1998, increasing interest in the KM in the region. As the kuna was freely convertible in the market, the conversion of kuna to KM, through DM if necessary, could be accomplished fairly easily.

With our prodding, amendments to the Federation Internal Payment Law (one of Ben Geva's babies) in the summer of 1998 required the termination of domestic payments through the ZAP and the ZPP in DM and kuna by the end of 1998. The goal was to limit domestic payments through the domestic payments system (now the CBBH and the payment bureaus) to the domestic currency (i.e., KM) and thus to remove all foreign currencies from the payment bureaus.[4] The Bosnian Croat authorities became very nervous about this requirement, and its implementation was delayed until October 1, 1999.

I always suspected that Jure Pelivan's worries about "uncovered" liabilities of the NBBH had their origin in these central bank functions being performed by the Mostar ZAP. If the ZAP had the DM and kuna bank notes it claimed to have had, it should have been able to unwind its monetary activities without difficulty. However, if the commercial banks had been insolvent, these operations could have forced the exposure of that insolvency. I undertook to analyze this situation more carefully to ensure that we were not overlooking potential problems and in order to share our understanding with the authorities and assuage their fears.

If the ZAP had to stop accepting and holding foreign currency, the implications were different for DM than for kuna. The withdrawal of DM bank notes or their exchange for KM was straightforward and simple, both because all such deposits with the payment bureaus were fully backed with DM bank notes and because the CBBH may buy them directly for KM. Thus, the implementation of the amendments to the Federation Internal Payment Law did not need to be delayed with regard to the DM on this account. At the end of 1998, these DM deposits with the ZAP and ZPP amounted to KM 312 million (almost three times the opening balance sheet of the CBBH).

There was an issue of what those depositors would do with the funds they would withdraw from the ZAP and ZPP, and there were good reasons for not depositing too much of it in banks until the banking sector was strengthened. In fact, I argued that the public should be allowed to deposit DM cash with the payment bureaus and transfer them in domestic payments well into 1999 in order to allow time for the banking sector to strengthen (the DM deposits with the payment bureau are essentially risk free as they are held as cash) and to allow the public's confidence in the new KM to be better established voluntarily.

The situation with regard to the kuna deposits was somewhat more complicated because they were not fully backed by cash and because they could not be directly exchanged for KM at the CBBH. If the public continued to hold the same level of kuna deposits with their banks (HRK equivalent to KM 89.5 million at the end of 1998), the kuna then held by banks with the ZAP (about KM 25 million) could easily be transferred to Croatian banks and/or to their own vaults. However, there seemed no reason for banks to want to continue holding what had been in effect a 45 percent reserve requirement, when they would then be free to lend out some of it. If there were not enough prudent kuna lending opportunities in Bosnia, they could place the funds in Croatia (a capital outflow). Banks might wish to use some of the freed resources to increase their holdings of KM with the CBBH (using DM purchased in the market with kuna) to provide additional liquidity.

In addition, the mission repeated its recommendation that the Federation Banking Agency impose a liquidity requirement on kuna deposits that would have the same effect as the CBBH's reserve requirement (which, however, is regrettably limited by law to KM deposits). This requirement would be met by holding additional KM balances in banks' reserve accounts with the CBBH. One way or the other, the operation should have been easy and potentially expansionary.

But we hoped the public would convert some of their kuna deposits and cash into KM. A problem could have arisen if the public had wished to convert its kuna deposits with banks into KM at too rapid a rate. Forty-five percent of the deposits could be converted immediately by withdrawing the kuna bank notes from the ZAP. However, the ability of banks to convert a larger amount would have been limited by the maturity and hence timing of the repayment of their existing kuna credits and other assets, their ability to sell "non-liquid" kuna assets for cash (bank notes or deposits), and the extent to which the kuna deposits withdrawn by the public would be replaced with KM deposits. While a rapid liquidation of kuna deposits and their replacement with KM deposits would have created a currency mismatch between banks' assets and liabilities (until kuna assets matured and could be replaced with KM credits), it would not have created a liquidity problem for banks since liquid KM reserves could have been used to cover new KM deposits. Thus, banks should have been able to manage the closing of kuna deposits with the ZAP and whatever withdrawal or conversion of kuna deposits the public was likely to demand, without difficulty.

Because it had to be done in the market, a rapid conversion of kuna to KM (or DM) could also have put pressure on the kuna exchange rate. I discussed this issue with Marko Škreb, the Governor of the Croatia National Bank in Zagreb. Marko had risen from the ranks. He was Director of the Research and Analysis Department of the CNB from 1992 through 1995. After serving as Economic Advisor to the President of the Republic of Croatia for four months he was appointed Governor in March 1996. He was widely respected and always a pleasure for me to deal with. Marko had no problems with the proposed termination of the Mostar ZAP's kuna operations and was prepared to monitor the foreign exchange market for kuna in order to prevent undue exchange rate pressure from any conversion. The CNB had more than enough dollar and DM reserves for this purpose.

We recommended that the transfer of kuna and DM deposits for domestic payments via the ZAP should be ended by June 1998 and that the use of the ZAP as a depository for kuna and DM bank notes should be phased out by June 1999. In fact both steps were taken at the same time, but not until October 1, 1999, in both the Federation and in the RS. It is interesting to note that the DM 324 million in foreign currencies withdrawn from the payment bureaus between September 30 and December 31, 1999, were used predominantly to buy KM and thus wound up with the CBBH, whose foreign currency holdings rose almost DM 450 million over that period.

REPUBLIKA SRPSKA

We expected a number of factors to increase the use of KM in Republika Srpska and we were eager to encourage them. The overwhelmingly dominant currency in the region was the Yugoslav dinar (YUD), which was not freely convertible. This situation reflected the historical, economic, and political ties of the RS to the FRY. The greater soundness of the KM (more stable value and freely convertible) had become a strong incentive to hold and use it in the region. In addition, the RS Government issued an instruction that, effective July 1, 1998, KM became the official means of payments in the territory of the RS. Starting with the 1998 budgets, KM was used as the unit of account in the presentation of all governmental budgets. However, the actual conversion to KM in the RS suffered from the lack of DM (or other freely usable currencies) with which to buy them.

The government could not spend in KM unless it received revenue in KM (or DM with which it could buy KM). The public could not pay its taxes in KM (or DM) unless it received income in KM, etc. The conversion would have to be incremental. As an example, the portion of the RS government staff's salary paid in KM was 50 percent in December 1998,[5] 70 percent in January 1999, and became 100 percent soon there after.

The shortage of DM was artificially exacerbated by an overvalued, fixed exchange rate for the YUD. Few were willing to pay YUD obligations with DM at that exchange rate. On November 6, 1998, the RS Government abandoned the Federal Republic of Yugoslavia's (FRY's) official exchange rate of 6.0 YUD = 1 DM, and moved instead to 7.5 YUD = 1 DM, a rate broadly in line with the prevailing market rate in the RS and FRY at the time. In response to this change in policy, the furious authorities in the FRY closed the access of the SPP to the NBY and to banks in the FRY. As a result, it became impossible to continue the practice of making payments between the RS and the FRY by submitting payment orders to the RS or FRY branches of the Serbian payment bureaus (SPP and SDK)[6]; and efforts to shift to cash payments were frustrated by an increasing shortage of YUD bank notes in the RS. The effort of the public to convert their YUD deposits into cash in order to make payments in the FRY confronted the inability of banks to pay out bank notes both because of the limited supply of YUD bank notes in the RS and because of banks' own lack of liquid assets with which to buy bank notes.

As we discussed this amazing development with the technical staff of the SPP during our February 1999 visit to Banja Luka, more layers of the payment bureau onion were peeled back. When the SPP was turned into a state bank to take over from the NBRS, I had assumed that the bank's reserve accounts and balances with the NBRS (as a branch of the NBY) had been transferred to the SPP along with the NBRS's claims on the NBY. With some embarrassment, Gjorge Mikes, the tall, chain-smoking, former basketball player from Sarajevo, who now headed the IT department of the SPP, explained to us that since the formal closing of the NBRS in June 1998, the transfers between banks' reserve accounts had been implicit rather than "actual."

Reserve accounts with the NBRS/NBY had not been transferred to the SPP and were, implicitly at least, still with the NBY. However, the SPP had continued to carry a claim on the NBY (in place of the claim it had previously carried on the NBRS) and to record all increases or decreases in its banks' implicit reserve account balances with the NBY resulting from payment transactions between the RS and Yugoslavia. It had been assumed (but not verified) that the NBY and/or SDK had been doing the same thing and that the records of the two systems showed the same results of payments between the two areas. These reserve balances in Belgrade had been frozen with the separation of the RS from the Yugoslav payment system in November 1998.

I am satisfied, but not certain, that we understood correctly what was going on. The difficulty we had in understanding each other had less to do with our respective mother tongues being English and Serbian, than with the conceptual differences in the organization of the Yugoslav payment system and those of most other countries.

Unfortunately, the RS Government was subsequently forced by its parliament to reverse its exchange rate decision. Nonetheless, the government wished to use the market rate quoted by the CBBH as the basis for official calculations, such as for taxes due (which were denominated in KM but still paid in YUD). In fact, at a meeting in February 1999 on other topics, Finance Minister Kondić asked me how to arrive at an appropriate measure of the parallel market exchange rate for the dinar. His question caught me totally by surprise. I offered some general guidance but promised to consult with experts, which I promptly did.

It was easy to understand the advantages to the RS government of using an exchange rate calculated by the CBBH. It would be very difficult for the CBBH to do it, however. Typically, a central bank will publish a reference rate that reflects either (a) its own dealings in the currency concerned; or (b) by cross-calculation from the official pronouncement of another central bank; or (c) based on credible data collected from commercial banks that allow the calculation of a market average.

It was not feasible, in this instance, for CBBH to use methods (a) or (b). The key issue was therefore whether credible data were available from commercial banks daily. Unofficial discussions with the Banking Agency in RS suggested to us that such data were not currently generated. Following the advice of our foreign exchange experts, we strongly advised CBBH not to become involved in publishing or giving some degree of official status to a reference rate, if the rate were based solely on some sort of sampling of market transactions through unofficial ("street") outlets. The idea was dropped; but the RS government adopted its own, street-based rate, which was the best they could do under the circumstances.

Cutting the RS out of the Yugoslav payment system (and thus freezing their deposits in Belgrade) complicated an already difficult situation. While it helped speed up the adoption of the KM, it worsened a systemic liquidity crisis, which risked triggering a systemic banking crisis. David Whitehead brought this problem forcefully to my attention. In early February 1999 we met for dinner at "The Castle" in Banja Luka to discuss his concerns and ideas.

The RS was already well into the process of gradually replacing YUD with KM as the primary means of payment within the RS. By the end of January 1999 the KM deposit component of the money supply had risen from zero in June 1998 to KM 11.4 million. However, at the end of 1998, these banks held YUD 419 million (or KM 79 million at official rates) in deposits with the SPP,[7] most of which were thought to be deposits of bank customers.[8]

We had argued previously that as KM came more into demand with growing confidence in its value and increased use in official and other transactions, the market would replace YUD with KM. While KM could not be purchased directly with YUD from the CBBH, they could be purchased in the market; and YUD could be used to purchase goods and services in the FRY. Thus, emphasis had been placed on measures to increase the public's demand for KM. The KM's real competition were with DM, not YUD. The problem in the RS was that there was not enough DM with which to buy KM.

Unlike the KM (or DM and kuna), however, the YUD was not a freely usable currency; and a street rate had emerged that was increasingly depreciated with respect to the official exchange rate of 6.0 YUD/KM. By the end of January 1999, the market rate of YUD had fallen to over 8 YUD/KM.

The accumulation in the RS of YUD bank notes held by the SPP and by the public and of YUD deposit with the SPP,[9] derived from the transfer of real or financial resources to the FRY. The return of those bank notes and deposits (claims on the NBY) to the FRY would require the reversal of the original outflow of resources from the RS—i.e., it would require an inflow into the RS of Yugoslav goods and services or hard currencies. Other things equal, the repatriation by the FRY of its YUD from the RS would also be inflationary for the YUD and would tend to depreciate its exchange rate further. Thus there was a short-term incentive for the FRY to prevent the return of the YUD held in the RS.

The separation of the Serbian payment clearing system into separate RS and FRY components made it impossible to use YUD deposits with the SPP to pay for goods and services in the FRY. As a result, the public began to withdraw YUD deposits from the SPP and to use the YUD bank notes received to make such payments. However, this possibility was limited by the amount of bank notes held by the SPP and these had by then fallen to low levels. There was some suspicion that YUD bank notes being received by RS exporters to the FRY were being kept out of the SPP (i.e., banks) out of concern that it might be difficult to withdraw them when needed. Thus the largest part of these deposits (about YUD 419 million) could not be withdrawn in cash. Furthermore, they could no longer be used to make payments in the FRY, either. The decision by the government of RS to require taxes and other payments to the government in KM would further limit the uses of these deposits.

These unusable YUD deposits with the SPP constituted a cost to the banking system and an impediment to the smooth function of the payment system.[10] The YUD deposits were a claim on balances with the NBY that were now frozen. David was rightly concerned about the situation and was looking for ways to resolve it. Basically he was proposing the obligatory conversion of YUD assets and liabilities into KM as we had done with the BH dinar in the Federation.

Unfortunately David's approach was not viable for the RS. If all YUD assets on banks' balance sheets were performing, it would seem that both assets and liabilities could be converted from YUD into KM as of a specified date without major financial disruptions. However, one class of those assets consisted of bank claims on the SPP. The YUD assets held by the SPP against these claims (their frozen claims on the NBY) obviously could not be converted into KM or DM the way BH dinar claims had been (by transferring the equivalent value of DM from the NBBH to the CBBH). It was not inconceivable that donors would provide the DM needed to replace the frozen YUD claims on Belgrade. However, a major difficulty in the Republika Srpska was that most assets in banks' balance sheets were non-performing, and, in particular, not just their claims on the SPP. In this situation, converting all YUD deposits into KM would be a formality lacking substance because it would not address the fundamental problem: many bank assets would remain non-performing or frozen, irrespective of the currency of denomination.

After considerable further thought, I attempted to spell out in clear language just what the problem was and to formulate what I thought were sensible and practical approaches to dealing with it. The problem had three aspects: the YUD liabilities of the preexisting monetary authority (now the SPP), the YUD liabilities of the RS banks, and the YUD obligations of everyone else in the RS. The first two of these might be called the "high powered money" problem, and the "bank money" problem. The third was an exchange rate problem and was already being dealt with by the RS government's adoption of "market" exchange rates for the Yugo dinar rather than the official rate in Belgrade.

As explained above, the SPP (or the government) could not just replace its YUD liabilities with DM or KM, because it didn't have enough DM or KM. Their conversion would have to be more gradual. I suggested that the government of RS take over the SPP's YUD liabilities to banks and its currently unrealizable claim on the NBY (of the same amount). This would enable the SPP to remove YUD assets and liabilities from its "books." It would also facilitate the government initiating legal action against Yugoslavia to collect its claim. The RS government could then accept a limited amount of the tax payments of enterprises in YUD. These payments, which would be made out of YUD balances with banks, would be debited to the government's deposit liabilities to banks taken over from the SPP and eliminated. This operation would need to be limited to the amount "deposited" with the SPP. Over time, these steps would fully remove any YUD from the payment bureau, which would then operate solely in KM.

Obviously the YUD collected from the public that were impounded would not be available to finance other government expenditures. Thus the size of the operation each period would have to be limited to what the Entity government's budget could afford. The amount could be larger, of course, if international donors were willing to pay for some or all of it and we offered to explain to donors the virtues of spending some of their money in this way. The use of YUD to pay taxes would need to be spread over time. For example, 5 percent of enterprise tax payments would fully use up the YUD 419 million now "deposited" with the SPP within one to two years (depending on the market rate of YUD for KM over that period). Thus the cost of the uncollectible claim on the NBY would be shared to some extent by depositors holding YUD (because of the delayed use and the probable depreciation in its exchange rate) and by the RS government. At the time of this operation, the government would need to announce that the SPP would no longer accept YUD bank notes or new deposits (which in these circumstances could only come in the aggregate from a reopened payment relationship with the NBY/SDK in Yugoslavia), in order to prevent the operation from becoming a way for Yugoslavs to convert their YUD into DM.[11] For administrative convenience, the ability to pay some taxes in YUD had to be limited to enterprises or maybe even to large enterprises. Others with YUD deposits would be allowed to transfer them to such enterprises in payment of obligations or in exchange for KM.

The removal of all YUD deposits with the SPP in this way would necessarily run into the constraint that the public's YUD deposits with banks exceeded banks' YUD reserve deposits at the SPP. RS banks had, after all, used some of their YUD deposits to make loans. Under "normal" circumstances faced by a country that was eliminating the use of a foreign currency (for example, undollarizing), a bank that was experiencing deposit withdraws of the foreign currency greater than its reserves in that currency, would need to sell other assets in order to restore sufficient reserves. In the RS's case, banks would need to buy enough YUD (by liquidating other assets) to cover the entire stock of its YUD deposit liabilities in excess of its YUD deposits with the SPP.

In this way, the entire stock of YUD deposits could be withdrawn in tax payments to the government. However, this was not possible because YUD were not freely tradable, and RS banks could not buy them from the NBY in Belgrade. In any event, the authorities were not keen to increase their claims on Belgrade even if they could have done so. This would have been a problem even if many of these banks had not been insolvent to begin with (i.e., not able to finance total deposit withdraws in any currency).

There was no way around the fact that the SPP (or government) would wind up with the whole bag (frozen claims on the NBY) if depositors were to get all of their money back (whatever the currency). The question of who would bear this loss—the government or depositors— could not really be separated from the strategy for resolving the banks' insolvency more generally. The "bright" side seemed to be that the excess of the public's YUD deposits beyond the YUD 419 million with the SPP seemed to be modest.[12] Banks' assets were predominantly in KM or DM already.

Nonetheless, we knew that the continued existence of YUD deposits that could not be used would further weaken public confidence in RS banks. We argued that banks should be allowed to transform YUD deposits into KM at an exchange rate acceptable to their customers, subject to prudential guidelines on open exchange positions established by the Banking Agency. Furthermore, bank borrowers of YUD could be required to service and repay these credits in accordance with their terms, in KM, using the market rates for YUD/KM at the time of each operation. (Where would they get the YUD to service their debt anyway?)

We opposed David's forced redenomination for several reasons. First and foremost a forced conversion of YUD to KM would have to have been accompanied by the imposition of limits on KM deposit withdrawals from insolvent banks, which would have undermined the credibility of the new KM. In and of itself, this risk would have been serious enough to have warranted the consideration of alternative approaches. I also think it would have provoked a stronger negative public reaction from those who felt they had lost in the forced conversion. The international community would have been blamed for what were really previous losses of the banks.

Typical of David, he had already discussed and promoted his scheme with the RS Prime Minister and Finance Minister before discussing it with me. Thus we were forced to mobilize a campaign with the government to kill the idea. In April 1999, Juan José sent a letter to Prime Minister Dodik and Finance Minister Kondić setting out the proposals I have outlined above. He argued that there were at least four advantages associated with this gradual approach over one that involved the forced, one-time conversion of YUD deposits: (a) there would be some sharing of costs between the budget and enterprises, as the depreciation of the YUD would reduce the KM value of the Giro accounts over time; (b) banks would be able to voluntarily transform YUD deposits into KM on the basis of availability of performing KM assets on their balance sheets (This would avoid the situation where banks that do not have performing KM assets, or do not have them in appropriate quantities, would be obliged to convert all their YUD liabilities into KM— a serious drawback of the forced conversion approach); (c) there would be no need to set an official exchange rate to be applied to the conversion—a very difficult task, subject to a substantial margin of error—because banks would negotiate the rate bilaterally with their customers; and (d) possible governance issues would be minimized because the government would have time to assess the legitimacy of the YUD Giro accounts. He also noted that the approach proposed in his letter would eliminate YUDs from the banking system relatively rapidly. The government accepted our recommendations.

I returned to Bosnia with a full team in late June, and we again drove to Banja Luka to press for the expansion of the use of KM. The new political team in the RS was much more cooperative than the previous one, and we were more hopeful than before. I arranged to meet with one of the intellectual leaders in the RS who was an informal economic advisor to the new government. There was some speculation that he might have an important position in the new government. He agreed to meet us for dinner at the Hotel Bosna in Banja Luka at 8:00 p.m.

Juan José was preparing for the Executive Board discussion of the Standby Arrangement and called me from Washington just as I was preparing to meet our guest in the dining room. The call lasted for over half an hour. I was sure that our guest was being adequately entertained by the other members of my team. However, by the time I arrived, he claimed rather gruffly that it was too late for him to dine with us and that he had to leave shortly. I was a bit surprised and disappointed. But as the conversation began, his anger seemed to subside. By 9:00 p.m. he seemed to have forgotten his need to leave shortly. However, he again turned aside my suggestion that we order dinner. I was hungry and could see that my team was too. The conversation seemed to have gathered considerable steam, but our guest would not think of dinner. By 10:00 p.m. the ever-resourceful Kim Rhee quietly ordered large quantities of hors d'oeuvres and a clandestine dinner was enjoyed by all as the conversation rolled on till midnight. Progress was in the air.

The countrywide adoption of KM gathered momentum. The monetary liabilities of the CBBH (currency in circulation and bank reserve deposits) rose rapidly from the stagnating level of KM 123 million at the end of June 1998 to KM 254 million by the end of that year. By the end of 1999 this figure had leapt to the astonishing level of KM 837 million. As already noted, a big part of this jump came from terminating the foreign currency deposits at the payment bureaus.

On May 15, 2002, the CBBH issued a new larger denomination note. The 200 KM note broke further new ground in that it had only one version and had been adopted by the CBBH Board and approved by the Joint Presidency without controversy. The writer on this note was none other than Ivo Andrić, whose name had been misspelled on the never-issued RS version of the one KM note. Ivo Andrić is the only Bosnian every to receive the Nobel Prize for Literature. By the end of 2002, the CBBH's monetary liabilities had exploded to KM 2.35 billion. These were covered by KM 2.46 billion in foreign currency assets. The CBBH was succeeding in the multiple roles seen for it in the Dayton Accord.

In April 2003 I attended a conference in Sarajevo hosted by the CBBH and presented some of this "ancient" history. To my great surprise (and delight) most people there, including the newer employees of the CBBH, were not even aware that there were two versions of each bank note in circulation. Our efforts (especially Peter's) to make the notes as much alike as possible had worked.

Thus, with the successful introduction of the new bank notes and interregional deposit transfers, all of the elements of a national monetary system seemed to be in place. What remained was to modernize the payment system and clean up the banks.

9 PAYMENT BUREAU REFORM

I t was clear to all of us that the banking system would not develop properly and the CBBH would not be free from the risks dramatized by the NBBH problem until the payment bureau system was replaced with one in which the public received payment services from banks. The ZPP, ZAP, SPP monopolies on domestic payments had to go.

By law, all business payments had to be made by deposit transfers except for the wage payments to their employees. Because all non-cash business payments were made through the bureaus, they were also very efficient tax collectors and the sources of very useful data on business activities. The problem of the payment bureaus was complex because it involved much more than just payments.

From my earlier experience with the Yugoslav system in Croatia, I knew that the payment bureau management would fight hard to preserve as much of their power as possible. The payment bureaus in Bosnia and Herzegovina employed more people than the entire banking system and Central Bank combined. They were a powerful political force. Furthermore, they worked and in their way were very efficient.

Beginning in February 1998 we began, almost subtlety, to outline the basic features of a future bank-based payment system. As the year progressed, we devoted more attention to the subject as it moved up our priority list. We needed not only to reform the payment system, but to dismantle the payment bureaus as institutions. Our basic strategy was to move the non-payment functions performed by the payment bureaus to the Ministry of Finance and a National Statistics Agency and to privatize the remaining clearinghouse functions to the banks. The clearing functions would also need to be completely redesigned in order to put banks in direct relationship with their customers and with the Central Bank. The cash handling and safekeeping functions could be absorbed by the CBBH or sold to banks. I was hoping for a cooperative role for the ZPP, ZAP, and the SPP in the reform process.

The reform of the payment system and of the payment bureaus became a highly charged issue between the regions and among the donors. Every bit as much as the common currency, an integrated payment system for deposits of that currency was an essential element in the reunification of the country economically. The payment bureau of the country had been broken into three at the time of the war as part of the attempted breakup of the country itself. Those who were still not reconciled to the preservation of the country were not eager to put the system back together again.

Not everyone felt that way of course. I was strongly impressed by the first meeting we held with the technical level payment system officials of the ZPP, ZAP, and the SPP. Almost a year earlier, in the Spring of 1997, I had asked Governor Serge Robert to request each of the three payment bureaus to send the head of their computer departments for a technical discussion of the requirements for countrywide transfers of the new money using a common payment order and electronic communications. We chaired the first such technical working group meeting near the end of our February visit in Sarajevo. I was expecting the same kind of venting that usually took place at the beginning of meetings among officials of the three regions. To our great surprise, as the representatives of each payment bureau arrived from their respective cities for the meeting, they embraced one another with tears in their eyes. For most of their careers they had worked together. When the war began and the bureaus split, they did not see or hear from one another again until that day, a period of four years. These men were proud of their technical abilities and of the capabilities of the payment systems they were part of. They greeted each other warmly and tearfully and were eager to put Humpty Dumpty back together again.

The bigger problem with payment system reform actually came from the reluctance of the payment bureaus to give up their powerful positions in the system. Even while conceding that "Western" ways would need to be adopted, the managements of the ZPP, ZAP, and SPP desperately wanted and expected to remain at the center of the new system. While they knew they would have to allow banks to provide payment services directly to their depositors, the payment bureaus expected to remain the back offices of the system. The related issues were to become a source of considerable tension with the bureaus and among the donors. We also needed to approach delicate political issues carefully, such as whether successor clearinghouses should be organized as one central system or three regional ones.

Though I was never in a position to know for sure, I had always believed that Maruf Burnazović, chairman of the Federation payment bureau, and Ranko Travar, Director of the RS payment bureau, had dealt with us honestly. We had had too many fights to think otherwise, and the CBBH would not have opened without Maruf's cooperation. While I was committed to the thorough modernization of the system, I believed that a careful transition, which gave the bureaus a fair chance to compete, was essential. In addition, the existing system needed to function properly until it could be replaced. I believed that the blueprint for reform needed to evolve gradually from a process of discussion in which the existing bureaus were involved.

THE TRANSFORMATION STRATEGY

My February 1998 mission recommended that BiH develop the general payment system structure found in developed market economies in which banks provided domestic payment services by dealing directly with their depositors and by transferring their customers' deposits as their own: (a) directly to the banks of payees with immediate settlement with banks' reserve account balances with the central bank (when immediate finality of settlement is important), or (b) by clearing payment

LVTS, RTGS, and Net Settlement systems

Economies use many payment systems. Most banks rely predominantly on two quite different systems. One settles each payment through banks' reserve accounts at their central bank (gross settlements) and the other accumulates payments between banks and settles the net amounts due to or from other banks periodically, e.g., daily (net settlements).

The first of these, used for important large value payments, are called Large Value Transfer Systems (LVTS). Several decades ago such payments in the United States were made over the Fed Wire system operated by the Federal Reserve Banks. However, with the technology available in those days, these individual gross payments could not be settled "real time." The individual messages were recorded over the day and actually processed each evening. Because large, money-center banks issued payment orders to debit their accounts with their Federal Reserve Bank each morning as they repaid overnight Fed funds borrowings from other banks, their Fed accounts were in fact overdrawn for part of the day. Because these gross payment orders were only processed bulk in the evening, this was not seen during the day.[1]

—continued on page 247

instructions through a clearinghouse with delayed net settlement. This required developing a large value transfer system (LVTS) between banks and the CBBH and could include converting the payment bureaus into clearinghouses. The development of new retail (or wholesale) payment instruments should be at the initiative of banks and other payment service providers.

This very general blueprint could have been achieved in a variety of ways. My team recommended the creation of a national payments council (the BiH Payments Council) for the purpose of discussing the strategy for transforming and modernizing the payment system. Any transformation of existing payment arrangements had to be undertaken in a way that did not disrupt the ongoing payment activity, without which the economy could not function. Our advice in the payment area to date had been consistent with the gradual evolution toward the above types of systems, while continuing to rely on existing structures. We suggested a transformation strategy along the following lines:

BY END MARCH 1998

- Establishment of one central bank and a single currency;
- Settlement of net end-of-day clearing balances of banks at the payment bureaus with the reserve accounts at the CBBH;
- Establishment of direct use by banks of their reserve accounts at the CBBH. This will be the genesis of a large value transfer system;

- Establishment of the BiH Payments Council.

By end 1998

- Amendment of domestic payments laws to permit banks to provide payments services and to establish a clear legal relationship between depositors, banks, the Central Bank and payment bureaus (as third-party service providers);
- Direct provision of payments services by banks. This will begin as individual banks are prepared to undertake such new services. Payment orders will be submitted to banks, which must accept responsibility for the adequacy of the depositors' funds. Banks will probably hire some of the new staff needed for these new activities from the payment bureaus. Customers submitting their payment orders to their banks will not have Giro accounts at a payment bureau, as their payment order will be debited to their banks' Giro account (if cleared through the payment bureau);
- Transfer of non-payment processing clearinghouse functions of the payment bureaus (e.g., government treasury services, government auditing) to other agencies.

1999

- Develop and adopt comprehensive modern clearinghouse rules and procedures for each clearinghouse (payment bureau);

Continued from page 246

Improvements in data processing and telecommunications have resulted in almost all LVTS becoming Real Time Gross Settlement (RTGS) systems. These systems settle (debit and credit) banks' reserve accounts at the central bank in real time. This has the great advantage that individual payments can be rejected (or cued for later settlement) if the bank does not have sufficient funds in its central bank reserve account without disrupting the system as a whole. Gross settlements are individual events.

Net settlement systems come in several versions (Automatic Clearing House—ACH, Giro, etc), but have the common feature that many payments between banks (and their customers) are accumulated and netted before they are finally settled on banks' reserve accounts with the central bank. These have the advantage of minimizing the number of actual settlements and thus can reduce the cost of payments. Their potential disadvantages are that the finality of their settlement can only be known with a delay and that they are "all or nothing" in nature (see pages 58 and 206). The failure of one bank to have sufficient funds can disrupt the settlement of all banks. Net settlement systems are generally used by small, not time-critical payments.

- Install modern large value transfer technology;
- Privatize the ownership of each clearinghouse (banks should be the main or sole owners).

2000

- Adopt new, modern domestic payments law.

DOMESTIC PAYMENTS LAW

We argued that an early step in implementing the above strategy was to modernize the domestic payments law. The domestic payments law in RS had been satisfactorily modernized several years earlier, and the drafting of a new law was nearing completion in the Federation. The amendments to the law in the Federation, however, were being made primarily to reflect organizational changes designed to integrate the ZAP and the ZPP into one Federation institution and also to accommodate the replacement of the Bosnian dinar by the Convertible Marka.

The reform strategy outlined above envisioned immediate amendments to existing laws sufficient to implement a bank-based payments system and the later adoption of a full-fledged, modern payments law once the environment was more settled and understood. During an earlier mission, June 11 to 24, 1997, Ben Geva had prepared drafts of two versions of a payments law. One proposed what we considered the essential minimum provisions to move forward, and the other was full-blown. During our February 1998 mission we agreed that the shorter of the two earlier drafts could be adopted as an amendment to the Domestic Payments System Law of each Entity. It permitted individuals and legal entities to open accounts in Convertible Marka and to use them to make and receive non-cash payments. It required that such accounts be kept in banks only.

We recommended that both Entities adopt amendments (1) clarifying that an inter-Entity payment is domestic, (2) providing that banks (and payment bureaus on their behalf) will not be required to keep records for a payment transaction with respect to which no dispute has been brought to their attention within a year after it took place, and (3) clarifying that an individual or legal entity be permitted to open more than one account and in more than one bank.

Because the existing Domestic Payments System Law of the Federation did not have many of the more modern provisions that were in the RS law, we recommended that the Federation law also be amended to allow customers to initiate and receive payments at their banks rather than only at the payment bureau. We did not propose to preclude customers' access to the payment bureau. Instead, we proposed to permit banks to provide direct payment services to their customers, if they wished to. This controversial feature reflected our view that the evolution to a modern system needed to be gradual enough to ensure the continuous functioning of the system throughout the transition.

Our recommendations at that time included the very modest proposal that a representative of the Central Bank be made a member of the Governing Board of the ZPP. To the same end, the mission further recommended that on matters of policy pertaining to the evolution of the payments system, the Governing Board, the General Manager, and his Deputy should regularly consult with, and seek the advice of, the Central Bank and the Payments Advisory Council, which was then being established. We wished to improve the mysterious governance of the payment bureaus during their reform.

The measures to promote the use of the Convertible Marka (KM) by ending the wartime practice of permitting the use of DM for non-cash payments through the payment bureau that I discussed in the previous chapter were also to be adopted as a part of these amendments. In addition, we made several specific suggestions for improvements to the language of the Federation Domestic Payments System Law that would make it more consistent with the CBBH Law.

ROLE OF THE CBBH

The CBBH's role in the payments system derived from several provisions in the CBBH Law, but above all from its authority over the opening and use of reserve accounts. The strict prohibition against the CBBH extending credit of any kind required it to ensure that payment settlements with reserve account balances could occur without Central Bank credit.

There are four major areas where a central bank could be involved in payments systems: the oversight (supervision) of payments systems, the provision of payments services, participation in payments systems, and leadership in payments systems modernization.

We recommended that the provision of payments services by the CBBH be limited to overseeing the printing, safekeeping, and initial distribution of currency notes, and the provision of reserve account balances (the large value transfer system). It is the provision of such deposit facilities for banks that makes a monetary authority a "central bank." The CBBH needed to establish the rules for banks' use of their reserve accounts, including their use for settlement of banks' net clearing balances with the payment bureaus. I had already drafted rules governing the use of these reserve accounts to satisfy the reserve requirement in the Central Bank Law. We also suggested that until the two Entity banking agencies developed sufficient expertise in the area of payments services and systems, the CBBH might also provide limited oversight of bank and clearinghouse payments procedures and risk-management systems.

The question of the proper role of a central bank in payments systems is an interesting one, given the monopoly every central bank has in issuing currency. Currency, however, is becoming less and less important as a means of payment in modern economies. The issue of the proper role of the central bank has recently been debated in the context of whether and how to regulate electronic money. My view is that central banks have a natural monopoly in the provision of the unit of account but not in the provision of means of payment. Thus I preferred to keep the CBBH out of the business of developing and providing retail payments services beyond supplying the currency.

Payments systems have many of the properties of money itself. Their value as a means of payment rests to a large extent with the universality of a payment instruments acceptance. For this reason, currency has become a monopoly of each country (of its central bank) that issues its own currency. Retail payment instruments, those used by you and me, have partially overcome this impetus toward monopoly by the payment industry's development and acceptance of common standards and protocols for designing and processing (clearing and settling) competitively provided payment instruments. We have long since overcome the potential problems of thousands of different issuers of checks (banks). The days of each oil company issuing its own credit card, which could only be used at its gas stations, have given way to a relatively few issuers of multi-use credit cards. In fact, mimicking checks to some extent, there are now actually thousands of companies issuing credit cards, but only a few consortia under whose rules and procedures they are issued (Delta Visa Card, United Visa Card, Bank of America Visa Card, etc). The debit card and ATM cards of tens of thousands of different banks are accepted at most point of sale readers or ATM machines, using a handful of clearing and settlement services (e.g., Cirrus, Plus, Star, The Exchange). (For more on this subject see Appendix III.)

Any transformation of existing payment arrangements in Bosnia needed to be undertaken in a way that did not disrupt the ongoing payment activity, without which the economy could not function. Our advice in the payments area had been consistent with the gradual evolution toward the above types of systems, while continuing to rely on existing structures. In addition to the steps already taken to move final settlement of interbank payments from the payment bureaus to the books of the Central Bank under the control of the CBBH, a transformation strategy could have proceeded by modernizing the payments law and improving the efficiency and risk management of the clearing functions of each payment bureau, while building up the technical efficiency of banks' direct access to their reserve accounts (LVTS). Such an approach could have allowed a modern system of payments to develop alongside the continued use of the existing system and would have permitted the continued use of payment bureau clearing services for as long as they remained competitive.

Maintaining payments systems that keep up with the needs of its users requires careful and visionary foresight. Much time, effort, and money has been lost as a result of inadequate forethought. Building a new payments system might be thought of as constructing a building. Someone first has a vision or a dream of what the building will be like (what it is for and how it should look). Next, that person hires an architect, or possibly an artist, to put the dream on paper to assure it is what the builder has in mind. Only after the conceptual dream is documented and agreed to (user requirements), can the architect begin to develop a model of what the building might look like. Later, detailed blueprints are prepared before construction starts. All this effort is considered part of the development process for a new building. A similar process is used to formulate an electronic payments system.

We recommended that the CBBH play a leadership role in the development of the blueprint for the modernization of the payments system in BiH. The CBBH would lead and coordinate the efforts of the private sector to develop efficient and secure means of payment for their customers. New payment instruments developed in the private sector needed to achieve the widespread, if not universal, acceptance that would be at the core of their usefulness. This invariably required industry agreement on standards and protocols. To facilitate the process of adopting such standards and the other roles of the CBBH in the payments system, Governor Nicoll appointed a payments system coordinator, who reported directly to him.

The Governor appointed Anka Musa to this new position. We all greatly respected and liked Anka. She headed the Mostar ZAP and was very knowledgeable about payments system needs. She was later appointed Director of the Mostar Main Unit of the CBBH and still later became a Vice Governor. Her cooperation was essential. In the past it had been rather difficult to meet with her in Mostar or in Sarajevo because of the three-or-so-hour drive. Her new position helped finance more frequent trips to Sarajevo and ensured that her wisdom was more fully utilized.

NATIONAL PAYMENTS COUNCIL

The development of the payments system should reflect the needs of the users and providers of payments services. In the past, the payment bureaus had exercised a disproportionate influence on payments system development. To provide a broader representation and a more appropriate balance of views, we recommended that the CBBH establish a national payments council—the BiH Payments Council. We began pressing for the establishment of the council during our February 1998 mission.

In addition to the normal challenges of reconciling the interests of all players in the provision of payments services, Bosnia and

Herzegovina had the extra challenge of reconciling the interests of the three regional payment bureaus. During the several years of the war, the ZPP, ZAP, and SPP had evolved separately and in somewhat different technical directions. These differences had to be overcome in order to reintegrate the systems. We saw the BiH Payments Council as the most promising vehicle for this purpose.

Assuring settlement of payments cleared through the payment bureaus without Central Bank credit (which by law the CBBH is prohibited from providing) needed to be one of the highest Payments Council priorities. Dealing with inadequate funds in a depositor's account at its bank was one thing. Dealing with inadequate funds in a bank's reserve account at the CBBH was another. There were many possibilities for creating measures to assure settlement should one of the banks not have sufficient funds in its account and not be able to garner enough funds in the marketplace to meet its short-term liquidity requirements. Techniques developed in other countries included loss sharing arrangements, pools of money for contingency purposes, and bilateral credit arrangements among banks. These all required policies and procedures to accommodate their implementation and to deter abuse by the participants in the arrangement. However, the participants in any settlement arrangement had to agree on the approach and assess the impact of that approach on the users of those specific payments services.

The process of developing payments systems required a lot of learning by the market and from the market. We wanted the process to get underway but didn't want it rushed.

INTERNAL TECHNICAL ENHANCEMENTS OF THE ZPP

An important and difficult question was: What technical enhancements should be undertaken by the payment bureaus during the transition period to a new institutional structure? The systems and state of technology in each payment bureau were different. The system in place in the RS was considerably more advanced over the system used by the ZPP and ZAP because the SPP had continued to upgrade its software along with Belgrade during the war, while the software used by the ZPP and ZAP had been cut off from the company that had created it. In the RS, the issue was simply whether to upgrade the system software as new versions were offered by the vendor. Thus we focused on this question only for the ZPP because it was most in need of technical upgrading. The issue was difficult and sensitive because while technical improvements were clearly needed, such improvements risked locking in a future system architecture that might not be appropriate for the market environment we wished to encourage. We were also aware that the ZPP had a strong incentive to design and implement a technical system that kept them in control of clearing and settlement as much as possible.

The ZPP consisted of a head office in Sarajevo; ten branches in regional centers (which handled larger volumes of transactions and developed daily settlement figures); thirty-eight units in larger sites (which disbursed cash and received payment orders, maintained participant accounts, collected and disbursed public revenues, and used PCs with modems for transmitting and receiving information); and four smaller offices without PCs.

The ZPP computer hardware consisted of an IBM 4381 for processing. Some branches had terminals connected to the 4381 and provided data entry points for payment orders. Fax messages were used between the ZPP offices for account consolidation.

The ZPP had very reluctantly given in to moving the final daily settlement between banks to the CBBH. The operating rules called for settlement information to be presented to the CBBH by 1800 hours. Because of the outdated technology in use, the ZPP was having difficulty meeting the schedule. During our February mission we noted that the ZPP settlement information did not usually arrive at CBBH until 2000 hours or later. Processing at CBBH took about two hours after receipt of the settlement balances. Banks were advised of their balances about one hour after receipt by the CBBH.

The hardware at the ZPP was old and not readily adaptable to current technology offerings. However, there were some innovations on the market that would improve the capabilities of ZPP. These could be implemented with modest expenditures and the use of vendor-supplied software. New hardware with faster processing and more reliable telecommunications and efficient data transfer would help the ZPP meet settlement deadlines.

This approach would allow for more efficient processing with some modestly improved functionality while the BiH Payments Council defined a strategy for the future payments system of the country concurrently with defining the roles of the CBBH and the payment bureaus. In the longer term, the Council would need to establish more uniformity and standardization in software functions among the payment bureaus once it had a better understanding of the overall architecture of the system.

However, as already discussed above, the role of the payment bureaus was expected to change in the near future. As they operated in 1998, the payment bureaus provided a means for the exchange of payment orders between banks after the bureaus had determined that the customer had sufficient funds in its account to execute the payment order instructions. In the future, the payment bureaus could continue to provide the means for these retail type payment orders to be exchanged between banks and to provide settlement information to the CBBH for finalizing the net settlement of systemwide payments, but the responsibility for checking the balance in a customer's account would belong to its bank. Thus in the future the ZPP would only deal with banks.

In addition, as banks increasingly took over the provision of domestic payments services, they would need a larger branch network. Over time, the need for the large number of ZPP offices would need to be reexamined. In some cases they might offer concentration services to the banks for exchanging payment orders and in other cases ZPP offices might be closed. Such office spaces could be sold to banks or other business ventures. We did not have a fully developed plan for the transition. It was rather like building a new super highway while having to keep the existing one working in the interim. But we wanted the cooperation and involvement of the ZAP, ZPP, and SPP to the extent possible.

Privatizing the retail payments functions of the payment bureaus (with the banks becoming owners) would allow them opportunities to seek new initiatives and foster new payments approaches for the public. It would be open to the transformed bureaus (business or financial service centers) to develop new services. These might include back-office credit card services (e.g., providing authorization access for merchants), billing, accounting, and net settlement services for banks. Other areas might include currency distribution services for banks and/or retailers and the operation of an on-line ATM (Automated Teller Machine) network for banks. We believed that initiatives in developing retail payments instruments and services should come from the private sector.

PAYMENTS SYSTEM TA COORDINATION

Payments system infrastructure is expensive and potential donors were beginning to take payments system issues more seriously. The World Bank and EU were separately preparing reports on the reform of the system. Help from the donor community was essential, but there was also the risk that if each donor developed its own strategy, the payment bureau managements could play off one donor against another in their efforts to maintain control. The process could also become unnecessarily expensive.

Coordination is the key to preventing such problems. All donors wanted to see a good reform and generally welcomed a cooperative approach. Someone had to lead, however, or it wouldn't happen. I began to allocate more time to bringing the various interested donors together to develop a strategy cooperatively.

When I returned to Sarajevo in April 1998 to further address the ongoing NBBH problem on my way to Bulgaria, I also met with Graeme Hunter (World Bank), Bryan Roberts (Economic Department of OHR), and Erik Somerling (EC Phare) to discuss coordination of payments system assistance. It was agreed that we would be guided at this point by the general high-level blueprint for payments system development in my team's April Technical Assistance report to the CBBH that had been prepared during our February mission. Mr. Roberts (and OHR) would provide Secretariat services in Sarajevo and hold periodic coordination meetings of parties interested in providing payments system technical assistance, and would circulate minutes and relevant documents to a roster of the interested parties (including the IMF Resident Representative and my department). We agreed that the interested parties, which included USAID, should also share their project proposals and related documents at the earliest feasible moment for comment and/or information. Mr. Roberts agreed to prepare, for comment, a draft list of areas of potential interest and assistance (subdivided aspects of payment system reform and modernization) and a list of the interested parties assigned to each project.

The OHR held the first two of its Roundtable Discussions on Payments System in BiH in June and July of 1998. They revealed considerable ignorance among some donors of the CBBH Law and regional experience with the Yugoslav system of payments. One participant proposed changes in the reserve requirement and the use of subsidies to encourage liquidity management practices that were not allowed by the CBBH Law. He also recommended copying the centrally directed so-called Interbank Money Market in Croatia that we were trying to get rid of. It stifled the development of a genuine interbank market. But the meetings were useful because they rapidly raised the level of the donor communities' understanding of payments system issues.

MOSTAR AND DUBROVNIK

Following my April visit to Sarajevo, I traveled on to Bulgaria. In early May I made short trips to Croatia and Hungary and returned to the Kyrgyz Republic later in the month for the first time in four years. There I was one of the honored guests at the fifth year celebration of the creation of the Kyrgyz som. The som is the Kyrgyz currency introduced on May 10, 1993, to replace the Soviet and Russian rubles then in use in the former Soviet Republics. President Akaev bestowed on me the Certificate of Honor for my help in launching the som. Still higher honors were bestowed by the President on Michael Camdessus, the Managing Director of the IMF, and John Odling-Smee, Director of the European II Department of the IMF. It was a wonderful conference and a grand moment for me.

I returned to Sarajevo June 22 for the launch of the KM bank notes. The next day I drove with Peter Nicholl to Mostar where Peter held a press conference on the new currency.

While in Mostar, Peter and I joined the meeting of a payments system technical working group organized by Anka Musa and also attended

by the CBBH branch managers. Anka had relinquished her post as Director of the Mostar ZAP several months earlier to become the Director of
the Mostar Main Unit of the CBBH and Governor Nicholl's advisor on
Payments Systems. Among the issues discussed at the meeting were the
organization and rules governing daily settlement of payments orders
cleared through the payment bureau (clearinghouse).

There was still considerable sensitivity about the centralization of
central banking functions. Aside from issuing currency, the main operational function of the CBBH was the operation of banks' reserve
accounts with the Central Bank. These balances were primarily used by
banks to buy currency and for interbank payments settlements. Legally
the CBBH had one set of books. Economically and legally no significance or meaning attached to whether the reserve accounts of Mostar
banks were "kept" in the Mostar Main Unit or in Sarajevo. However,
psychologically it mattered a lot to those in Mostar and in the RS. Thus
in designing the operational work of managing reserve accounts, we
placed the responsibility and staff with each Main Unit. Banks whose
headquarters were in the area of the Mostar Main Unit would contact
that office and open their accounts with it. Their messages to debit or
credit their reserve accounts would be sent to their Main Unit. We
explained these arrangements to those assembled, to their obvious great
relief.

During this meeting, the technical working group concluded the
Protocol Agreement and the Implementation Agreement between the
bureaus of Mostar, Banja Luka, and Sarajevo for settlement of payments
across regional boundaries. We had been working with the group for
almost a year to agree on common message formats and standards among
the three bureaus to facilitate interregional payments. The first inter-
Entity transaction under this new system took place on September 22,
1998, on the basis of fax messages. An electronic file-transfer message
system using the new standards was finally implemented February 1,
1999. The old system was changing one step at a time.

Following these meetings Peter and I met privately with Anka. She
expressed strong concern that the amendments to the Federation Internal Payment Law currently before the Parliament did not incorporate
the changes recommended by my previous mission. She maintained that

the latest draft incorporated potentially dangerous changes to the draft we had seen earlier, some of which could endanger the integrity of the CBBH's currency board arrangements. She was also concerned that the proposed treatment of kuna as a foreign currency would force too quickly a 100 percent reserve requirement on kuna deposits with the ZAP. We arranged for an English translation to be sent to me in Dubrovnik, my next stop.

That afternoon Peter and I drove on to Dubrovnik for the Fourth Dubrovnik Conference on Transition Economies sponsored by the Croatian National Bank. The theme that year was: "Central Banking and Monetary Policy: Major Issues and Implications for Transition Economies." I was presenting a paper on: *The Central Bank of Bosnia and Herzegovina: Its History and its Issues,* which has since grown into this book. The conference's Scientific Committee and godfathers were: Marko Škreb—Chairman and Governor of the Croatian National Bank; Pero Jurkovic, former Governor of the CNB; Robert A. Mundell, Columbia University and soon to receive the Nobel Prize for Economics; and Mario I. Blejer, my colleague at the International Monetary Fund and later the Governor of the Central Bank of Argentina.

Dubrovnik was the weekend escape of choice for the expatriate community in Sarajevo. It was another two-hour drive from Mostar. The City-Republic of Dubrovnik had been the first state to recognize the United States when it declared its independence from England. At that time it had already enjoyed a long history as a spectacularly beautiful medieval trading port. The old town of Dubrovnik, mercifully only superficially damaged in the recent war, was truly breathtaking when viewed from the mountains above.

One of the best views is from the site of our conference, in the Hotel Argentina just south of the old city. Looking down from the terraces of the Hotel Argentina, we saw a medieval, walled city with its all-marble streets surrounded on three sides by the crystal clear, turquoise blue water of the Adriatic Sea. When you look down on it, it is immediately obvious why this southern tip of the Dalmatian Coast of Croatia is called the Pearl of the Adriatic.

Peter and I drove south along the coast, past the old city and up the hill to the Argentina. The Argentina itself is a marvel. Its rooms are rather small and tired and in need of renovation (subsequently received), but its grounds are magical. The hotel starts half-way down the mountainside. The entrance is near the top floor with the rest of the hotel built down the steep mountainside ending with a beautiful swimming pool on the edge of the sea. The walk down to the beach twists and turns with many terraces and hide-a-ways along the way. The mountainside and its fauna are bathed in the arid Mediterranean sun. The 1950s movie, "The Magic Garden" came to my mind. I could picture the happy young daughter of a wealthy trader skipping rope on one terrace, playing jacks on another, and running the rest of the way down for a swim in the shinning blue water. Children could explore the grounds for days without boredom. Next door was the villa that had been owned by Elisabeth Taylor and Richard Burton some years earlier. It was now boarded up and empty.

This was not the first time I had visited the city. One year earlier, at my first participation in these conferences—the Third Dubrovnik Conference on Transition Economies—I had been introduced to the old city in the grandest style. At the end of our first full day of that conference, the conference participants gathered in front of the hotel and walked down the long hill to the old city. As we walked, my conversation with one of the participants was suddenly interrupted by a shout from the city wall above the entrance. The drawbridge had been pulled up to close the entrance. The speaker, a sentry in medieval dress, was addressing us in Latin, the medieval language of the city. Our guide replied to the sentry and then reported to us that the sentry had blocked our entry because we had no passports to the city. Marko Škreb, the Governor of the Croatian National Bank and our host, appealed to the sentry, who promised to petition the mayor for permission to enter. In a few minutes, herald trumpets sounded a fanfare and we were bid entry. We were led by the procession of sentry and trumpeters down a torch-lit path through the marble streets of the old city to the palace entrance. We were asked to wait and enjoy the entertainment to be provided while the mayor considered our petition.

We sat in the palace ballroom sipping our cocktails for the next hour to the sight of dancers, lutists, singers, magicians, and other entertainers, all in medieval dress. We were delighted and charmed beyond words. At last the mayor's greeting and ruling were delivered with much fanfare, and we were escorted to dinner overlooking the harbor. The tourists wandering through the town stared at us in wonderment. For a while I forgot that the bloodiest war since WWII had taken place here and in the region, killing a quarter of a million people and displacing several millions from their homes.

Our dinner was served to the accompaniment of a Croatian band and singing quartet. When I had concluded that I could not be more amazed than I had been for the last hour, Božo Prka arrived. Božo was Croatia's Finance Minister. I had met with him formally twice before in Zagreb. Without even sitting, he grabbed one of the ladies in our group and began dancing. When the song was finished Božo took the microphone from the lead singer and began singing. In the midst of his song he turned to Marko Škreb, with whom I was sitting, and sang, *"Oh, Mister Governor, . . . won't you please, . . . Give me your seigniorage."* I was actually witnessing the Finance Minister singing to the Central Bank Governor and asking for his profits. I couldn't stop laughing. I could not believe what I was hearing.

Later in the evening Božo took the microphone again with Ricardo Lago, Deputy Chief Economist of the European Bank for Reconstruction and Development, and sang what became the theme song of the Dubrovnik conferences:

"No Bridge Financing"
(sung to the tune of the Spanish song *"Cielito Lindo"*)

Every year in Croatia
There is a forum
On the transition
You should come
To Dubrovnik
And you will learn
The main issues

Ay ay ay ay
No bridge financing
For once the money is gone
The loan is water
Under the bridge

For stabilization
You must remember
Robert Mundell
He said that
For each target
You always need
One instrument

Ay ay ay ay
No bridge financing
For once the money is gone
The loan is water
Under the bridge

In the fight of inflation
There are some lessons you need to follow
Zero domestic credit
A balanced budget
And no bail out

Ay ay ay ay
No bridge financing
For once the money is gone
The loan is water
Under the bridge

Steering the external sector
Requires to manage
The exchange rate
You can either fix it
Or else float it
Or dollarize

Ay ay ay ay
No bridge financing
For once the money is gone
The loan is water
Under the bridge

Two years later—at the Fifth Dubrovnik Conference on Transition Economies—Božo again took a microphone and sang. By that time he was President of Privredna Banka Zagreb, the largest state bank, which was being prepared for privatization. We were returning to Dubrovnik by bus after the hydrofoil that had taken us to one of Dalmatia's many Islands had broken down. We were returning to the mainland by regular boat several hours north of the Hotel Argentina. After Božo completed his song he insisted that Bob Mundell sing. Bob sang five verses of "Ghost Riders in the Sky" without missing a word. Still prodding the group on, Božo then insisted that Jacob Frenkel, Governor of the Bank of Israel, sing. Without any hesitation Jacob regaled us with a lengthy passage from "La Traviata." Dubrovnik and the wonderful people of the Croatian National Bank continue to have a very special place in my heart.

But in June of 1998 I was not given much peace to enjoy the conference. While attending the conference I received an English translation of the draft Payment Law Anka Musa was so upset about. I made arrangements for it to be reviewed urgently in Washington and by Ben Geva, who had been working with me on the payments laws and who had drafted the model law we hoped would be adopted eventually. Following my review and the more careful one by Ben, I sent the following memo to Scott Brown.

 *Office Memorandum*

To: Scott Brown   July 3, 1998
From: Warren Coats
Subject: **Federation Internal Payment Law**

The IMF's advice on the Law on the Internal Payment System contained in our earlier reports and communications has been guided by two primary goals. The first goal is to achieve the objective of the Dayton Agreement of a single central bank and monetary system for Bosnia and Herzegovina. This objective requires that the authority of the Central Bank of Bosnia and Herzegovina (CBBH) to regulate banks' use of their reserve accounts with the CBBH not be compromised or weakened by any other laws, such as the internal payments laws of the Entities. The settlement of net payments processed by clearinghouses, such as the several payment bureaus in Bosnia and Herzegovina, by transferring bank balances with the CBBH must be under the control of the CBBH. Payments between the Federation and the RS are not naturally or easily governed by the Entity Internal Payment Laws and should be governed by the CBBH.

The second goal is to establish a legal foundation for the gradual development of a modern, market-economy system of payments. This objective requires that the relationship between the public (depositors), banks (depositories), and the payments bureaus (third-party processors such as clearinghouses), and the finality of payment be very clearly established in the law and that banks be permitted (eventually at least) to provide payments services. In particular, it must be clear that the payment bureaus do not accept deposits (with the limited, temporary exception of kuna and DM deposits fully backed by kuna and DM bank notes). They oversee the transfer of customer deposits with banks. Banks should be free, subject to CBBH regulations, to operate their deposits with the CBBH directly, i.e., without going through the payment bureaus. This is the foundation of the Large Value Transfer Systems found in all market economies.

While the proposed amendments to the existing Federation Law on Internal Payments introduce some improvements, the law as amended would not provide the foundation needed to reform and modernize the payments systems of Bosnia and Herzegovina and continues to conflict with the authority of the CBBH to administer the unified KM payments system common to the entire State as provided for in the Dayton Agreement. These deficiencies warrant a reconsideration of the Law on Changes and Amendments to the Law on Internal Payment System now before the Parliament. The most important of them are:

1. The KM Payment Transaction Law proposed in our July 1997 report would establish the above principles (e.g., payment finality, and the payment bureaus as third-party processors) and was to be incorporated as a chapter of the existing law. For some reason it was dropped from the list of amendments, and this should be reconsidered. Without these provisions the foundation for reform will be missing.

2. The necessary authority of the CBBH as established by the Central Bank Law is challenged in several places. For example: Article 2 of the Draft Bill replacing Article 8 of the principal law is drafted as if it (rather than the CBBH Law) is the basis of the CBBH's powers.

3. By not deferring specifically to CBBH regulations on matters relating to payments instructions by banks and from bank accounts, the Federation law potentially challenges the unity of the payments system and provides basis to challenging its operation, and possibly, indirectly, the currency board arrangement.

4. The CBBH's authority to regulate banks' use of their reserve accounts seems to be contradicted by Article 5 of the existing law (in the Federation, but not in the RS's internal payment law). Does the requirement of Article 5 that all legal entities must "make all [KM] payments through ZPP," conflict with AND OVERRIDE the CBBH's regulations requiring banks to buy and sell

KM against DM directly with the CBBH and that permit banks to transfer their reserve account balances to other banks by orders sent directly to the CBBH (LVTS)?

5. Rescinding of the war-time arrangements for domestic payments in DM (Articles 59-61) would be unwise at this time until KM is more firmly established in practice and in the confidence of the public. We recommend delaying that step for one year. Furthermore, as this law incorporates the activities of the Mostar ZAP into the ZPP, such provisions must be extended to the kuna as well. The current formulations of these Articles are unclear to us or are inappropriate. Cash held on deposits with the ZPP for transfer in domestic payments, should not be "assigned" as the liability of a bank. It should belong to the depositor, with the ZPP acting as trustee (almost like a safe deposit box).

6. The proposed changes in Article 35 of the principal law, which would limit the ZPP's domestic payments activities to KM, while appropriate, would create adjustment problems for kuna deposits with banks that are reflected in Giro accounts at the ZAP. A reasonable transition period should be granted to banks with kuna deposits for withdrawing them from the ZAP/ZPP (perhaps one year, but no sooner than the end of 1998).

cc: Governor Peter Nicholl
    Contributor: Ben Geva

Four days later Scott replied.

To: Warren Coats, MAE, IMF
     Dan Berney, Federation Banking Advisor
From: Scott Brown, EU1, IMF
Subject: Latest Amendments to Federation Payments Law

Warren,

Attached per our conversation are the latest amendments to the Draft Law on Amendments of the Federation Payments Law, which were sent to us by the Federation Finance Ministry today. I looked them over against your comments, and then consulted with Anka Musa. The impression we have is that they have done very little to address your concerns about providing for the future evolution of the payments system. A couple of the inconsistencies with the Central Bank Law were also addressed. They have provided for a longer transition period for the use of kuna and DM in the payments system.

If the opportunity arises, we will seek to assess whether Article 5 of the existing law presents any legal obstacle to direct transactions, either in KM or DM, between the Central Bank and the commercial banks. If there were any question, and the opportunity arose, we would ask the Ministry to add language indicating that this article does not present any such obstacle.

As I indicated, neither Anka nor I interpret the actions of the Ministry as holding out much prospect of consultation on this draft before its consideration in the Federation Parliament. The Federation Parliament begins its meeting tomorrow. There has not been any direct consultation between the FMOF and CBBH. There was not any written reply to the earlier letters that you, Anka, or Governor Nicholl wrote to the FMOF. The response to the letter that I wrote, and my face-to-face conversation, was to provide me (today) with the attached pages, but nobody at the FMOF is available today to discuss our reactions.

Best regards,
Scott

In the end we were not very happy with the law that was enacted, though some further improvements were made. It dealt far more with the ZPP as a quasi-governmental body than with payment system rights and obligations. Enough of the legal provisions needed for the reform of the payment system were included to allow us to proceed, but a new payment law would be needed before the new system could be fully implemented.

Over the summer, work continued by various interested donors. By sharing and commenting on each other's drafts, we hoped to deal with the ever-present danger of one donor or another drifting off in conflicting directions. The major issues were how gradual to make the modernization of the systems, how to transition from the existing systems to the future bank-based one, and what roles would be played by the SPP, ZAP, and ZPP. There were also technically and politically important issues of how centralized or decentralized to make the system and whether to build the existing payment bureaus in or out. The issues of the governance and organizational restructuring of these three monsters were only gradually coming into focus.

The first of the donor drafts to be circulated for comment was the EC PHARE study of the large value transfer needs and solutions by Eric Somerling. My IMF colleague Tony Lybek and I reviewed it and offered the following comments.

Erik Somerling   August 8, 1998

Dear Erik:

Thank you for the opportunity to review your draft report on a Large Value Transfer System (LVTS) for BiH. While waiting for the World Bank report on the ZPP and Simon's report, we (my colleague, Tony Lybek and I) would like to offer some comments and suggestions for your consideration.

1. It is not clear whether your report is in keeping with the general approach suggested in the IMF's TA Report on payments earlier this year or is proposing a different approach. We had recommended that banks operate their reserve accounts directly with the CBBH on a real time gross settlement (RTGS) basis, while payment orders submitted through the payment bureaus would be settled on a net basis at the end of the day as is already in operation. The direct operation of bank reserve accounts (FX transactions with the CBBH and interbank payments) would provide competition to the payment bureaus, which would be expected to offer retail payment processing (clearinghouse) services. An RTGS operation of reserve accounts could be operated by and/or through the payment bureaus as you seem to suggest in some places in your report (otherwise there is no need for "derivative accounts"), but this would perpetuate the monopoly position of the bureaus. In addition, the RTGS approach we had recommended would be more easily truly national rather than regional. Your approach might also weaken the CBBH's control over settlements of reserve account payments.

2. Assuming that you have in mind the direct (non-payment bureau) RTGS operation of reserve accounts we have recommended, questions remain about the domain and phasing of the BHIPS [Bosnia and Herzegovina Interbank Payment System] you have proposed.

   a. Payment orders from banks should be received by the CBBH at its branch that maintains that bank's reserve account. Thus a first order of business is for the CBBH to develop an efficient telecommunications/computer link between its branch accounts (computers) and its Main office accounts in Sarajevo. This internal system will provide the core of interbank payments between payment bureaus and branches of the CBBH.

   b. BHIPS would address how messages from each bank reach the CBBH at the appropriate branch of the CBBH. It may well be privately owned as you suggest. Furthermore, it should not be precluded that the ZAP, ZPP, or SPP would be the successful bidder to technically build and/or maintain the network. It may also be that the same network would be used to link branches of those banks not wishing to develop their own networks, to direct retail payment orders to clearinghouses rather than to the CBBH reserve accounts (it is not clear what your report has in mind when it refers to one system), and to exchange other information among banks. For some time (several years), however, the delivery of payment orders directly to the CBBH can be left to banks on the basis of message standards that must be established by the CBBH. Fax, telex, and hand-delivered diskettes could meet the very low volumes now involved for some time while the Payments Council and the banking sector increase their understanding of the options and of their needs. We think that it would be unwise to make the decisions on an automated RTGS (or a telecommunications network—BHIPS/BANKNET—too quickly (i.e., sooner than two or three years from now).

3. The report recommends on page 15 that bank branches directly access the LVTS, arguing that many banks will otherwise have to invest in their telecommunication for their branch network. Banks will sooner or later have to consolidate their branch network anyway, and it is preferable that each bank has one consolidated settlement account with the Central Bank. Otherwise it will be difficult for the banks to manage their liquidity on a consolidated basis, which is important for the efficiency of an RTGS system.

4. It is recommended on pages 12–13 that the LVTS use SWIFT as communication carrier. The functions mentioned on page 13, in fact, suggest that the BHIPS also provides other services by operating a Wide Area Network (WAN) for the banks. The WAN could also be used as the message carrier, although the message may still use the SWIFT format. Some countries use SWIFT as message carrier for their RTGS systems (e.g., Croatia), but the report should elaborate on the costs and risks of using an alternative carrier. To really compare the pricing of SWIFT (page 18), an assessment of the number of transactions—however rough it may be—and the costs and risks of developing its own communication carrier (in particular, if the WAN will be established anyway) should be discussed.

5. Although the report rightly refers discussion of details to future work on the design of the RTGS system, its argumentation can be strengthened. Pricing and competition policies are hardly discussed, although the costs of the system are important. Potential linkages to a securities depository system and possible future linkage with TARGET are not explicitly mentioned. Finally, the report could provide a more balanced view supporting its conclusions.

Specific comments [Omitted]

Very truly yours,

Warren Coats
Advisor
Monetary and Exchange Affairs Department
International Monetary Fund

At about the same time, August 1998, we repackaged and consolidated the relevant sections of our earlier technical assistance reports in order to give a comprehensive statement of our understanding and strategy for payment system reform. This document was circulated to the authorities and donor community.

In early October we received the report of Ashok Kumar Lahiri, a World Bank consultant. The objective of his report was "to assess the work done to date for reform in the context of the current system and examine if the transition implied would not be too disruptive to the economy." The report was well done and provided an excellent overview of the situation and the general strategy thinking up to that time.

USAID was also preparing a report on payment system reform under the direction of David Whitehead. We were struggling to provide different focuses to each report in order to maximize their value added. As each report had gotten underway before we had increased our efforts to coordinate, this was a challenging task and generally required some adjustment to the original purpose of each report. David's report was to illuminate the functional and governance aspects of the payment bureaus as organizations. We were hoping the report would deepen our understanding of the bureaus' inner workings. I saw a preliminary draft in September and was disappointed and worried.

DAVID WHITEHEAD

David had become convinced that the payment bureaus were major impediments to economic development and that the only way to reform them was to kill them off as quickly as possible. He had obtained USAID funding to prepare a report in which he would make his case and elaborate on the need for the donor community, under his leadership, to take over the reform process. I, on the other hand, continued to believe that we needed, or at least should seek, the cooperation of the payment bureaus in the reform process.

David attributed evil political control and motivations to the continued operation of the bureaus. For all I know, he was right. He believed that the management of the bureaus should be excluded from the reforms, which should be directly controlled by the donors. I urged him to use his report to build a more solid information base from which we could all assess the appropriate strategy for reform. The preliminary draft I saw was more a polemic, one that I thought would be of limited use.

When I returned with my team October 21, 1998, it was clear that donor interest in payment system reform had moved to the top of the list. A big fight was brewing over strategy and the blueprint for a reformed system. David wanted to head a Donor Steering Committee that would dictate the reforms. I strongly believed that our local counterparts needed to be involved in the process and on board. For one thing they were in a position to easily sabotage any plan we had if they chose to do so by bringing the existing system to a halt before a new one could be implemented. For another, they had knowledge of the existing system and potential transition problems that we did not. This knowledge could be valuable in designing and implementing a smooth transition.

In an effort to head David off at the pass, we formulated a summary of the general thinking at that point, drawing on my earlier MAE mission reports and reports by Erik Somerling, financed by the EU, and Ashok Kumar Lahiri, financed by the World Bank, as well as David's USAID project draft. Our summary outlined the desired reformed system, the transition strategy for getting there, an action plan for the authorities, and the related projects for which donor support would be needed. This document was intended to facilitate coordination among donors interested in assisting with payments reform and to build support among our counterparts.

We discussed the strategy document at the first meeting of the Bosnia and Herzegovina Payments System Council. Peter had convened this meeting so that my team could be there. The meeting had very high level representatives from the payment bureaus, banks, and Ministry of Finance from both Entities. Among the locals, many of the banks were eager for the adoption of the basic features of the reforms we proposed (competitive, bank-based payment services). They were beginning to become a pressure group in favor of reform. The payment bureaus themselves seemed to have accepted the need to change, but, as I noted earlier, wanted to protect a strong role for themselves. Our strategy document was well received by the Payments System Council.

The real showdown came at a meeting on November 1 in Sarajevo with the representatives of the donor community interested in payment system reform. Eighteen people attended in addition to my team. David was adamant that the donor community needed to take strong control of the process. It was also clear to everyone that he was intent on leading the donor committee that would have that responsibility. The issue, simply put, was whether the donor community would dictate reform through a Steering Committee without payment bureau involvement, or sell it and assist it via a coordinating committee with payment bureau input.

Again, I was disturbed by the prospect of cutting the bureaus out of the process after all of the help they had given and their strong desire to remake themselves in order to survive. And I was offended by David's very hard push to take over the process. David's interest was clearly more focused on dismantling the bureaus as organizations than on the details of a reformed payment system. Thus I saw an advantage in separating the two projects, giving the CBBH responsibility for oversight of payment system reform, which Peter would insist on anyway. I discussed these thoughts with Peter in advance of the big meeting with donors, and he agreed.

I had met in advance with many of the participants in this donor meeting and was reasonably sure they would support the approach outlined in our strategy document. The meeting itself was full of interagency tension at a multilateral level. It was chaired by Mike Sarhan, USAID. Mike was highly respected by me and the entire international donor community. He placed the success of the reconstruction and reform program we were all a part of above petty politics. During the meeting I received the strong endorsement for our strategy that I had hoped for. David was visibly unhappy during the meeting. He continually tried to resurrect his preferred International Steering Committee, but Mike kept him in check. The group accepted Mike's appointment of David to provide secretariat services for a new advisory group on the payment bureaus' organizational dismantling. Kim Rhee was appointed by Peter to oversee the reform of the payment systems themselves.

In addition to keeping the reform on track, the meeting and our strategy paper served to identify specific tasks and projects for which donor assistance would be needed. It provided a list of responsibilities donors could sign up for. These would be coordinated by the new International Advisory Group on Payment Bureau and Payment System Reform, the name finally settled on for the group David would lead (under Mike Sarhan's chairmanship). I was asked by the group to return in January or February to further refine the strategy and its work plan after they and their governments had studied the current draft more carefully. I promised to do so.

These maneuverings were all in preparation for a large donor conference on Bosnia to be held in Madrid in December, for which David had big plans. We all generally agreed that the payment bureaus should cease to exist as organizations in their current form within two years. This timetable was subsequently strongly endorsed by the Madrid meeting. I recommended to my management at the IMF that key elements of the reform strategy be supported by World Bank and IMF program conditionality. These included the complete separation of the payment bureau in the Republika Srpska (RS) from the Serb Development Bank, of which it was currently a part; the elimination of the German mark from internal non-cash payments through the payment bureau in the RS (as was to be done in the Federation by the end of the year); the

Temporary foot bridge where the famous "Old Mostar Bridge" had been before it was destroyed in the war. From left to right: stranger, the author, and Len Fernelius.—February 1997.

quick amendment of the Federation Internal Payment Law to improve the governance and transparency of the Federation payment bureau (ZPP); and the adoption in both Entities of a modern payment law (along the lines we had recommended earlier) by the summer of 1999.

I left Sarajevo on November 3 thinking that we had finally put David's plans to rest and brought the international community and our counterparts together around a common view of the reform path ahead. However, while good progress had been made, victory was not yet quite in hand. David continued to fight a rear guard action that seemed to ignore the agreements just reached at the November 1 donor meeting in Sarajevo. When David circulated the latest draft of his report following that meeting, I felt the need to comment extensively and publicly (within the donor community).

> To: Bosnia payments system reform donor group   December 12, 1998
> From: Warren Coats
> Subject: Comments on USAID study on Payment Bureaus in Bosnia
> and Herzegovina: Obstacles to Development and a Strategy for Orderly
> Transformation
>
> This is an impressive study, which assembled a lot of useful information in a short period of time. It makes a positive contribution in the on-going process of reforming the system. In my opinion that contribution will be greater if the report (especially the executive summary) can adopt a more constructive tone and if allegations that are not substantiated are either substantiated or removed. It would also be useful if the executive summary summarized the key findings and recommendations (I appreciate that this is still a draft).
>
> Starting with the recommendations and next steps given in the report (Section V), I suggest that Table V.2 be modified in two fundamentally important ways that reflect what I understand to be the strategy for developing and implementing the reforms agreed to by the donors. I suggest that the table drop the comparisons with the "World Bank Plan" and the "IMF Plan," and that it limit the elements ("Reform Steps") to those in the area addressed by the report (payment bureau reform in a somewhat narrow way).
>
> The current presentation could give the incorrect impression that there are competing World Bank and IMF (and USAID) plans. This is not the case. The reform steps in the World Bank study and those in the IMF report (still being finalized) represent the state of play at the time each was written. In fact, the formulation of the strategy and rough timetable in the IMF report is meant to be the distillation of thinking among the donors at the time it was prepared, not a

competing IMF Plan. Thus it would be more useful for the USAID report to compare its proposed timetable to the prevailing consensus in the IMF draft. If we all agree to the adjustments recommended then the consensus document would be amended and updated. We see our role, in this particular respect, as that of the secretariat for the overall effort.

In the same vein, the USAID report is deepening our understanding of the payment bureaus themselves and increasing the information available to help design and carry out their actual reform. Thus it should not propose new dates for other areas of the overall project. For example, the item "Inter-entity settlement done in CBBH" is a separate project from anything coming out of the USAID study. Table V.2 says that the IMF Plan targets that for August 1999. In fact, such payments started in October 1998 and we target upgrading the system to a SWIFT messaging system by Spring 1999 (the project specifications will be developed during my Jan/Feb 1999 visit and will be circulated for comments to the donors and the Payment Council).

As another example, the report contains a paragraph in its recommendation section (page 63) on "ending the legal monopoly on payments clearing by the PBs." We are all completely agreed on this. The current strategy (if I may refer to the current draft of the strategy and the project matrix in the draft IMF report in this way) lists three projects for achieving this in a meaningful way: 1) the preparation of a new payment law for each Entity; 2) preparation by banks and the CBBH/BHPSC (with TA) for providing customer payment services; and 3) development by the Banking Agencies of prudential criteria for approving bank provision of payment services. As a matter of procedure, I think that we will make more rapid progress if the details of the projects in each of these areas is developed by the donor that takes responsibility for each (with the rest of us commenting on the project TOR). It may well be that other ways of packaging the work in this area would work better and whenever that seems to be the case, proposals to do so should be made. I hope that our meeting with donors in Sarajevo the first week of February will provide an intense examination of the project matrix.

In the same spirit, and as another example of a recommendation that is really beyond the scope of this report, the report sets out the principles that should guide the design of new clearing mechanisms. I agree with all of them, but aside from applying them to the interim enhancements that the ZPP desperately needs to make in the next few months (see below for further comments), they are premature and out of place in this report and should be developed by the donor team that accepts responsibility for the project on "modernization of clearing function."

The USAID report's recommendations for restructuring the PBs are contained in pages 60–64. Those that deal with the immediate operations of the PBs and with their organizational restructuring are contained in three paragraphs on pages 61–62. The recommendation to improve the "governance and control over the internal activities of the PBs" and the recommendation to improve "transparency in the operations of existing PBs" are the subjects of the project "Implementation of good governance and transparency" in the current strategy document (under 1.A.3 ZPP Financial aspects and 1.B.3 SPP Financial aspects, in the project matrix). To some extent, the paragraph on page 62 dealing with transparency mixes that issue with improving the payment law (which has nothing to do specifically with the payment bureaus), which is the subject of the project under Legal issues in the matrix.

It would be very helpful if this report could be more specific about the elements that *should* be addressed or undertaken as a part of the project "Implementation of Good Governance and Transparency in the Existing Payment Bureaus." It would be helpful if it could indicate a tentative start date, provide an estimate of the length, and suggest the components of the project (composition and powers of the governing board, fee structure, publication of financial statements, etc.). In short, if it is to help us move on to actual reform it should provide as much of the input as possible for the TOR for the project on "Implementation of Good Governance and Transparency in the Existing Payment Bureaus." We think that the timetable for this project should be and can be sooner than seems to be suggested by the USAID report. But in any event, we hope that a donor, presumably USAID, can be found to commit to the project ASAP. This donor should develop a detailed TOR of the actively involved for the review of the donor community in January or February at the latest. It would seem to me that the amendments to the Federation Internal Payment Law and the RS Internal Payment Law that come out of this project and the new fee structures, etc., could be ready for implementation within two to three months of that.

The report also proposes a functional audit of the PBs in order to determine more clearly what they each do, and how they are organized to do it. We agree that this information will be needed to guide the relocation of non-clearinghouse functions out of the PBs. This is, of course, a very different project, or series of projects, than the one discussed above and will take some time (one, two, three years?) to fully implement. The projects to relocate non-clearinghouse functions are listed in the "Government functions" (1.A.1. and 1.B.1) section of the project matrix and the projects to modernize the clearinghouse functions and prepare the PBs (consisting only of the clearinghouse activities) for privatization are contained in the "Payment system function" (1.A.2. and 1.B.2) of the matrix. These projects may well not be the best packaging and I would welcome suggestions for improvement in this area. The USAID report will be helpful in this regard. It seems logical and efficient to have the PBs themselves prepare the documentation of their functions and organization. In fact, I recommend that they be asked to prepare recommendations for their own reorganization. This could then be subject to donor review and/or comment and counterproposals by outside experts. I personally think that the best and quickest product from this project would result from collaborative discussions between the PBs and experts to fashion reorganization plans on the basis of descriptive information first drafted by the PBs.

Much (but certainly not all) of the criticism in the report of the level and quality of service provided by the PBs, and especially the ZPP, reflects the very antiquated equipment and software of the PBs. Yet the report is silent in its recommendations on this area. We support a modest modernization of telecommunications and computing systems (new computers and software are needed in part to overcome Y2K problems) for the ZPP and recommended in our report that a donor-funded expert evaluate the ZPP plans to ensure that they are compatible with the future design of the system as contained in the current strategy. This strategy has been endorsed, at least in the general form it now takes in the current strategy document, by the BHPSC in its November meeting in Banja Luka. I consider it an important and urgent matter to provide that assistance, which has also been requested by the ZPP.

Detailed comments on the report

I fear that the tone of the executive summary will undercut the effectiveness of the report and the value of the descriptive material presented in its main body, which generally has a more objective tone than the executive summary.

The report is misleading about the credit creation resulting from PB loans (e.g., pages 6 and 10). As we all know, credit was created as a result of overdrawing the NBBH's reserve account at the CBBH. However, the occasional loans from the ZPP (and perhaps other PBs) to the Federation government do not create credit in any way different than when the government would spend the profits of the ZPP had they been transferred to the government as the USAID report properly proposes. I am assuming, of course, that the funds loaned by the ZPP were its own funds (i.e., retained earnings) and the USAID report provides no evidence to the contrary.

Similarly, the statement on page 28 that the ZPP (why not the SPP?) "has the potential to affect the quantity of money," is very misleading. All banks, enterprises, and the public have the same potential and the ZPP has no special potential (other than permitting overdrafts of reserve accounts against the rules). The implication seems to be that the payment bureaus use bank deposits (that are reflected in the Giro account balances of the public maintained by the PBs) or cash deposited with the PBs to make loans, but no evidence of this is offered in the report and I seriously doubt that that has happened. Even then, the statement on page 6 that "Creation of credit by the PBs is particularly disturbing, because this would directly undermine the Currency Board mandate of the Dayton Agreement, . . ." is no more correct for PBs making loans than for banks making loans. When the ZPP processed payment orders of NBBH depositors that overdrew its reserve account, it was the CBBH that extended credit not the ZPP. . . . There are a number of places where the study basically reports rumors or unsubstantiated claims. This is potentially unfair and runs the very high risk of discrediting the more solid parts of the report. Examples are:

1. The executive summary states on page 7 that "requirements for businesses to receive approval from a PB for every transaction they make inefficiently raises the costs of conducting normal business activity." The requirement that the payer have sufficient funds on deposit with its bank (as reflected in the Giro balance at the PB) is a proper control and will be taken over by banks when they provide payment services. No other requirements are convincingly documented by the report. The fact that individual employees may occasionally violate the PBs rules and abuse their position is not to be doubted. And the monopoly position of the PBs and their relationship with the government increase the prospects of such abuses, but I think this requires a somewhat different tone and presentation in the report than is used.

2. The report on page 30 states that "It is suspected, but not yet definitively proven, that some funds could be transferred to the accounts of the political parties . . ." It is very questionable that such statements belong in a study of this type. Even more objectionable is the statement on the top of page 36 that "there is the probability that ZPP is using these funds [cash deposits] to generate, but not report on, additional cash flows through illegal lending and investment activities." This is totally unsubstantiated in the report and I strongly doubt that it is true. The report might usefully draw a clearer distinction between the operational rules and practices of the PBs (some of which are quite objectionable), violations of these rules by individual employees (some examination of the adequacies of internal controls would be useful), and inappropriate uses of net income by senior management or political bosses (which I am ready to believe if it can be proven).

3. The claim on page 37 (picking winners . . .) that some banks receive loans from the PBs (assuming that it is not from the SDB) is a potentially serious revelation and needs to be better understood and documented (or dropped). The claim in the next paragraph that the unassigned depositors (whose deposits were assigned to the NBBH because they had not designated banks to hold them) were reassigned to banks by the ZPP (thus opening the possibility of favoritism) should also be verified. I had understood letters had been sent to all such depositors that they must designate banks to transfer these funds to.

The report makes a few incorrect (or perhaps misleading) statements, which should be corrected. The factual statements in the report should be vetted by the PBs. These include (though in the short time we have for review of this draft we no doubt missed some):

1. The statement in the middle of page 13 (and bottom of page 30) is incorrect, ("If a business operates according to law within the PB system, it has no need for a commercial bank account ..."). All account balances with the PBs, except those from the safekeeping of cash, are actually liabilities of banks for which purpose accounts with banks must be opened and maintained.

2. In the report's findings on the qualitative costs of the PBs (page 13-4), it lists "Encouraging imports at the expense of domestic producers ..." and "Increasing payments system risk ... and creating legal barriers to problem resolution." The report should explain the reasoning behind these claims.

3. "Float" (page 32 near the bottom) is usually defined as the money or credit created by mismatches between debits and credits (not the "return" earned as a result).

4. The cash deposited with the PBs (throughout it would be helpful if the report more clearly distinguished cash deposits—what we have called in our reports the custodial or lock box deposits of cash—and the Giro account balances that simply mirror funds deposited with banks) increases the cost of the system (forgone seigniorage), but it is misleading to say (footnote 16 on page 36) that there is a loss from reduced money creation. Such money creation, which is no different than the printing press, would be inflationary if it were not offset by the Central Bank or by capital outflows as would tend to happen with a currency board).

In the interest of better balance, the report might note (page 7) among the side benefits of the PBs, that they provide a safe place to deposit cash at a time when the banks cannot be trusted. Furthermore (page 34 and elsewhere), while it is useful to point out the inefficiencies of the payment system compared to modern market economy systems (which is a desirable goal for BiH), compared with the systems of the FSU and many other Central European countries it has provided a very efficient and safe system. The tax performance of former Yugoslav countries would be envied in Russia.

On page 34 (middle), I have argued above that the development of an effective interbank market should also be beyond the scope of this study.

The report would contribute more to the reform if it provided more information on its recommendations. For example, the recommendation to "abolish overnight ceilings on cash" (table on page 16) might indicate the law or regulation that needs to be changed.

What is meant by the "capital infusion from the IMF" on page 29? Also on page 29, the statement that Article 37 of the Federation payment law was changed to remove the power of the "ZPP to compel a bank to replenish its reserve account. . . ." is written in such a way that it leaves the impression that there was something inappropriate about that change (which was made to reflect the fact that this is a power and responsibility of the CBBH not the PBs).

Why is gross settlement "quite complicated"? It is net settlement systems that tend to be complicated.

The report sometimes lapses into hyperbole. The discussion of "acceptance orders" and liens and blocked accounts on page 40 is an example. These practices need careful study and some practices probably need to be reformed (whether we are speaking of PBs or banks). It is rarely the case that "When the account is blocked, the company literally ceases to function." (Trade credit in the form of arrears is well known and practiced.) It is hard to take seriously the statement on page 41 that a foreign investor shut down his company for 20 days, "losing a multi-million DM client as a result," rather than pay a disputed 40 DM to the PB. Similarly, the statement at the bottom of page 48 that "the financial wealth of firms and households held with the PBs can be confiscated arbitrarily at any time . . ." is a gross overstatement. The careful analysis of shortcomings in the laws, rules, and practices of the PBs in this area that could help with the reform is missing.

The cash (custodial) deposits at the PBs are estimated at 400 million DM on page 35 and at 350 million DM on page 48.

Pages 49 to 51 summarize the income statements for 1997 provided by the PBs. The lengthy discussion of the plausibility of the figures is rather insulting. One sentence in a footnote might be all right if there are serious suspicions that the books are cooked. It would be more useful to elaborate on the shortcomings for analysis and monitoring of the presentation of the figures (in a way that could help improve the reporting). I can't follow the point in the middle of page 52. Is it that some capital expenditures were incorrectly included as current expenditures deducted (inappropriately) from net income??

On page 46, without disputing the excessive costs and poor service of the ZPP, it is not credible to attribute low financial depth to these factors over the poor and unsafe banks those deposits must be held in. A more balanced statement is found on page 54 and I found the regression analysis very interesting and suggestive.

The December 16, 1998, Madrid Declaration of the Peace Implementation Group had focused everyone's attention on the determination of the international community to achieve rapid and dramatic payment system reform; and the mission encountered strong support for and cooperation with those goals. Even the payment bureaus themselves seem to have accepted the reform as inevitable.

Soon after the Madrid meeting, Bruno de Schaetzen, our resident representative in Sarajevo, sent me the following letter:

Warren,   December 29, 1998

Last Friday I had a long and somewhat tense conversation with Mike Sarhan on the reform of the payment bureaus. This is what he said.

There is growing frustration on the part of the U.S. over the slow pace of progress on the economy. In spite of more than one billion in U.S. assistance, there has been little private sector response and unemployment remains extraordinarily high. This is retarding progress on key political issues such as refugee returns and ultimately on full implementation of Dayton. It is now the strongly held view of the U.S. that a dominant factor in this failure is the continued existence of the payment bureaus and their control over businesses. Therefore the U.S. has now resolved at the highest level to launch a massive effort to abolish these institutions.

There will be three main lines of attacks. First the U.S. will provide the resources necessary to develop Treasury functions for the State and the Entities as quickly as possible. Second, ways will be found to strengthen the banking system. For instance, under consideration is a program whereby local banks would be paired with U.S. banks, which would send staff to Bosnia and also train local staff. Third, there will be large scale efforts to improve accountability and transparency of the system along the suggestions and timetable set out in the USAID draft report. Performing a functional audit of the system will be the essential starting point for this line of efforts. Finally, those three specific approaches will be supplemented by a large-scale campaign conducted at the highest U.S. diplomatic level to put pressure on the authorities to eliminate the payment bureaus.

The U.S. recognizes the expertise and responsibilities that the multinational organisations, especially the Fund and the Bank, have in this regard, as well as the interest of other donors. However, in view of the importance of this undertaking for the overall strategy of the U.S. in Bosnia and the amount of resources that the U.S. is prepared to commit, it intends to have a significant leadership role. In this regard, they welcome Kim's appointment. They especially consider that her drive, and managerial, organisational and diplomatic skills will allow her to make a significant contribution to the process. However, there is concern that she might not have enough experience and background to provide the vision and overall leadership that is needed for this complex task. There is full confidence that you and your MAE colleagues can, of course, be counted on to provide the necessary expertise and leadership. However there is concern that your occasional visit will not be enough to maintain the required pressures. They consider that what is needed is a daily involvement at a high level. In fact, some in USAID and among its consultants consider that the slow progress in other ex-Yugoslav countries might be due to the fact that in between MAE visits there is little motivation on the part of the authorities to keep the reform momentum going.

I said that you and Juan José would strongly welcome joint effort to try to accelerate the reform process. We all agreed that the bureaus had to go as soon as prudently possible. The fact that the U.S. was prepared to commit large amounts of assistance (tens of millions of dollars) would certainly help speed up things, especially on the treasury side. But as you had said many times, one should be careful not to create chaos. I noted that in Russia the quick elimination of Gosbank had been a major factor in the collapse of fiscal revenues. I explained your proposal that the functional audit could be performed by the bureaus themselves under the supervision of Kim and the international community. Sarhan thought that this was a good idea and he will consider it in more depth. Finally, I said that at the time of your next visit you would propose a detailed strategy to the authorities and that we could then allocate the tasks among the different donors. Meanwhile, I could pass on to you any specific proposal they had for your consideration. Sarhan agreed and we will meet in early January to discuss their plans for the timetable, which I will send to you. Finally, I commented on their report along the lines of your comments, stressing in particular the inaccuracies such as the threat to the currency board, and that the very hostile tone of the report probably did not serve any good purpose. They intend to take virtually all your comments.

On another matter, Juan José now tells me that he will be arriving with his mission in Banja Luka on January 27 to finalize the first review. I am concerned that if both of your missions arrive at the same time that this will overload the authorities and my logistical capabilities. Would it not be wise to try to advance the dates of your mission by one week?

Merry Christmas and happy New Year.
Bruno

I wasn't sure whether to be encouraged or alarmed by this new statement of U.S. intentions. It reflected many of David's views. It was clear that Mike was under great pressure from David and from home. At the same time Mike is a careful and thoughtful guy.

On January 7, 1999, I sent David the following letter:

Dear David,

We eagerly await the final version of your payment bureau report and with it a clearer statement of the next steps forward in the two separate but related projects to reform the PBs (1. the project to immediately improve governance and transparency of the PBs, and 2. the project to prepare them for privatization as clearinghouses). You asked for our further thoughts on the steps ahead in this area, so here they are.

1. General approach:
   a. We think that the desired results will be more quickly and economically achieved if the reform of the PBs is undertaken cooperatively with them. The experience in other former Yugoslav republics supports this view. Thus the description of PB functions and the allocation of staff to functions, and proposals to transfer these functions to other agencies should be developed in the first instance by the PBs in consultation with USAID experts.
   b. The future clearinghouse(s) should be built from the existing ones. Not only will building on the existing infrastructure of equipment, procedures, and expertise achieve our goals more quickly and at much lower cost, but it will also maximize local political support (i.e., minimize local political resistance) for the reforms.

2. The governing boards of the PBs:
   a. A single statewide governing board for the PBs (which you suggested was under consideration) is a good goal and is legally possible if both Entities agree to adopt the necessary laws. However, we see several reasons for making it a medium term rather than immediate goal. (1) Such a body, which would be responsible for PBs only, is likely to detract from strengthening the CBBH's role in the payment system, which is the more promising approach to an integrated nationwide monetary and payment system. (2) It is likely to take longer to develop the political support needed for this more radical approach than to amend the laws with regard to the existing governing boards. (3) The cooperation from management and staff of the PBs, without which will be very difficult if not impossible to reform them, will be much more difficult to obtain for a state board than for Entity boards. We would even argue that given the total failure to integrate the ZAP and ZPP under one board, the Federation law should acknowledge and reestablish officially separate boards for these two organizations (though perhaps we are out of date on the state of play in this area).
   b. The composition of the governing boards (whether there is one, two, or three) that you have suggested seems appropriate.

3. Other immediate reforms:
   a. Other accountability and transparency provisions (specific provisions on the approval of the PBs' budgets, use of net income, publishing financial statements and fee schedules, etc.), and the elimination of inconsistencies with the CBBH law should be enacted by both Entities. Ben Geva, our payment law expert, will offer some suggestions in these areas.

b. Consideration should be given to putting all of the PBs' own funds in accounts at the CBBH (these funds now take the form, we assume, of deposits with other banks, or cash) where their use can be more easily monitored. This should be simple for the ZPP where its cash and deposits will be in KM and DM and relatively easy for the ZAP, which no doubt holds kuna as well, but may be more problematic for the SPP which surely holds YUD as well.

c. Fee schedules should be rationalized, and the PBs should be required to post them in every office.

David sent me a new draft of his report in mid-January. It was an enormous disappointment. I was getting tired of reviewing his drafts with such little benefit. On January 25 I sent David the following letter in which I used very strong language:

To: David Whitehead
From: Warren Coats
Subject: USAID ZPP study

These comments on the January 15, 1999, draft proceed in the order in which statements appear in the draft. I understand that the report is still a draft, but it continues to fall so short of normal professional standards (in some sections at least), that I question whether it should be issued at all. It is not clear what purpose it would serve at this point. The draft continues to seriously misrepresent the operations of the PBs and says little that is useful to payment bureau reform.

Executive Summary

The executive summary makes many statements that are not substantiated by the subsequent report. I am not sure, for example, what is meant by the statement that "The PB system seriously represses the flow of funds in the Bosnian economy." Despite its inefficiency relative to modern market economy systems, the PBs have provided relatively rapid and secure payments clearing and settlement and have avoided the large automatic overdrafts that plagued the systems in the FSU for a number of years.

Main Report—Parts I and II

1. At the bottom of page 11 the report states: "Implications: The ability of the PB to extend or create credit is in direct conflict with the concept of the Currency Board...."

The paper does not establish that any PB has "created credit," which I understand to mean behaving like a bank (i.e., lending deposit resources). In any event, doing so would not violate the concept of a Currency Board Arrangement (CBA). The ZPP apparently did extend credit to the Federation Government out of its own resources. This is undesirable. It would be better for such resources to be transferred directly to the government (transfer of profits) rather than lent, but in either case it is of no consequences for the CBA, which doesn't enjoy any control over how Entity governments use their resources. I don't understand what is being said in footnote 1.

2. On pages 13–14 there is a list "of regulations on commercial business activity." The interesting question is why these regulations exist. That question needs an answer before making any recommendations. Presumably they serve to compute and enforce payment of taxes. If so, any recommendation to relax these regulations must indicate how their tax function will be performed.

3. Also on page 14 and in a number of other places (such as page 28) it is incorrectly stated that "If a business operates according to law with the PB system, it has no need for a commercial bank account. . . ." The same sentence is repeated at the top of page 30. The report continues to misrepresent (or fails to understand) the nature of "accounts" maintained by the PBs. While the first paragraph on page 30 notes that "businesses must have accounts with banks," it incorrectly goes on to say that "their deposits are completely controlled by the PBs." The report needs to clarify the nature of the accounts maintained with PBs. These accounts (aside from cash—lock box deposits) are simply accounting records of what is on deposit in businesses' banks. Banks have full use of these resources, just as they do in normal banking systems. They are not able to manage these deposit resources as efficiently as in normal systems because they do not see the result of the day's net payment activity until after the end of the day. PBs do not control the use of these funds in any way. They do, however, ensure that payment orders are not accepted that would overdraw these accounts.

4. I do not believe that the discussion in the middle of page 35 ("(1) Intermediation of DM Deposits") is correct. Deposits of cash by businesses would give rise to increases in their deposits with their banks (their banks receive credit to their reserve accounts at the CBBH and the ZPP holds the cash—now out of circulation—as agent for the CBBH). My understanding is that the DM 400 million or so is placed in the PBs by households who do not have accounts with banks. Such "custodial" accounts offer the public a safe place to hold money (and the service of transferring it) for those who do not trust the banks (a very reasonable view under current circumstances). Thus if the PBs were no longer allowed to hold cash for the public, it is unlikely that much, if any, of it would be placed in banks.

5. My understanding of the changes to articles 36 and 37 of the Federation payment law (I don't have my copy of the payment law with me at the moment)

is that they were necessary to reflect the authority of the CBBH in the area of reserve requirements and accounts. Instructions from the CBBH require the payment bureaus to report net clearings of banks each day and to reject any payment orders that would overdraw a bank's reserve account with the CBBH. You should reexamine the third paragraph on page 28.

6. The report does not do justice to the differences between the PBs. Most of it describes only the ZPP without really saying so and there are big differences between the PBs.

7. The Action Plan (pages 17 and 59) continues to list some items that have already been done for August 1999. In general, more discussion is needed of the timetable. As it stands it asserts a timetable without explanation.

8. In terms of actual substance, the report proposes two near term steps: "The plan begins with the establishment of a new Governing Board for the Payment Bureaus. . . ." And it calls for a functional audit of the activities of the ZPP in August 1999. If the functional audit is only of the ZPP, is the new Governing Board also only for the ZPP? The need to improve governance is broader than a new governing board for the ZPP. This report has even less information on this important next step than the very sketchy discussion in our last report. This is very disappointing. I continue to believe that a functional audit, prepared with the help of the three PBs (we must get beyond talking only of the ZPP) can and should be completed in the next few months. Why wait until August?

9. The action plan is given without serious discussion. I would like to discuss each entry with you in order to have a better understanding of what you have in mind. For example, what is the meaning of the item: "Organization of alternative clearinghouses"? This sounds like a different proposal than the one endorsed by the Payment Council and reported in our last report (i.e., converting the existing PBs into privately owned clearinghouses), yet there is no discussion of such an idea anywhere in the report. This is not an appropriate or useful way to introduce new ideas (if that is what it is).

10. On page 60 (second paragraph) the report states that banks can begin clearing on-us and intra (I assume you mean inter) bank payments, after a new tax collection system is put in place during 1999 and 2000. I basically agree with that sequencing, but I hope that the adjustments in computing taxes that are needed in order to eliminate the PBs monopoly can be developed and implemented sooner than that so that banks may begin providing payment services sooner than you propose. This will need to await the finding of the project in that area. However, the report seems to contradict this paragraph at the bottom of the same page by saying that some banks claim to be clearing payments on themselves and with some other selected banks already.

Annex I: Payment Bureau Procedures and Practices

This annex potentially provides factual information that should be helpful in designing the reform of the PBs. However, it suffers from a number of serious shortcomings. My disappointment with this section is so acute that I will provide a fair amount of detail on the shortcomings of one or two sections.

1. Though the section is headed **ZPP/ZAP/SPP procedures and practices,** the description pertains only to ZPP and there are dramatic differences between the three with regard to the subjects discussed in this section. Furthermore, many, if not most, of the inefficiencies described will be corrected by the installation of new equipment and procedures that are now planned. It is a serious shortcoming that the report is silent about this.

2. The opening section on deposits fails to make the most fundamental distinction, which is between deposits of the public that are with banks and those of cash that are held as cash by the BP (custodial deposits). Thus the first sentence: "No interest is paid on funds on deposits," is strange. Whether interest is paid or not is a matter of the policies of the banks with whom the funds are kept. We have all known for a long time that the PBs hold no funds against these kinds of deposits, which are simply accounting entries that mirror the amounts held by banks. The report occasionally acknowledges this but seems generally to forget or obscure it. With regard to custodial deposits, one would expect a service charge for the safekeeping services rather than interest but the report does not reveal whether such a charge is levied or not.

3. With regard to "Settlement times," (page 68) the impressionistic nature of the data seems hard to justify. Exact figures are surely available from the PBs. I simply do not believe the statement that payments between ZAP and ZPP "require from 15 to 45 days. . . ." At a minimum, the report should acknowledge that these payments are now being made same day or in one day using the procedures for CBBH settlement that started operating last September.

4. The presentation of the information in this annex (which again pertains, implicitly, only to ZPP) would benefit from a clearer distinction between customer payment services (which will be taken over by banks and thus potentially improved under competitive pressure), requirements of the tax authorities—such as limits on cash withdrawals and cash payments (which will continue to exist even if banks provide the service unless the approach to taxation is changed)—and inter-bank payment clearing and settlement, for which a clearinghouse will still be needed.

5. The report makes conflicting statements about ZPP fees (it says little about ZAP and SPP fees). In some places (e.g., page 38) it is stated that there is no

known fee schedule, but on page 76 the published fee schedule is reproduced without comment.

cc: IMF/MAE mission members

Fortunately USAID never issued David's report.

I returned to Sarajevo January 28 to February 8, 1999 to further refine and advance the payment system reform strategy, as well as to provide technical assistance to the CBBH in several other areas. The executive summary of Volume II of our technical assistance report summarized the reform strategy spelled out in detail in the report as follows:

Objectives, Architecture, Transition, and Work Plan

The goals of modernizing the payment systems of Bosnia and Herzegovina are to: better integrate payments throughout the country; promote the use of KM in domestic transactions; increase the speed and ease and reduce the cost of making payments without the use of Central Bank credit; improve the efficiency and soundness of banks; and adopt standards that will facilitate integration with the world, and particularly European economies.

The system of domestic payments to be developed in Bosnia and Herzegovina will resemble the systems found in other market economies, particularly those of the European Union. Banks will provide payment services directly to their customers, clearing payments to customers of other banks bilaterally or through clearinghouses of their choice and settling them on the books of the Central Bank. Interbank payments will be settled using deposits with the Central Bank accessed directly (ultimately with a real time gross settlement system). The payment bureaus will transfer their functions to other agencies, wind down and terminate their teller window services (including the acceptance of payment orders), and sell (if they are valuable in the new system) their clearinghouse infrastructure and related assets to new clearinghouses.

While undertaking immediately to improve the administration of the payment bureaus and to move their functions to other agencies over the next two years, the payment bureaus' monopolies on providing payment services will be eliminated, and banks will be permitted to provide payment services directly to their customers as and when they and the banking agency that regulates them determine that they are capable of doing so. These banks may continue to use (for as long as they exist) the clearing services of the payment bureaus. Other banks during this transition period will direct their customers to continue using all of the payment services of the payment bureaus (teller services, payment order processing, and clearing). Thus, the shifting of payment functions to banks will be gradual and orderly.

The technical aspects of operating banks' reserve accounts directly will be improved as warranted by the needs expressed by banks and the CBBH. The standards and method of using reserve accounts for interbank payments will be established and technically improved. A modern real time gross settlement system (RTGS) for interbank and CBBH payments will be designed and implemented only after the future structure of the real economy and the banking sector are more clearly established.

A bank owned company(ies) will acquire any useful clearing assets from the existing payment bureaus before they are liquidated. The systems for clearing customer payment orders (and the development of new instruments) will develop and clarify over time on the basis of experience and discussion within the Bosnia and Herzegovina Payment System Council (BHPSC). Thus, the reform of the remaining payment functions of the payment bureaus will be largely market determined.

The mission worked with the donor community and the BHPSC to document the above strategy. The strategy, summarized in Appendix I of this report, was endorsed by the International Advisory Group on Payment Bureau and Payment System Reform at its meeting February 7 and will be discussed by the BHPSC (which endorsed the November version of the strategy at its December 1998 meeting) at its next meeting in March. The strategy and its action deadlines have also been endorsed by the Council of Ministers of Bosnia and Herzegovina and by the Prime Ministers of both Entities and will become a part of the Memorandum of Economic and Financial Policies underlying the standby arrangement supported by the IMF.

The strategy will be refined over time as the reform progresses. The IMF has provided a resident payment system advisor to coordinate donor assistance to the reform and modernization projects in the payment system areas and to work with the CBBH's Payments Coordination unit. USAID has provided resident advisors to provide secretariat support to the International Advisory Group.

KIM RHEE

With David Whitehead shackled to the secretariat of the IAG for the institutional aspects of the reform (spinning off the non-payment functions of the PBs and their liquidation), the reigns of payment reform were taken up by Governor Nicholl and Kim Rhee. For this purpose Kim took up full-time residence in Sarajevo for another eighteen months. My involvement ended in 1999. Peter and Kim led the reform of the payment systems project to a spectacular success. Both are stubborn and determined leaders and were simply not prepared to fail. Thus I was surprised in 2001 when Mladjan Dinkic, then the Governor of the National Bank of Yugoslavia, told me that Yugoslavia would not make the mistakes of Bosnia when it reformed its payment systems (the SDK).[3] He never fully clarified this remark, but I think he was focusing on Bosnia's experience with dismantling its payment bureaus and the resulting dislocations and unemployment, rather than on the reform of its payment systems.

The reform of the payment systems led to the sorts of systems outlined in the strategy we had proposed as summarized above. However, there were important differences in the migration from the existing to the new systems from what we had recommended. Our proposed strategy, while radical in proposing the dismantling of the PBs as institutions (something that was not done in any other former Yugoslav republic), was more gradual and incremental in the migration from PBs to banks and in the build up of the technical infrastructure (the RTGS and small value clearinghouse).

Peter, with Kim's support, decided to accept a USAID offer to fund the development of full blown RTGS and Giro clearinghouse systems. This decision was approved by the CBBH Board in February 2000 and endorsed by the National Payment Council. It provided for the CBBH to own and operate these two systems; to oversee their development and implementation; and for a one-day switch-over from the old PBs to the new systems, on January 5, 2001. There would be one national RTGS located in Sarajevo (with a back-up facility in Banja Luka) and three regional Giro clearinghouses in the regions previously served by the SPP, ZAP, and ZPP. Logica won the tender to install the RTGS, and Logica and Halcom of Slovinia jointly won the tender for the three regional, small-value net settlement systems. This was a very bold undertaking. It succeeded brilliantly thanks to the determination, energy, and skills of Kim and Peter, the support of the political authorities, and the willingness of the existing PBs to cooperate with the process.

Three thousand employees of the PBs were replaced by 14 staff at the CBBH devoted to operating these two payment systems and a modest number of staff at the MOF and statistical bureau. In their first year of operation almost 12 million payment transactions were made by the two systems combined with a total value of almost 17 billion KM. In 2005 these had more than doubled to almost 25 million transactions, with a total value of almost 39 billion KM. The cost of making payments was reduced (and will be reduced more as volume increases) and the efficiency significantly improved. Bosnia had a fully modern system compatible with Europe and the rest of the world and considerable capacity to grow. And the CBBH proved that very significant reform was possible.

10 FAREWELL SARAJEVO

With the addition of Kosovo, Serbia, and Turkey to my intensive countries, it had become impossible to keep up properly with the demands of Croatia, Bulgaria, and Bosnia. I decided to drop Bulgaria and Bosnia and on November 30, 1999, just five days after returning from my second visit to Turkey in one month, I took off on my final flight to Bosnia to introduce my replacement, Delisle Worrell, a former Deputy Governor of the Central Bank of Barbados. By taking United's late afternoon flight from Washington to Munich, I could connect with a Lufthansa flight on December 1 and arrive in Sarajevo without a stopover.

By the time we were airborne, almost 5:00 p.m., it was dark as we were rapidly approaching the shortest day of the year. The temperature, which had generally been very mild in Washington up to that point, had dropped to the low 40s. The night air was crisp and crystal clear.

I always find sitting in an airplane very relaxing. By that point, whatever preparation was needed for a trip has been done or not done, packing was behind me, and there was no longer any worry of missing the flight. On this occasion I enjoyed a glass of Dom Perignon, and marveled at the beauty of the lights of the cities and towns below glistening through the clear night air. I switched to a nice Robert Mondovi Chardonnay and

291

reflected on what a lucky man I had been. The red wine was a disappointment as were the two movies; and I fell asleep in the middle of "Blue Eyes"
something or other with Hugh Grant, until I was awakened by the spectacular airborne sunrise over the snow-covered Alps behind Munich. In
the first morning soft-lit, bluish glow, the snow-covered ground was peaceful and Christmas-like. Though a bit cloudy, the air over Germany was
also exceptionally clear (especially for Europe). Then the sun began to
make its morning presence more dramatically felt as it streamed through
the clouds over the peaks of the Alps. The sky to the East turned spectacular shades of orange, yellow, and red. The sight was so breathtaking that
the flight steward announced it as an event of rare beauty.

Kim Rhee was also on the flight, and we went to the Senator lounge
together for the three-hour layover in Munich, during which she briefed
me on the most recent developments in Bosnia. She had returned to her
Potomac, Maryland, home for Thanksgiving with her family and was
returning to her post at the CBBH in Sarajevo.

My final arrival into Sarajevo contrasted sharply with my first. On
that occasion I had been sitting in the cockpit of a Hercules C-130
NATO troop transport descending into the fog of the Sarajevo airport,
wide-eyed and full of eager curiosity. On my final trip, I had slept all
the way from Munich (normally a one-hour flight, which had turned
into two) in the relative comfort of a Lufthansa Boeing 737-500. Again
we landed in fog (after a half-hour delay on the ground in Munich and
an extra hour in the air waiting for the fog to thin to acceptable minimum levels in Sarajevo); but this time my mind, in its half-slumber, was
reminiscing about the last three-and-a-half years of work there.

When we finally touched ground, I was amazed at the changes at
the airport. I had been impressed with the changes at each of my many
landings there, but this was the most dramatic. In the five months since
my last visit in late June, a new departure terminal had been completed
and the exterior of the old terminal (now the arrival terminal) was new,
removing all traces of the war's damage. The old jet ways—which had
been destroyed during the bombardment of the airport and which just
dangled there useless for several years—had been removed a year earlier, leaving a cleaner look. But the two openings that had connected
them to the terminal building on the second floor were clearly visible

where plywood boards covered the holes. I had never seen the interior of the still-unused second floor and would not on this occasion either. The new interior was just getting underway, both on the unused and unseen second floor and on the ground floor with which I was familiar. The Stability Pack summit and President Bill Clinton's recent visit had clearly forced the pace of reconstruction with fairly dramatic effects, visually at least.

The old central market of Sarajevo was even more charming than before, despite the temporary absence of the hundreds, if not thousands, of outdoor café tables and chairs. In the spring—and miraculously on any warm day during the winter—they would reappear in an instant. Spurred on by the deaths of two young people the previous spring from falling chunks of building facades along the pedestrian walkway, the building facades had been repaired and painted.

I settled into my hotel; and Delisle Worrell arrived from Vienna soon thereafter. We all went to the Central Bank and met directly with Peter for about two hours of discussion of recent events. That evening Kim, Delisle, Bruno, and I were his guests for dinner at his home. Glynyss had started a very upscale restaurant in their home, which, while being a bit odd, was really wonderful.

Delisle and I had meetings with various department heads and the Vice Governor in order to introduce him around, and at 2:30 p.m. we met with the Governor and the management board for my farewell. Very nice words were said by all. Kasim Omićević, Governor of the "former" NBBH and Board member of CBBH, spoke the longest. He reminisced about our three-and-a-half years work together. Sadly, Kasim was under indictment for the foreign exchange reserves of the NBBH deposited with Promdi Banka. Promdi was now under liquidation in Croatia and the President had been shot dead in his home. The NBBH deposit of about DM 14 million had never been returned.

Words cannot capture what we had shared during my three-and-a-half years of hard work on behalf of Bosnia and Herzegovina and the CBBH, but I was touched by their expressions of gratitude. My efforts to express my own feelings of shared enterprise and comradeship were no more successful, but I hope equally appreciated. The Board presented me with a beautiful oil painting of Sarajevo.

That evening we dined at Kim's with the two Vice Governors, Dragan Kovačević and Ljubiša Vladušić, and Bruno and Maria. By dining the previous evening at Peter and Glynyss's and on this one at Kim's, we had dined at what are commonly acknowledged as two of the three best kitchens in Sarajevo (the third being the Swedish embassy). It was wonderful to observe the warm relationship that had developed between Dragan and Ljubiša only four years after the war that had divided them.

My final full day was rather anticlimactic. In the early afternoon I met with the chief accountant to try to clarify the complicated accounting required to reflect Bosnia's financial dealing with the IMF, in order to break the blockage that had kept the CBBH from taking over the accounting function for the government from the now-liquidated NBBH (the problem being to protect the currency board arrangement from the usual requirements of the IMF when it lends to member countries). In addition, we met with Dan and Dale, the USAID/Barents (now called BearingPoint) banking supervision advisors who had been in residence in Sarajevo for three years and who gave a very depressing account of the efforts by the Prime Minister to block the privatization of the state banks and other banking sector clean-up problems. Finally, in the late afternoon we met with Vicki Petersen, the financial sector specialist at the World Bank.

On this, my final evening in Sarajevo, Ann Schwartz, U.S. Treasury lawyer, hosted a birthday party dinner for Kim and Vicki. The guests, in addition to us, were other international advisors and experts who helped make up the international community in Sarajevo, most of them from USAID. The food was very good, as was the millennium champagne. But as the evening progressed, my mind was saying goodbye. One theme that weaved its way through several conversations was the difficulty of combining the postwar reconstruction with transformation from central planning to a market economy in an obstructionist environment of Bosnian, Croat, and Serb political leaders who continued to hate one another and whose primary concern was how to hang on as long as possible to the privileges they enjoyed under the old regime. The next generation of leaders waiting in the wings promised to be better, but not that much better. What hope there was, was with the young and the desire of most people for normal lives.

Bruno's popular joke of the night before was repeated for the new audience with equal appreciation. "What is the same about a bikini on a well-endowed young lady and the government of Belgium (or France, or Germany, etc.)?—You wonder how it holds together and you hope it falls." Kim, Delisle, Vicki, Maria, and I walked together back to our respective residences from Ann's. It was about a twenty-minute walk that took us through the old town. Kim and I walked arm in arm wondering where we might work together next.

The next morning I flew home, experiencing a flood of emotions I don't have the talent to describe.

11 LESSONS LEARNED

Technical assistance to new or developing central banks has many common features and many that are unique to the country receiving it. Technical assistance to post-conflict countries, especially during the first months and years, is a unique experience. Prioritizing the urgency of money and payment needs is of the essence. Helping to prepare a paper for the UNDP on the minimal requirements for money and payments in post-conflict countries and the technical assistance that I had provided in several former Soviet republics had helped prepare me for what we did in Bosnia.

I learned additional lessons in Kosovo, West Bank and Gaza Strip, Serbia, Afghanistan, and Iraq. Advance planning and preparation make a very big difference and should always be possible. Advice at the stage of peace negotiations can be particularly helpful in providing a solid foundation for subsequent development of sound monetary arrangements. Early planning can also help minimize and deal with turf battles and donor coordination issues. These and other lessons are summarized below.

PLANNING AND DONOR COORDINATION IS REQUIRED

The donor resources available for post-conflict reconstruction are limited and need to be used effectively. In addition, policy advice and reform strategies are less likely to be adopted and implemented if the donor community does not speak with more or less one voice. To a large extent, financial policy leadership is provided by the International Financial Institutions in accordance with well-established competencies. Such broad agreement on the assignment of leadership responsibilities has generally made it possible to settle rather quickly and easily the marginal turf battles that inevitably exist at the beginning of each new post-conflict reconstruction experience. Mechanisms of coordination, such as Donor Consultative Groups, are very important. These mechanisms are generally well understood, but need to be rebuilt with each new post-conflict case.

A highly successful example of coordination of work somewhat outside of the ordinary is provided by the reform of the payment bureaus in Bosnia and Herzegovina. Two-and-a-half years following the Dayton Peace Agreement, donors applied considerable pressure on the Entity governments to dismantle the payment bureau successors of the Yugoslav SDK, which gave the reform of the payments system a high priority. Though relatively efficient from a technical standpoint, the payment bureaus of the three regions had been powerful instruments of state and political control of the economy and were thought to be slowing the economic reform and integration that was expected to contribute to the development of the new political arrangements. The payment bureaus also undercut the development of banks, which in other countries provided many of the payments services provided by these bureaus.

Many donors were very eager to contribute to this effort. Sharply different viewpoints emerged among them over how to proceed. The main difference, which was more among individuals than donor organizations, was over the extent of donor or local control of the process. One group pushed for a donor steering group to control the process to ensure that the reform "was done right" and expeditiously. Another supported a donor advisory group with implementation control with the locals, arguing that a smooth transition to a modern payment system was not likely without local ownership and support. The IMF took the leadership in preparing a draft strategy document, which set out the proposed elements of the future payment systems and the means for developing them while dismantling the existing payment bureaus (SPP, ZAP, and ZPP). The document was first discussed among the donors (World Bank, EU, USAID, U.S. Treasury, and others) and revised accordingly. With an agreed donor position, the revised document was discussed in a series of meetings of the Bosnia and Herzegovina Payment System Council (which had representatives from all three ethnic regions). Once agreement was reached, the document became the blueprint of reform, with individual donors assigned specific responsibilities for assistance. Control of the project was with the locals (the CBBH, SPP, ZAP, ZPP, and respective Entity finance ministries). Rather than a donor steering group, the donors established an International Advisory Group on Payment Bureau and Payment System Reform. Payment system reform was assigned to the CBBH (and IMF). Other donors were assigned to payment bureau reform with respect to its other functions and organizational structure. Two years later, on January 5, 2001, the CBBH launched a Real Time Gross Settlement system and Giro clearinghouse and such activities through the payment bureaus ceased. These systems have been a spectacular success. The transformation of the payment bureaus as institutions was less successful in handling the employment impacts.

SHORT-TERM NEEDS AND LONG-RUN DEVELOPMENT

The solutions to the immediate needs for a new government to have a currency and to make payments need to be considered in the light of the best approach to the long-run development of the monetary and banking system of the economy. Generally, existing facilities and staff should be used initially but this may contribute to the perpetuation of approaches that are not appropriate in the long run. Advanced planning by experienced experts and a clear but evolving strategy for development are the antidote.

The most important short-term decisions with respect to long-run options are:

a. the choice of currency and monetary policy regime;
b. the extent to which existing institutions, facilities, and laws are used initially; and
c. the extent of modernization of state banks destined to be privatized or liquidated.

In **Bosnia and Herzegovina** the advanced agreement on the monetary regime in the Dayton Peace Agreement was an enormous advantage that allowed reconstruction and reform to focus on the institutional establishment of a new Central Bank and the liquidation of existing ones and on the very challenging task of reforming the highly centralized payment bureau system of domestic payments. Reliance on the existing payment bureaus in the beginning assured immediate continuity of domestic payments, but it may have prolonged the period of transition to a new modern, bank-based payment systems. Nonetheless, the modernization of the core payment systems and development of the banking system proceeded steadily in an orderly fashion without disruptions. Bosnia was the first former Yugoslav republic to completely replace the old SDK-type centralized domestic payment monopoly, despite starting later.

In **Kosovo** the United Nations Interim Administration Mission in Kosovo (UNMIK) quickly agreed to establish the German mark as a legal tender (along with the existing Yugoslav dinar) and to use it exclusively for domestic payments (temporarily) through the existing payment bureaus. This endorsed what was already in place and facilitated focusing on developing the limited-purpose Banking and Payment Authority of Kosovo (BPK) and developing the banking system with modern bank-based payment systems. However, the immediate replacement of the SDK payment bureau system imposed a hardship on the Serbian population, which continued to use the Yugoslav dinar extensively and needed payment services in dinar.

Afghanistan faced bigger challenges because of a more complicated, multiple currency situation. A number of factors favored dollarization, including the speed with which a foreign currency could have been introduced and the ease of managing it. However, for historical and statebuilding purposes the authorities chose to issue their own currency. This proved to be quite costly in terms of delay, direct costs, and corruption. However, they were able to take advantage of earlier, partially completed work to issue a new currency in just eight months. A new central bank law protects the value of the new currency from the inflationary effects of central bank lending to government, but the choice of a market-determined exchange rate monetary policy regime has placed heavy demands on the central bank's capacity to manage monetary policy, which it is not yet fully able to fulfill. The government also continues to rely on the central bank's branch network and commercial operations as well as the hawala (money changers and remitters) to facilitate government payments. The government had a difficult choice of whether to quickly expand the activities of the state banks or to continue to use the services of the central bank. Its choice to use the central bank and hawala system for payments should result in a more carefully considered strategy for the state banks going forward. However, such a plan has not yet been developed.

Iraq, on the other hand, faced very difficult currency choices and decided to issue a new currency (technically a new note series of the same currency) in order to increase the depleted note supply with notes without Saddam Hussein's picture and without dollarizing. Though economically advantageous, the Coalition Provisional Authority (CPA) decided that dollarization would not be acceptable politically. As an emergency interim measure, U.S. dollars were imported and used in government salary and stipend disbursements, and additional Saddam dinars were printed until the new notes could be produced and issued. Though the stability of the new notes would depend on the monetary regime adopted, no clear decisions on a monetary regime were taken by the time the new notes were exchanged for the old ones. The currency exchange itself was very successful, but the propensity of the CPA to focus on fire fighting has resulted in quite limited development of the Central Bank of Iraq's own capacity. Four years after the toppling of Saddam's Ba'athist regime, the U.S. Embassy and military remain heavily involved and focused on cash distribution around Iraq. The lack of security continues to overshadow everything else.

THERE ARE NO BLANK SLATES

The world has no blank slates. Every society has existing institutions, customs, and attitudes, which are ignored at the new government's (or its advisors') peril. The Central Bank of Bosnia and Herzegovina was legally a new institution but it took over the buildings, systems, and some of the staff of predecessor central banks. The Banking and Payment Authority of Kosovo was a radically new institution, but it took over the buildings, systems, and some of the staff of the National Bank of Kosovo and of the Kosovo branch of the Yugoslav payment bureau. New systems and ways of operating needed to be built from existing bases. They were not constructed on a blank slate and dealing with existing staff posed many serious challenges.

Though the **Palestine Monetary Authority** had no predecessor nor any existing buildings, staff or systems, there were existing arrangements in place for banking and payments, which provided the experience and frame of reference from which new approaches and systems needed to be built. In some instances a new institution may be easier to develop than reforming an existing one, but not always. In any event, the management of the new (or old) institution will be working with the human capital and experience available, and change and new knowledge take time to develop properly.

Progress in developing the **Banking and Payment Authority of Kosovo** was slower than it needed to be because when establishing new systems and procedures, we underestimated the difficulties of overcoming earlier training. Not enough effort was made to obtain local buy-in to the need for the new systems. Also, training in the new systems was inadequate.

In all cases, political sensitivities and conflicts need to be understood and dealt with. The time and resources required are easily underestimated.

POLICIES MUST REFLECT CAPABILITIES

Some policies are more demanding than others. What is possible will depend on what is in place and what resources can be drawn on.

Dollarization can be implemented quickly and easily, but with its own limitations and political drawbacks. **Bosnia and Herzegovina** relied extensively on existing institutions for several years and the Currency Board arrangements minimized the demands on the new Central Bank while it focused on its establishment and on reintegrating the monetary and payment systems. This was as much a political as a technical challenge and gave the time needed for the gradual reestablishment of inter-regional trust. Dollarization in **Timor Leste** provides a similar example.

The adoption of a new accounting system at the **Banking and Payment Authority of Kosovo** also proved a major challenge to the staff. The difficulties in modernizing information systems even in the United States (take the recent example of the $100 million dollars spent by the FBI on a new case management system that failed and was abandoned), illustrates the difficulties even in favorable environments.

The monetary regimes adopted in **Afghanistan and Iraq** are much more demanding, with much less by way of usable existing systems to draw on. Serious errors in implementing monetary policy have been avoided by the protection established in the new central bank laws against central-bank lending to government and by the current adequacy of donor-provided international reserves with which to stabilize the exchange rate. The results have not been as good, though it is still early. The security situation, especially in Iraq, has prevented much of the development and capacity building at the central bank that might otherwise have been possible.

The design and introduction of a new currency is a once-off undertaking for which relevant local experience is not likely to be found. Foreign assistance will invariably be needed and was effectively used in Bosnia and Herzegovina, Timor Leste, Afghanistan, and Iraq.

POLITICAL SUPPORT FOR REFORMS IS NEEDED

Other than for purely technical matters, reforms in the financial sector are difficult to implement without local understanding and support and are less likely to take root and survive.

304 ONE CURRENCY FOR BOSNIA

Even in the presence of NATO troops, the local political leadership in **Bosnia and Herzegovina** would not agree on and accept a new countrywide currency for over two years after the December 1995 Paris signing of the Dayton Peace Agreement. The three Joint Presidents did not agree on a new central bank law creating the Central Bank of Bosnia and Herzegovina until May 1997. The CBBH opened its doors on August 11, 1997. The new bank notes were not issued until June 22, 1998. However, the very slow pace of these steps built sufficient local support so that the new central bank and its currency became an enormous success in a bitterly torn country with few successes in its recent history.

Though heavy-handed compared with Bosnia and Herzegovina, the process by which the central bank and banking laws were adopted in Kosovo by the **United Nations Interim Administration Mission in Kosovo (UNMIK)**—one of the few other instances, along with East Timor, of post-conflict reconstruction lacking a sovereign counterpart— included serious discussion with and among Kosovars.

The goal of government and enterprise efficiency, which was important for economic development and thus ultimate success in statebuilding, often conflicted with short-term needs to maintain household income and security, which was also important for public support of the state. For this reason the steps to shed redundant workers and thus make institutions more efficient were often implemented slowly and with delay. The slow pace of the downsizing of the BPK in Kosovo is an example. However, such delays also ran the risk that padded staffs and poor work ethics would be ingrained or perpetuated for a long time. This also illustrates the tension between short-term and long-term considerations. The difficulties in implementing the Universal Teller Window systems and new accounting systems in Kosovo also illustrate the impossibility of reform without local support.

A number of the reforms adopted in Iraq by the Coalition Provisional Authority with minimal local consultation and buy-in were simply ignored once sovereignty had been returned to Iraqis. Thus the merger of three of the state banks into a fourth and the resolution of the central bank's claims on the government adopted by the CPA were never implemented.

POSTSCRIPT

After this "final" visit, I went back one more time. (Well, it's the Balkans after all.) On April 11, 2003, I attended a conference hosted by the CBBH. The conference on "The Monetary Policy Role of Currency Boards: History and Practice" was a celebration of the first five years of the CBBH and was primarily the result of the work and inspiration of Marko Škreb, the former governor of the Croatian National Bank. Marko had been hired by the IMF as an advisor to the Research Department of the CBBH.

Scott Brown, who had planned to attend from the IMF, was preempted to work on the planning for the post-conflict reconstruction of Iraq. I delivered his regrets for him and later visited him in Baghdad while on mission to Iraq in July 2003. One month later, when a terrorist/insurgent explosion destroyed the UN headquarters in Baghdad, the Canal Hotel, and killed Sergio Vieira De Mello, Scott was seriously injured. He permanently lost much of the use of his left arm but miraculously survived the loss of almost half of his blood from head wounds. The closing two paragraphs of my remarks "modestly" proclaimed:

"The CBBH has continued to develop its capacities. The public's acceptance and confidence in its currency has grown significantly. One of the most dramatic demonstrations of that confidence, to my mind, was the fact that when German mark bank notes held by the public in Bosnia and Herzegovina were converted at the beginning of last year, about one-third of the total of DM 4.3 billion was deposited in local banks, one-third was exchanged for KM bank notes and only one-third was kept as foreign currency (euro). The success of the CBBH that we celebrate today can only be fully appreciated by remembering the difficulties that it had to overcome in its beginning and early years. The CBBH has developed into a solid foundation for the economic rebuilding of Bosnia and Herzegovina. It has also contributed impressively to the rebuilding of trust and cooperation between Bosnia's ethnic groups, a job far from finished. It has helped demonstrate that a level playing

305

field, cooperation, and fair economic competition can serve mutual self-interests. It is a great honor for me to be here to celebrate this great accomplishment with you."

Peter had hoped to announce at this conference the successor arrangements for the CBBH, but it was not to be. The Dayton agreement had specified a currency board arrangement for six years and the six years would be up in August. After that time the government of BiH was free to adopt any monetary arrangements it wanted. The Joint Presidency had, however, announced that the currency board arrangements would continue. The mystery over the new Governor and Board, however, lasted a few more months.

The following email exchange seems an appropriate place to conclude these few years of history.

July 28, 2003

Peter,

Marko Škreb brought to my attention your designation as best CB Governor of the area in Financial Magazine. Wonderful. Congratulations.

Warren

Peter's reply:

August 13, 2003

Warren,

Thanks very much. The CBBH was also recognized as the best central bank in the region. As you can imagine, my staff are very proud of that—and justifiably so. It is good to see their efforts being recognized outside the country and it is also good for BiH to get some positive publicity for a change.

The first six years of the CBBH came to an end on Sunday. That meant there had to be a new Board of five Bosnian citizens and a Bosnian Governor. The new Board had its first meeting on Monday, 11 August. Manojlo has been reappointed (but not Kasim or Jure), I continue as a member (now that I am a Bosnian citizen) and Kemal Kozaric has become a Board member, while continuing as a Vice Governor. So we have a good degree of continuity. Of the two new members, one was until last week a member of the State Council of Ministers. But she resigned in order to come onto our Board—as she had to do under the very good

CBBH Law!!!

Just to show that not everything goes completely smoothly in BiH, the 5th position is still vacant. The first person the Presidency nominated (a Serb) was removed by OHR before he started. The Presidency have suggested someone else (also a Serb) but OHR aren't too happy with him either and have not yet given their approval. But we can operate with 4 members so we proceeded on Monday. I was asked to defer the meeting but declined to do so and the meeting proceeded without problems.

The Board appointed the Governor for the next 6 years: me for the period to 31/12/04 and Kemal Kozaric for the period 1/1/05 to 10/8/09. So we are now in the second phase of the CBBH—and things look much the same. I think it has been a very successful transition—almost a non-event which is how central bank matters should be.

Regards,
Peter N

APPENDIX I
THE MAIN MONETARY POLICY REGIMES

There are several fundamentally different ways that a country can pursue a price level (purchasing power) objective for its currency. One is simply to administer prices in accordance with that objective. This approach requires (ultimately, at least) state-administered investment, production, and distribution, and has historically been associated with central planning, inefficiency, low levels of income, and long lines for poor-quality goods. The desire to allocate resources on the basis of the profit incentive and market-determined price signals of consumer demand and the cost of production require the abandonment of administered prices. This note discusses control of the value of money when the prices of goods and services are determined by the market.

When individual prices are market-determined, the aggregate price level (i.e., the value of money) is determined by the market so as to equate the public's demand for money with the banking system's supply of it. The achievement of an inflation target, therefore, requires a quantity of money consistent with the public's demand for it at the targeted price level.[1] The three most common general approaches to determining the quantity of money are (a) to limit its creation by banks by directly controlling the amount of credit they may extend, (b) to fix the exchange rate of the currency to another currency or unit whose value behaves in the desired way and to allow the quantity of money to be determined by the public's demand for it at the value that has been fixed by the exchange rate, and (c) to limit the creation of money by banks by controlling the amount of reserves (central bank money) available to them.

The first of these approaches, which generally takes the form of an aggregate target for bank credit that is administratively allocated among individual banks, retains some of the features and disadvantages of central planning. By determining the growth in individual bank assets administratively, the incentive for individual banks to work harder to

309

deliver better services more efficiently (i.e., at lower cost) is greatly diminished. The market is not allowed to determine the relative growth of individual banks on the basis of their success in satisfying their customers. Economic efficiency and growth are, therefore, better served by indirect techniques of monetary control, i.e., approaches (b) or (c) above.[2]

The approach of a fixed exchange rate has considerable advantages: it is easy to administer and does not require knowledge of the public's demand for money, which is particularly difficult to estimate during periods of economic reform. This requires, however, that government borrowing be limited to amounts that can be raised from the public.[3] Fixing the value of money exogenously (e.g., to the dollar, euro, SDR, gold, or a commodity basket) is not only the easiest monetary policy to administer, assuming that the fiscal deficit can be appropriately limited, but probably provides the quickest way to establish the public's faith in the stability of such money's value. If the rules of a fixed exchange rate are followed, the value of money will be the same as the value of the currency or basket of currencies or goods to which the exchange rate of the currency has been fixed.

A currency board is the simplest monetary regime with an externally fixed value, and the simplest one to administer, and it has the highest credibility. A currency board simply buys and/or sells its currency in exchange for the currency or commodity(s) in terms of which its value is fixed. The rules of a currency board require the monetary authority to hold the asset to which the domestic money's value is fixed to the full extent of the currency it has issued (i.e., 100 percent backing). The monetary authority would accomplish this automatically by issuing its currency only by buying the currency (or other assets) to which its value is fixed. If anyone holding its currency wishes to exchange it for the asset(s) backing it, the monetary authority must redeem its currency at the currency's fixed price (only small margins—bid/ask spreads—are allowed).

These requirements—that the central bank must buy or sell its currency at a fixed price—ensure that the public has just the amount of the currency that it wants to hold at that price. In short, a fixed exchange rate as administered by a currency board supplies exactly the quantity of domestic currency the public wants to hold (i.e., equates the supply of and demand for money) by an automatic market mechanism, while ensuring aggregate price behavior equal to that of the unit to which the currency's value is fixed. There is no need for the monetary authority to estimate the public's demand for money in order to know how much it needs to supply to hit the desired price target.

Mention should also be made of the option of using someone else's currency (so-called dollarization) and having no national currency at all.[4] Dollarization works in the same fundamental way as a currency board to regulate the quantity of (foreign) money so that it is equal to the public's demand at its foreign-determined value. If, for example, dollar prices in Panama, which has no currency of its own, rise relative to dollar prices in the U.S., the dollars circulating in Panama will be spent in the U.S. and the cheaper goods imported. Panamanian goods will tend to be more expensive than similar goods in the U.S. or elsewhere and exports will fall. Larger imports and reduced exports will cause an outflow (or reduce the inflow) of dollars. This market-induced reduction in Panama's quantity of money will reverse (or prevent) the relative increase in dollar prices in Panama.

The advantage of a currency board over dollarization is that the monetary authority that issues its own currency will benefit from the profit of its currency monopoly (so called "seigniorage"). With dollarization, this profit goes to the foreign central bank whose currency is used. A national currency may also have nation building advantages.

A fixed exchange rate regime without the currency board restrictions would work in the same way to produce the quantity of money the public demands but would open the possibility for the central bank to buy and sell domestic assets as an additional instrument for influencing the quantity of money. The central bank's monetary liabilities would no longer need to be fully backed by foreign assets. This has the advantage of accommodating various demand and external supply shocks without the need for adjustments in the domestic price level. However, it is subject to abuse or misjudgment that can result in a domestic money supply that is not matched with demand. Such a mismatch would put pressure on the fixed exchange rate and could result in the loss of the ability of the central bank to defend the exchange rate as its foreign exchange reserves declined. For this reason fixed exchange rate regimes that are not fully backed with foreign currency can be subject to speculative exchange rate attacks.

An alternative market approach to equating the supply of and demand for money is to fix the money supply and allow the market to determine its value (i.e., to determine the price level). This approach contrasts with the fixed exchange rate approach in which the value of money is fixed and the market determines its supply, and obviously requires that exchange rates be market-determined. Fixing, or more generally, controlling the quantity of money in an effort to stabilize its value requires a reasonably good estimate of the public's demand for money and the ability of the central bank to control its supply. This is a challenging task for any central bank.

In most economies for which estimates have been made, money demand has been found to have a relatively stable relationship with nominal income and interest rates (or more exactly, with the opportunity cost of holding money—defined as the difference between the average rate of interest on financial market instruments and the average interest return on money). Estimates generally find a relatively stable relationship between real money demand (money deflated by a general price index) and real income (nominal or money income deflated by the same price index) and an interest rate. These empirical findings for medium-to-longer-run relationships are in keeping with economic theory. For a given level of real income and interest rates, the demand for money tends to be proportional to the price level, i.e., other things equal, doubling the price level will tend to double the demand for nominal money and vice-versa. A stable price level, therefore, requires that the supply of money grow at about the same rate as real income.

The alternative of market-determined exchange rates and central-bank-determined money supply often takes the form of adhering to a monetary target or rule. An example of such a rule is the so-called Friedman rule of a constant growth in M2 of 3 to 5 percent for the U.S. The Friedman rule was based on the historical long-run value of money demand (or its secular growth) in relation to income (velocity of circulation) and the historical growth rate for income (GDP) of about 3 percent per year in the U.S. If those values continued in the future on average over periods of several years, growth in M2 of 3 to 5 percent would produce stable prices (inflation of 0 to 2 percent per annum).

There is a large body of literature on the demand for money, and the subject will not be further considered here.[5]

The latest development in monetary policy thinking has been to anchor monetary policy directly to an inflation target. A growing number of countries with developed central banks have adopted "inflation targeting," which has the following features. The central bank accepts responsibility for setting monetary policy so as to achieve an explicit inflation target two or so years in the future (because of the lag in the response of prices to current monetary policy). While the central bank is thus made accountable for future inflation outcomes, which tends to anchor policy to the medium term, it is able to take into account all information currently available to it in determining what is needed and appropriate now. Actual inflation at any moment (which is the result of monetary policy in the past and thus cannot be changed with monetary policy now) may differ from the target for reasons other than past monetary policy (oil price shocks, etc.) and will need to be explained. But the central bank will have its eyes on the future. Full central bank transparency is key for inflation targeting. If its efforts to achieve price stability are credible in the market, market behavior will expect future prices to match the inflation target and will thus help the central bank achieve its targets with minimal real income disturbances.

APPENDIX II
THE QUANTITY THEORY OF MONEY

$$MV \equiv Pq,$$

where $M \equiv$ quantity of money;
$V \equiv$ the velocity of circulation of money (the inverse of the income elasticity of demand for M);
$P \equiv$ Price level; and
$q \equiv$ real national income.

The supply-must-equal-demand formulation of this famous equation results from replacing V (the number of times a dollar is spent per period) with its reciprocal, $k \equiv 1/V$:

$$M \equiv kPq,$$

The left-hand side of the equation is the quantity of money, which is controlled by the central bank, and the right-hand side is the public's demand for it, which depends on its value (the price level P), real national income, and k. Restating these relationships in growth rate terms gives, to a first approximation:

$$\Delta M/M = \Delta k/k + \Delta P/P + \Delta q/q$$

This expression says that the rate of growth of the quantity of money must equal the rates of growth of its demand, which largely reflects the rate of growth of real income and inflation. The central proposition of the quantity theory of money is that k (or the velocity of circulation) and real income (or its growth) are largely independent of the behavior of M. If so, M determines P, or the growth rate of the money supply determines the inflation rate (less the growth rate in real income and any trend change in k). A stable price level, therefore, requires that the supply of money grow at about the same rate as real income.

The modern world with banks is a bit more complicated because what we have come to mean by money also includes the public's deposits at banks. Central banks no longer control the quantity of money directly.

They control what we call the monetary base (sometimes called reserve money, or B), which consists of currency in circulation (currency held by the public, or C, plus currency in the vaults of banks, or VC) plus bank deposits with the central bank (R).

$$B \equiv C + VC + R$$

The money stock itself is made up of central bank money (Currency or C) held by the public and bank money (deposits or D) of the public:

$$M \equiv C + D$$

The quantity of money, defined as currency plus bank deposits, depends on the amount of "base money" created by the central bank (currency plus bank reserve deposits with the central bank) and the amount of deposits created by the process of banks lending out some of the currency deposited with them, some of which is redeposited with the same or another bank, which lends out some of it, and so on. This is described in Money and Banking textbooks as the deposit multiplier. The amount of deposits the public and their banks can make is constrained by the amount of base money created by the central bank. The relationship between the quantity of money and the money base is called the "money multiplier" (m).

$$M \equiv mB$$

Thus the central bank's control of the quantity of money involves controlling its own creation of base money in light of the influence it has on the money multiplier and its forecast of the influence of other factors on the multiplier. If you didn't take the sophomore class on Money and Banking in college, these are among the things you missed.

Controlling and/or forecasting the money multiplier is not always easy but historically has not been an important source of inflation (excessive monetary growth). Inflation is invariably the result of the excessive creation of central bank money (B) and this has most often been as the result of pressure to finance the government. Modern trends in central banking have attempted to protect central banks from such pressure in various ways. Dollarization, or use of another country's currency, is the firmest protection there can be. A very close second is to issue your own currency under currency board rules.

APPENDIX III
DESIGNS FOR KM BANK NOTES[1]

The Dayton agreement provided for a single central bank with *"the sole authority for issuing currency and for monetary policy throughout Bosnia and Herzegovina."* The IMF's negotiations with the tripartite political leadership in Bosnia and Herzegovina over the new Central Bank Law compromised on the meaning of a single currency and accepted that two versions of the currency would be issued. The two versions would have "common design elements as well as distinct design elements for the Federation of Bosnia and Herzegovina and the Republika Srpska."[2] The international community was determined that the two versions would look as much alike as possible, and each had to be acceptable to both Entities.

Discussions of note designs got underway soon after the adoption of the Central Bank Law in May 1997. Each "side" submitted designs for their Entity's version. The first RS designs had Serb patriots on one side. One was Gavrilo Princep, who shot Archduke Ferdinand in Sarajevo. These designs were rejected by the CBBH Board. As explained by then CBBH Governor Peter Nicholl: "On the reverse of that set was a very attractive painting—the most famous Serb painting of all they told me, 'The Retreat from Kosovo' in 1389. In a meeting with then RS president Krajisnek, I asked him what it was. When he told me, I pretended to be naive about regional geography and said I hadn't realized Kosovo was part of Bosnia. He said of course that it isn't—to which I said, "So why on earth do you think we will agree to put it on a CBBH Bosnian bank note when it isn't even part of the country?" He reluctantly removed the painting. But at a meeting in Pale a few weeks later, which the then-High Representative attended in order to try and make progress on the design issue, Krajisnek reintroduced the painting. I said that this had already been rejected as it had no relationship to Bosnia, and that it was a step backwards. To my surprise, and even more to Krajisnek's surprise, the High Representative stood up and said the President clearly didn't want to negotiate seriously—and walked out."[3]

The Federation members first submitted simple designs with plants, etc., and clearly marked as coupons. They were rejected by Governor Nicholl because the two designs bore no resemblance to each other.

Eventually the Serbs came up with a set of writers on their design. In late December 1997, the Federation Board members tabled a set of writers too, one of which, Mesa Selimovic, was the same as one the Serbs had submitted. At that, the Serb member said they would take the writers off their design—since they wanted the designs to be different.

In January 1998, President Krajisnek with some reluctance said he would agree to the designs that had been unilaterally developed by Governor Nicholl as long as the RS one had the entity Coat of Arms on it. The Federation Presidents didn't want the Entity Coats of Arms but said that if the RS had it on theirs, they would have it on the Federation's version too. That would have defeated the purpose of trying to get the two designs to be as similar as possible. Thus the High Representative took the decision not to include the Entity Coats of Arms. He also accepted Governor Nicholl's suggestion to remove "Coupon" from the designs.

The results, illustrated above with the 100 KM notes, were notes that looked very much alike except for different writers. In addition, the Cyrillic name of the Central Bank is on top for the RS version, and the Latin version is on top for the Federation version.

The Joint Presidents accepted Mesa Selimovic, who had been submitted earlier by both the RS and Federation on both the RS and

Federation versions of the five dinar notes finally issued. Meša Selimović was born in Tuzla on April 26, 1910, and lived at different times in Belgrade and Sarajevo. His first novel, entitled "Insulted Man," was published in 1947. Other novels included "Silences," which was published in 1961, "Dervish and Death" in 1966, "Island" in 1974, "Memories" in 1976, and "Circle" in 1983. He died in Belgrade in 1982.

The other writer, initially on both lists, was Ivo Andrić, who received the Nobel Prize for Literature in 1961. He was born on October 10, 1892, in Dolac near Travnik, but his parents lived in Sarajevo. He studied in Zagreb and lived at various times in Belgrade, Trieste, Marseille, Paris, Berlin, Brussels, and Geneva. When a 200 KM note was later added to the initial denominations there was only one version for the whole country with Andrić's face on it. This single version design was approved by the Joint Presidency.

APPENDIX IV
THE NATURE OF MONEY

The purpose of money is to facilitate trade. Even when transacting without money (barter), ancient traders sought means to lower the search and transaction costs of their activities. Hence central market places developed, with established locations of specific types of products. Camel caravans (unlike the later door-to-door salesmen) were composed of traders who knew what to deliver to those producing the goods they wished to acquire. "Money" was an important cost-reducing innovation that eliminated the need for transactors to seek out counterparts having what they wanted and who wanted what they had—the so-called "double coincidence of wants." Money was not wanted in its own right and was used only as an intermediate store of value between transactions for the goods and services actually wanted.

COMMODITIES

The initial monies were commodities that already had well-established market values and that had other convenient properties as well (see below). The early traveling traders (caravans) may have played an important role in the development of money as a result of their need to accept something in exchange for their goods that could be easily carried, i.e., that was portable and durable. Precious metals such as gold, silver, and copper met these criteria and were quickly adopted.

Standardization is a means of broadening the acceptability and lowering the costs of producing and/or using a product. Standardization has been important for the development of money. The time consuming and costly task of verifying the weight and purity of commodity monies was made easier by minting coins that carried the seal of the person (sovereign) vouching for the commodity content of the coin. Milling was developed to reveal and thus stop the practice of shaving metal from a coin. "Debasement" emerged as a form of fraudulently reducing the precious metal content of a coin. The history of money has never been without the need to stay ahead of counterfeiters.

BANK DEPOSITS

Initially, payments required the physical transfer of money. An important early development that lowered the cost of making payments was the use of written instructions as a means of transferring the ownership of gold without actually physically delivering the commodity. Storing commodity money and issuing warehouse receipt (bills) and bills of exchange (checks) as a means to transfer ownership of the commodity had a number of advantages (and disadvantages) that lowered the cost and increased the convenience of using money. The development of banking and the use of deposited money for loans and other investments (thus raising the return on deposits) further lowered the cost of using money but increased its risk and complexity.

The use of checks or other forms of authorization to transfer the ownership of bank balances also introduced other features that were attractive in some cases (e.g., record keeping, authentication of the genuineness of money,[1] and safekeeping). On the other hand, the "value" of a check (meaning the certainty that the stipulated amount of money will be delivered and the uncertainty over the length of time required to make delivery) is less certain than is the value of money physically delivered on the spot.

Transferring ownership of bank balances is now the backbone of all modern means of payment. Aside from currency notes, all other means of payment (even when combined with the extension of credit, as with the use of credit cards) involve the use of different technologies or legal approaches to transferring ownership of bank balances.[2]

BILLS/NOTES

Bills (currency notes) represented certificates of ownership of the underlying monetary commodity. Unlike bank drafts (checks), however, they tended to circulate from person to person without being redeemed for the commodity they were a claim to, unless the holder of the notes planned to travel to where the notes would not be easily recognized. The obligation of the issuer to redeem the note provided a market mechanism for regulating the quantity of notes issued.[3]

In its early days, the United States had many different currency notes issued by banks. There were one dollar bills from banks X, Y, and Z. Bank notes traded at different prices and tended to trade at a discount the farther they were used from their issuer (information traveled much slower in those days). The cost of evaluating the authenticity (counterfeit) and safety (financial soundness of the issuer) of each brand of dollar bill was considerable (but with today's technology would be much cheaper). It is estimated that about one-third of all notes in circulation in the U.S. during that period were counterfeit.

The complexity and cost of multiple currency notes created an opportunity to further reduce the cost of using money. The risk of loss from accepting a particular issuer's money could be eliminated by ensuring that all issuers are safe (e.g., by limiting the issuing of money to banks that operate in accordance with agreed prudential rules), by insuring the money that they issue (much like deposit insurance)[4] or by replacing the multiple issue with one "riskless" monopoly issuer (an official central bank). Government-issued currency (or base money—currency and deposits with the central bank) has become the standard in every country.

Thus the earlier obligation for issuers of bank notes to redeem them for "real" money, was replaced by a monopoly issue of currency notes by the official monetary authorities of each country (generally the central banks), that were made "legal tender," which obligated others to accept them in payment of all financial obligations. Currency notes are therefore no longer redeemable for anything and have become "real" money themselves. Everyone accepts them because "governments don't go bankrupt" (because of legal tender laws) and no special requirements (such as having a bank account or a membership in VISA) are necessary either to use or receive them. The physical delivery of currency notes (cash) constitutes final settlement of a financial obligation.

TOKEN COINS

The evolution of bank notes from warehouse receipts to fiat currencies occurred with coins as well. It was not so long ago that coins of cheap but durable metals, with a much smaller metallic than monetary value, began to replace their "full" valued cousins of earlier years.

Each new means of payment introduced a complex set of properties with advantages and disadvantages. This can be illustrated by the check, an example of what is known as a "debit transfer."[5] Despite the very high costs, risks, and uncertainties of check payments, checks are a very popular means of payment in the United States, because they can be presented as evidence of the intention to pay at the time of a purchase (both parties to the transaction get something on the spot).[6] Unlike Giro or payment order payments (so called "credit transfers"), which are issued by the payer to his bank, a check is delivered first to the payee (the merchant). This feature seems to be the source of the check's great popularity. But before the payment really takes place (until settlement is "final," as payment experts like to say), the check must be sent to the payer's bank (after having been provisionally deposited in the merchant's account with its bank). If the payer has sufficient funds in his account, the payer's bank issues instructions to its Federal Reserve Bank to debit its account at the FRB and credit the account of the merchant's bank with that bank's Federal Reserve Bank, etc.

The check might bounce for lack of funds in the payer's account. And worse yet, there is no fixed period over which it might bounce (though check processing rules require banks to credit the account of a depositor after a given number of days that reflects how far away the payer's bank is from the payee's bank). Thus the settlement cannot be known to be final until after a waiting period over which the probability rises that the check is OK as time passes without it bouncing. Very elaborate and costly systems have been developed to process (collect) checks. The Federal Reserve System maintains a fleet of airplanes to facilitate the physical transport of checks as rapidly as possible. Giro or funds transfers do not suffer from these problems because the payment instruction is sent to the payer's bank first, which never transfers funds to the payee's bank unless the payer has them in the first place.

Payment specialists hate checks (preferring "credit transfers"). And the public (in a few countries at least) loves them. Electronic payments, by dramatically compressing the time involved in transmitting and processing payment instructions will "virtually" eliminate the distinction between debit and credit transfers.

Two more recent innovations in payments—the credit card and the debit card—further illustrate the enormous variety of arrangements that are possible. The debit card is a kind of electronic check that is delivered in person. It is made possible by a number of modern technological developments, the most important of which is the ability of high-speed, dedicated, telecommunications lines to link a card reader on the premises of a merchant with the computer of the user's bank to verify that the card holder is who she says she is (that the Personal Identification Number—**PIN**—that she provides is correct for that card) and that her account with the bank that issued the debit card has sufficient funds for the payment.[7] The payment is deducted immediately from her account, and instructions are sent over Fed-Wire (another dedicated telecommunications line) to debit her bank's account with its Federal Reserve Bank and to credit the account of the merchant's bank with its Federal Reserve Bank, which in turn will credit the merchant's account. A debit card payment has the advantage that the merchant has almost no risk of non-payment. The card user, however, loses that amount of money from her bank account immediately; and unless she records the transaction in her checkbook, she may easily lose track of her current balance.

Debit cards have not been as popular in the United States as credit cards, in part because a credit card combines a payment (the merchant receives almost immediate payment, though the payer may contest the payments for up to two months—the card issuer acts as a trusted third party in resolving payment disputes) with an extension of pre-approved credit by the card issuer.[8] Thus the payment can be made without concern for one's bank balance up to an agreed credit limit and the user enjoys the interest free use of money if the balance is paid off each month. Credit card payments also produce an accounting report of transactions that many find more convenient than their bank statements.[9] Unlike cash payments, both credit and debit cards automatically create a record of each transaction. Cash payments create records only as a separate, conscious act.

Early monies were commodities with convenient properties. Modern money consists of cash issued by the monetary authority and bank deposits. Payment with money has always meant, and continues to mean, however, the transfer of ownership of the appropriate amount of money. Cash, bank deposits, debit cards, checks, payment orders, traveler's checks, digital cash, electronic purses, and stored value cards are all means of payment; but some are money and others are instruments (contracts, technologies, instructions) for transferring ownership of money. While economists generally define money as cash and bank deposits, only the currency and coins issued by the central bank are defined as legal tender in the laws of most countries. Bank deposits must ultimately be convertible into cash; and checks, payment orders, debit cards, and all of the new digital/electronic means of payment are ways of transferring the ownership of money. Thus the central bank is able to leave the creation and supply of bank money and means of payment other than cash to the private sector. Because of the growth in these modern means of payment (i.e., of transferring ownership of money) fewer and fewer payments are made directly with traditional money. Thus the share of central bank money in the total has steadily declined.

Modern technology and telecommunications are further changing these distinctions.[10]

Digital cash (prepaid, smart cards or computer chips) introduces something rather new to the lexicon of money. When providers of smart "cash" cards claim that they put electronic cash on the cards, they really mean that they have encoded messages on the card that give the owner of the message the ability to acquire a bank balance (whenever she wants to collect it).

Thus digital cash, in one sense, is a means of payment that involves an authorization to transfer the ownership of bank balances. Like a check, digital money could be seen as a means of payment that is not itself money. In this light, digital cash would be considered a new means of delivering money rather than a new form of money. However, I think that the prepaid feature of digital cash, which makes it a claim on the issuer (presumably a bank) rather than the current owner of the card, makes it more useful to add digital cash to the definition of money. Money would then be defined as paper cash, digital cash, and bank balances of the non-bank public. As a practical matter, the amount of digital cash in existence would probably be measured by banks' liabilities to redeem it. What form these liabilities take in the accounts of banks will depend on market and/or regulatory requirements attached to the issue of digital cash. For example, banks might be required to place to a general account all amounts collected (by debit to customers' deposits or by receipt of paper cash) against the issue of digital cash, in effect a 100 percent reserve requirement.

While digital cash, like paper cash, may circulate from hand to hand (or purse to purse) without being collected from the bank that issued it (redeemed), it is the requirement of issuers to redeem it on demand that makes it possible to leave the creation of digital cash to the market. Should that link ever be broken, direct central bank control over the issue of digital cash would be needed to preserve overall monetary control and price stability.

NOTES

Chapter 2
1. http://www.imf.org/external/about.htm.
2. "Financial Relations Among Countries of the Former Soviet Union," IMF Economic Review No. 1, (Washington: International Monetary Fund, February 1994).

Chapter 3
1. Karen Flamme, "A Brief History of Our Nation's Paper Money" 1995 Annual Report, Federal Reserve Bank of San Francisco.
2. Bank of England, "A Brief History of Banknotes," http://www.bankofengland.co.uk/banknotes/about/history.htm.
3. Committee of Scottish Clearing Banks. "History of Scottish Banknotes," http://www.scotbanks.org.uk/banknote_history.php.
4. Loans from the IMF to its members are operationally and legally conducted as currency swaps. The IMF sells the currency of a member with a strong currency for the currency of the purchasing member. Repayment (called a repurchase) takes the form of reversing the swap.
5. "The Amended Consolidated Indictment, submitted on 7 March 2002 pursuant to the Decision of the Trial Chamber dated 4 March 2002, generally alleges that, between 1 July 1991 and 30 December 1992, Momčilo Krajišnik, Biljana Plavsić and others, including Slobodan Milosević, Zeljko Raznatović aka 'Arkan' and Radovan Karadzić participated in the joint criminal enterprise, planned, instigated, ordered, committed or otherwise aided and abetted the planning, preparation or execution of the partial destruction of the Bosnian Muslim and Bosnian Croatian national, ethnical, racial or religious groups, in the territories within Bosnia and Herzegovina. The objective of the joint criminal enterprise was primarily achieved through a manifest pattern of persecutions as alleged in the Indictment." http://www.un.org/icty/glance/krajisnik.htm.

Chapter 4

1. Giro account systems found in Europe and the UK, often in post offices, are similar to the more recently developed ACH (Automated Clearing House) payments becoming more common in the U.S. Rather than paying a bill by sending a check to the vender, the customer with a Giro account issues a payment order to her bank to transfer funds to the vendor. This might be a standing order to pay monthly bills as they are received. Checks on the other hand are given to the vendor who deposits them in his account. But before he receives use of such funds, his bank must send the check to the customer's bank to verify that sufficient funds are in the customer's account (which is then debited and the vendor's account credited—through a clearing house or central bank).

Chapter 6

1. The flow of information and control in centralized systems is very different than in decentralized market systems. Soviet payment systems passed payment orders from each branch of each bank to the nearest office of the central bank. From there they went to the main branch of which that office was a part to the head office of the central bank. Information flowed in a straight line from the bank branch to the center. In decentralized market systems, payment orders from each branch of a bank flow to the headquarters of the bank and from the bank HQ to the central bank (often via the nearest branch of the central bank). This decentralized structure gives individual banks better control over the operation of their branches and of their bank-wide liquidity, even though it seems more roundabout in some respects.
2. The monetary base, or "base" money, refers to the monetary liabilities of the central bank (currency in circulation plus bank current account deposits with the central bank) that form part of the money supply (currency) or the basis on which bank money (deposits) is produced.

Chapter 8

1. Mr. Zubak is a member of the Presidency, Mr. Tomić is the Vice-Chairman of the Council of Ministers, and Mr. Pelivan is a member of the Board of the CBBH.

2. This department covers several areas: Human Resources, Legal, Budget and Accounting, Information Technology, and General Support.

3. This statement abstracts for historical claims that may still exist on the previous NBBH from the period of the recent war.

4. The exception would be the DM banknotes that the CBBH must maintain in order to honor its currency board obligations. As long as the payment bureaus bought as well as sold KM for DM with the public as agent of the CBBH, they would need to keep DM banknotes belonging to the CBBH on their premises.

5. The amount was limited by the government's holdings (and receipts) of KM (or of DM with which to purchase KM).

6. Until that moment, a payment from an RS enterprise or bank to a FRY enterprise or bank could be made by debiting the payor's account with the SPP and crediting the payee's account with the SDK. The reserve accounts of the payor's and payee's banks with the NBY were debited and credited respectively.

7. Prior to the opening of the CBBH, banks' YUD reserves were deposited with the NBRS (the branch of the NBY in RS); thus the statement that banks had deposits with the SPP should be read to mean that they had deposits with their central bank, which were reflected in their Giro account balances kept at the SPP. The closing of the NBRS has complicated this straightforward description (see the footnote after next).

8. Our understanding of the situation at the time was based on the monetary data reported by the NBRS, which was not fully reliable.

9. It was a common, if somewhat confusing, practice in former Yugoslav republics to refer to the accounting records kept by the payment bureaus as deposits in the payment bureaus. In fact, all "deposits" (with the exception of deposits of cash for safekeeping, which were held as cash by the payment bureau on behalf of the depositor) in these payment bureaus were merely accounting records of deposits with banks.

10. Of course, these deposits could be used to make YUD payments within the RS to the extent that banks and the public remained willing to accept them. But their complete delinking from the central

bank that created them would eventually turn them into an "asset" that no one would want to be left holding. Subsequently I learned that such a situation existed in the Kurdish regions of Iraq until their so-called Swiss dinars were replaced by a new, post-Saddam, national currency. Strangely the Swiss dinar continued to circulate (with a fixed supply) for ten years at an increasingly appreciated value to the Saddam dinar that replaced it in the south. I hope that someone is doing a Ph.D. thesis on this.

11. If the existing level of YUD deposits could have been increased and then used to pay taxes, taxpayers might have had an incentive (at some exchange rate) to buy YUD with DM for this purpose. If this were to occur, the government's claim on the NBY could have become larger than the SPP's current claim. This additional claim would have taken the form of an increase in the government's holdings of YUD banknotes.

12. The mission was not able to obtain reliable deposit data that would have allowed more exact estimates of remaining YUD deposits.

Chapter 9

1. See Coats and Frankel, 1980.

2. Frankly, and sadly, I have little confidence in the accuracy of much of what appears in the report. I think that it would be scandalous for USAID to put its name on a document that says things (without further support) like "there is the probability that ZPP is using these funds to generate, but not report on, additional cash flows through illegal lending and investment activities." (Page 35) And "It is suspected, but not yet definitively proven, that . . ." (Page 29). Not only has it "not yet [been] definitively proven," but no evidence is provided of any sort.

3. Yugolslavia, soon to become Serbia and Montenegro, chose to keep its payment bureau, the original SDK, but to transform its operations.

Chapter 11

1. Adopted from Coats, Warren, "Currency and Sovereignty: Why Monetary Policy is Critical" in *Peace and the Public Purse: Economic*

Policies for Postwar Statebuilding, James K. Boyce and Madalene O'Donnell, editors (New York, Lynne Rienner, 2007).

2. "FBI Pushed Ahead With Troubled Software," By Dan Eggen, *The Washington Post,* June 6, 2005, p 1.

Appendix I

1. For a more general discussion of these issues see any standard textbook on money and banking or monetary theory.

2. The advantages of indirect techniques of monetary control are discussed in greater detail in Johnston and Per Brekk.

3. A modest amount of borrowing from the central bank might be consistent with the monetary growth desired by the public under a fixed exchange rate, but allowing the government to borrow from the central bank has often been abused historically and lies behind all cases of very high or hyper inflation.

4. It is also important to keep in mind that the means of payment in modern economies extend far beyond traditional money (currency and bank deposits) to include: checks, travelers' checks, credit cards, debt cards, and other evolving electronic means of payment.

5. See, for example, the classic article on this subject by Milton Friedman (1969).

Appendix III

1. Based on material provided in personal correspondence from Peter Nicholl, former Governor of the CBBH.

2. Article 42.3 of the Central Bank Law.

3. Peter Nicholl, in personal correspondence.

Appendix IV

1. Early in the history of banks, it became accepted that deposit balances were not warehouse receipts (the contents of safe deposit boxes), but a claim to the indicated amount of legal tender. Thus a payment made by transferring the ownership of a $100 bank balance replaced the risk when making payment with cash that the currency notes are not genuine (or the purity and weight of gold/silver not as indicated) with the risk that the bank might not be able

to redeem the bank balance for $100 in genuine currency notes.

2. More recent innovations in payment technology, such as "PayPal" modify but do not fundamentally change this statement.

3. See Coats, and Selgen.

4. In a competitive market, merchants would charge a premium to accept money from riskier issuers, unless it was insured. It is easy to imagine that private insurance companies would rate the safety of each issuer and charge an insurance premium according to these ratings. This would provide a good market discipline to the behavior of issuers of money, and with modern technology would not be very costly or inconvenient to operate.

5. **Debit transfer** (e.g., **check** or **credit card**): A payment in which the payment instruction is given directly to the payee so that it initially moves in the opposite direction from that of the funds—from the payer to the payee, to the payee's bank, to the payer's bank, at which point the funds and instructions move together as with a credit transfer.

6. The payment of a bill by sending a check through the mail is convenient because the information needed is limited to the name and address of the payee. On the receiving end the payee can easily match the payment to the bill as both documents are received in the mail together. A payment order (funds transfer) requires knowledge of the payee's bank account and the payment is credited to his account without a clear link to the bill being paid unless an invoice number is also included with the payment document. Electronic billing and payment, now becoming common in many countries, overcome these limitations of Giro/payment order payments because the bank and account numbers are contained in the bill that is being paid. The electronic receipt of a bill and its electronic payment is as easy as responding to an e-mail message (click on "Respond" and say "OK pay").

7. Unlike the Internet, dedicated lines have well-controlled access that presumably makes them secure against third-party eavesdropping that could compromise a card number.

8. Charge cards, such as the American Express card, differ from credit cards. They must be paid in full when billed each month and are subject to different regulations than credit cards.

9. Some credit card issuers now allow their itemized charge records to be downloaded over a modem to a PC accounting package such as Quicken.

10. All generalizations in the monetary area seem to have exceptions. Thus the statement that a check is a claim on money rather than money itself is occasionally questionable when checks are passed from person to person in "final" settlement of financial obligations. In 1994 for a period, after the collapse of the national currency briefly issued by the National Bank of Republika Srpska, banks there were permitted to issue certified checks, which circulated like cash.

BIBLIOGRAPHY

Bank of England. "A Brief History of Banknotes," http://www. bankofengland.co.uk/banknotes/about/history.htm.

Coats, Warren. "In Search of a Monetary Anchor: A New Monetary Standard," *Completed Papers Number 48,* International Center for Economic Growth (San Francisco, January, 1994).

Coats, Warren. "Currency and Sovereignty: Why Monetary Policy is Critical" in *Peace and the Public Purse: Economic Policies for Postwar Statebuilding,* James K. Boyce and Madalene O'Donnell, editors (New York, Lynne Rienner, 2007).

Coats, Warren and Allen Frankel. "The Effect of Prohibiting Reserve Account Overdrafts," Research Papers in Banking and Finance Economics, Financial Studies Section, Division of Research and Statistics (Washington: Board of Governors of the Federal Reserve System, September, 1980).

Coats, Warren, Thomas Wolf, Daniel Citrin, and Adrienne Cheasty. "Financial Relations Among Countries of the Former Soviet Union," *IMF Economic Review No. 1* (Washington: International Monetary Fund, February, 1994).

Coats, Warren and Marko Škreb. "Ten Years of Transition Central Banking in the CEE and the Baltics," Surveys (Croatian National Bank, April 2002), http://www.hnb.hr/publikac/pregledi/s-007.pdf.

Committee of Scottish Clearing Banks. "History of Scottish Banknotes," http://www.scotbanks.org.uk/notes.htm.

Eggen, Dan. "FBI Pushed Ahead With Troubled Software," *The Washington Post* (Washington: June 6, 2005, p. 1).

Flamme, Karen. "A Brief History of Our Nation's Paper Money," 1995 Annual Report (San Francisco: Federal Reserve Bank of San Francisco, 1996).

Friedman, Milton. "The Demand for Money: Some Theoretical and Empirical Results," in *The Optimum Quantity of Money and Other Essays* (Chicago: Aldine, 1969).

Johnston, Barry, and Odd Per Brekk. "Monetary Control Procedures and Financial Reform: Approaches, Issues and Recent Experiences in Developing Countries" (unpublished, International Monetary Fund, June 2, 1989).

Hanke, Steve H. "On Dollarization and Currency Boards: Error and Deception," *Policy Reform,* 2002, Vol. 5(4), pp. 203–222.

Hanke, Steve H. and Kurt Schuler. *Currency Boards for Developing Countries* (San Francisco, ICS Press, 1994).

Lindgren, Carl-Johan. "The Transition from Direct to Indirect Instruments of Monetary Policy" in *The Evolving Role of Central Banks.* Patrick Domes and Reza Vaez-Zadeh, editors (Washington: International Monetary Fund, 1991).

Nicholl, Peter. "Payments System Reform: A Case Study of Bosnia and Herzegovina," Chapter 11 of *Central Bank Modernisation* (Bearing Point, 2006).

Selgin, George. *The Theory of Free Banking: Money Supply Under Competitive Note Issue* (Rowman & Littlefield, 1988).

World Bank. *World Development Report 1989* (Oxford University Press).

INDEX*

---

*Page numbers in italics refer to illustrations. Page numbers beginning with 331 refer to notes.